ABBOTTSFORD.

THE WORKS

OF

WASHINGTON IRVING.

NEW EDITION, REVISED.

VOL. IX.

CRAYON MISCELLANY.

NEW YORK:
G. P. PUTNAM, 532 BROADWAY.
1861.

NEWSTEAD ABBEY.

THE

CRAYON MISCELLANY.

BY

WASHINGTON IRVING.

AUTHOR'S REVISED EDITION.

COMPLETE IN ONE VOLUME

NEW YORK:
G. P. PUTNAM, 532 BROADWAY.
1861.

John F. Trow,
Printer, Stereotyper, and Electrotyper,
46, 48 & 50 Greene Street,
Between Grand & Broome, New York.

A TOUR ON THE PRAIRIES.

ABBOTSFORD.

NEWSTEAD ABBEY.

INTRODUCTION.

Having, since my return to the United States, made a wide and varied tour, for the gratification of my curiosity, it has been supposed that I did it for the purpose of writing a book; and it has more than once been intimated in the papers, that such a work was actually in the press, containing scenes and sketches of the Far West.

These announcements, gratuitously made for me, before I had put pen to paper, or even contemplated any thing of the kind, have embarrassed me exceedingly. I have been like a poor actor, who finds himself announced for a part he had no thought of playing, and his appearance expected on the stage before he has committed a line to memory.

I have always had a repugnance, amounting almost to disability, to write in the face of expectation; and, in the present instance, I was expected to write about a region fruitful of wonders and adventures, and which had already been made the theme of spirit-stirring narratives from able pens; yet about which I had nothing wonderful or adventurous to offer.

Since such, however, seems to be the desire of the public, and that they take sufficient interest in my wanderings to deem them worthy of recital, I have hastened, as promptly as possible, to meet in some degree, the expectation which others have excited. For this purpose, I have, as it were, plucked a few leaves out of my memorandum book, containing a month's foray beyond the outposts of human habitation, into the wilderness of the Far West. It forms, indeed, but a small portion of an extensive tour; but it is an episode, complete as far as it goes. As such, I offer it to the public, with great diffidence. It is a simple narrative of every day occurrences; such as happen to every one who travels the prairies. I have no wonders to describe, nor any moving accidents by flood or field to narrate; and as to those who look for a marvellous or adventurous story at my hands, I can only reply in the words of the weary knife-grinder: "Story! God bless you, I have none to tell, sir."

A TOUR ON THE PRAIRIES.

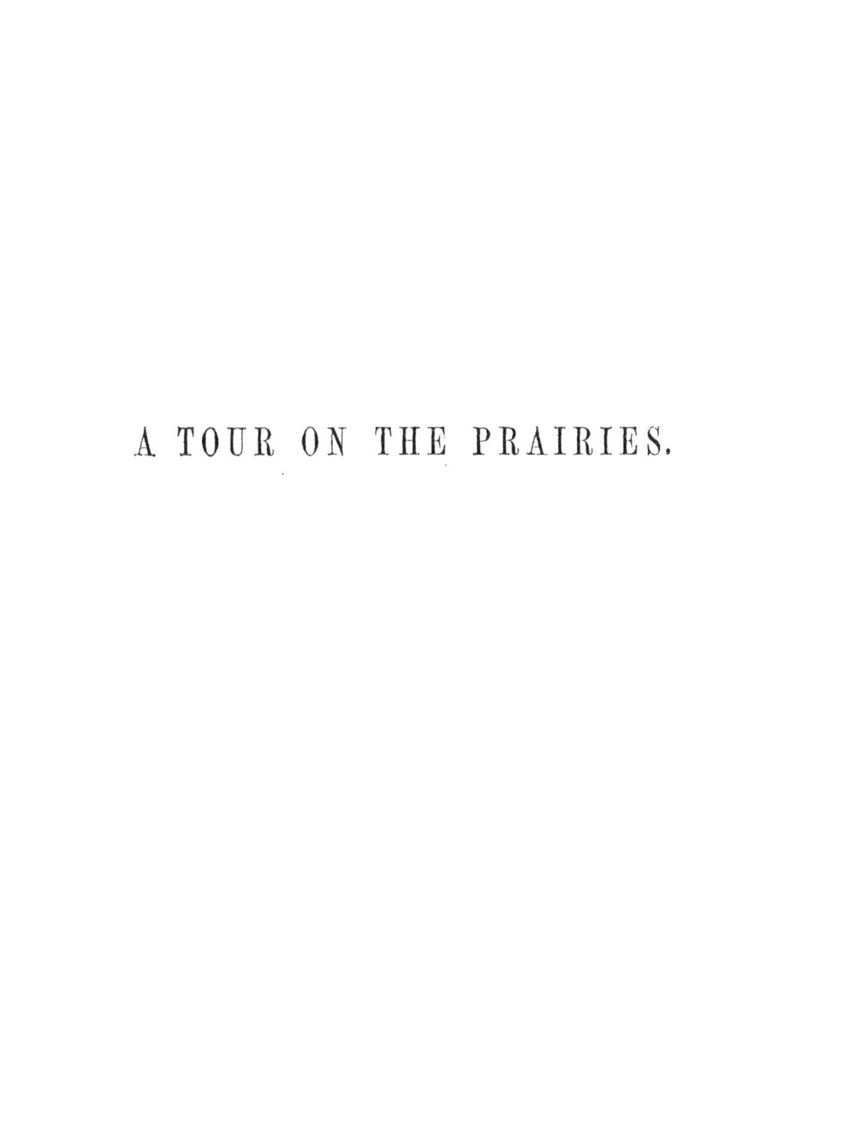

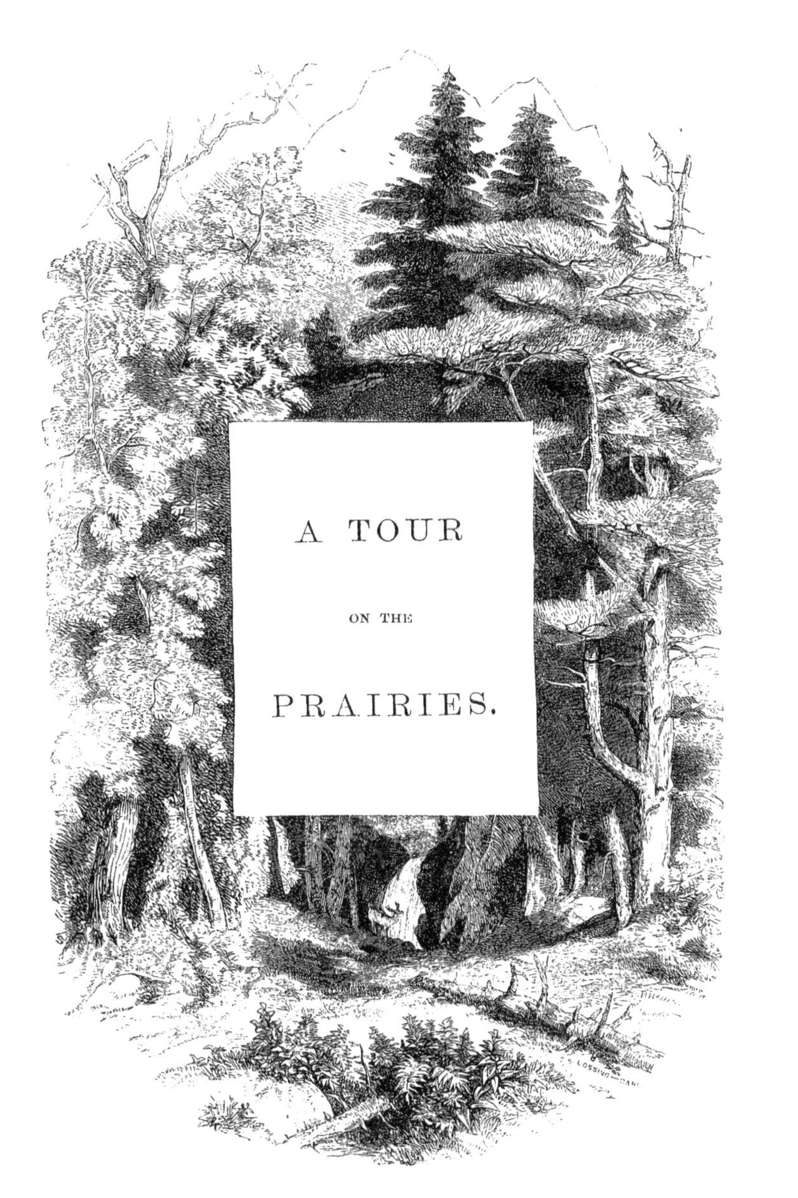
A TOUR
ON THE
PRAIRIES.

A TOUR ON THE PRAIRIES.

CHAPTER I.

THE PAWNEE HUNTING GROUNDS.—TRAVELLING COMPANIONS.—A COMMISSIONER.—A VIRTUOSO.—A SEEKER OF ADVENTURES.—A GIL BLAS OF THE FRONTIER.—A YOUNG MAN'S ANTICIPATIONS OF PLEASURE.

In the often vaunted regions of the Far West, several hundred miles beyond the Mississippi, extends a vast tract of uninhabited country, where there is neither to be seen the log house of the white man, nor the wigwam of the Indian. It consists of great grassy plains, interspersed with forests and groves, and clumps of trees, and watered by the Arkansas, the grand Canadian, the Red River, and their tributary streams. Over these fertile and verdant wastes still roam the elk, the buffalo, and the wild horse, in all their native freedom. These, in fact, are the hunting grounds of the various tribes of the Far West. Hither repair the Osage, the Creek, the Delaware and other tribes that have linked themselves with civilization, and live within the vicinity of the white settlements. Here resort also, the Pawnees, the Comanches, and other fierce, and as yet independent tribes, the nomades of the prairies, or the inhabitants of the skirts of the Rocky Mountains. The regions I have mentioned form a debatable ground of these warring and vindictive tribes; none of them presume to erect a permanent habitation within its borders. Their hunters and "Braves" repair thither in numerous bodies during the season of game, throw up their transient hunting camps, consisting of light bowers covered with bark and skins, commit sad havoc among the innumerable herds that graze the prairies, and having loaded themselves with venison and buffalo meat, warily retire from the dangerous neighborhood These expeditions partake, always, of a warlike character; the hunters are all armed for action, offensive and defensive, and are bound to incessant vigilance. Should they, in their excursions, meet the hunters of an adverse tribe, savage conflicts take place. Their encampments, too, are always subject to be surprised by wandering war parties, and their hunters, when scattered in pursuit of game, to be captured or massacred by lurking foes. Mouldering skulls and skeletons, bleaching in some dark ravine, or near the traces of a hunting camp, occasionally mark the scene of a foregone act of blood, and let the wanderer know the dangerous nature of the region he is traversing. It is the purport of the following pages to narrate a month's excursion to these noted hunting grounds, through a tract of country which had not as yet been explored by white men.

It was early in October, 1832, that I arrived at Fort Gibson, a frontier post of the Far West, situated on the Neosho, or Grand River, near its confluence with the Arkansas. I had been travelling for a month past, with a small party from St. Louis, up the banks of the Missouri, and along the frontier line of agencies and missions, that extends from the Missouri to the Arkansas. Our party was headed by one of the Commissioners appointed by the government of the United States to superintend the settlement of the Indian tribes migrating from the east to the west of the Mississippi. In the discharge of his duties, he was thus visiting the various outposts of civilization.

And here let me bear testimony to the merits of this worthy leader of our little band. He was a native of one of the towns of Connecticut, a man in whom a course of legal practice and political life had not been able to vitiate an innate simplicity and benevolence of heart. The greater part of his days had been passed in the bosom of his family and the society of deacons, elders, and selectmen, on the peaceful banks of the Connecticut; when suddenly he had been called to mount his steed, shoulder his rifle, and mingle among stark hunters, backwoodsmen, and naked savages, on the trackless wilds of the Far West.

Another of my fellow-travellers was Mr. L., an Englishman by birth, but descended from a foreign stock; and who had all the buoyancy and accommodating spirit of a native of the Continent. Having rambled over many countries, he had become, to a certain degree, a citizen of the world, easily adapting himself to any change. He was a man of a thousand occupations; a botanist, a geologist, a hunter of beetles and butterflies, a musical amateur, a sketcher of no mean pretensions, in short, a complete virtuoso; added to which, he was a very indefatigable, if not always a very successful, sportsman. Never had a man more irons in the fire, and, consequently, never was man more busy nor more cheerful.

My third fellow-traveller was one who had accompanied the former from Europe, and travelled with him as his Telemachus; being apt, like his prototype, to give occasional perplexity and disquiet to his Mentor. He was a young Swiss Count, scarce twenty-one years of age, full of talent and spirit, but galliard in the extreme, and prone to every kind of wild adventure.

Having made this mention of my comrades, I must not pass over unnoticed, a personage of inferior rank, but of all-pervading and prevalent importance: the squire, the groom, the cook, the tent man, in a word, the factotum, and, I may add, the universal meddler and marplot of our party. This was a little swarthy, meagre, French creole, named Antoine, but familiarly dubbed Tonish: a kind of Gil Blas of the frontiers, who had passed a scrambling life, sometimes among white men, sometimes among Indians; sometimes in the employ of traders, missionaries, and Indian agents; sometimes mingling with the Osage hunters. We picked him up at St. Louis, near which he has a small farm, an Indian wife, and a brood of half-blood children. According to his own account, however, he had a wife in every tribe; in fact, if all this little vagabond said of himself were to be believed, he was without morals, without caste, without creed, without country, and even without language; for he spoke a jargon of mingled French, English, and Osage. He was, withal, a notorious braggart, and a liar of the first water. It was amusing to hear him vapor and gasconade about his terrible exploits and hair-breadth escapes in war and hunting. In the midst of his volubility, he was prone to be seized by a spasmodic gasping, as if the springs of his jaws were suddenly unhinged; but I am apt to think it was caused by some falsehood that stuck in his throat, for I generally remarked, that immediately afterwards there bolted forth a lie of the first magnitude.

Our route had been a pleasant one, quartering ourselves, occasionally, at the widely separated establishments of the Indian missionaries, but in general camping out in the fine groves that border the streams, and sleeping under cover of a tent. During the latter part of our tour we had pressed forward in hopes of arriving in time at Fort Gibson, to accompany the Osage hunters on their autumnal visit to the buffalo prairies. Indeed the imagination of the young Count had become completely excited on the subject. The grand scenery and wild habits of the prairies had set his spirits madding, and the stories that little Tonish told him of Indian braves and Indian beauties, of hunting buffaloes and catching wild horses, had set him all agog for a dash into savage life. He was a bold and hard rider, and longed to be scouring the hunting grounds. It was amusing to hear his youthful anticipations of all that he was to see, and do, and enjoy, when mingling among the Indians and participating in their hardy adventures; and it was still more amusing to listen to the gasconadings of little Tonish, who volunteered to be his faithful squire in all his perilous undertakings; to teach him how to catch the wild horse, bring down the buffalo, and win the smiles of Indian princesses;—"And if we can only get sight of a prairie on fire!" said the young Count—"By Gar, I'll set one on fire myself!" cried the little Frenchman.

CHAPTER II.

ANTICIPATIONS DISAPPOINTED.—NEW PLANS.—PREPARATIONS TO JOIN AN EXPLORING PARTY.—DEPARTURE FROM FORT GIBSON.—FORDING OF THE VERDIGRIS.—AN INDIAN CAVALIER.

The anticipations of a young man are prone to meet with disappointment. Unfortunately for the Count's scheme of wild campaigning, before we reached the end of our journey, we heard that the Osage hunters had set forth upon their expedition to the buffalo grounds. The Count still determined, if possible, to follow on their track and overtake them, and for this purpose stopped short at the Osage Agency, a few miles distant from Fort Gibson, to make inquiries and preparations. His travelling companion, Mr. L., stopped with him; while the Commissioner and myself proceeded to Fort Gibson, followed by the faithful and veracious Tonish. I hinted to him his promises to follow the Count in his campaignings, but I found the little varlet had a keen eye to self-interest. He was aware that the Commissioner, from his official duties, would remain for a long time in the country, and be likely to give him permanent employment, while the sojourn of the Count would be but transient. The gasconading of the little braggart was suddenly therefore at an end. He spoke not another word to the young Count about Indians, buffaloes, and wild horses, but putting himself tacitly in the train of the Commissioner, jogged silently after us to the garrison.

On arriving at the fort, however, a new chance presented itself for a cruise on the prairies. We learnt that a company of mounted rangers, or riflemen, had departed but three days previous, to make a wide exploring tour, from the Arkansas to the Red River, including a part of the Pawnee hunting grounds, where no party of white men had as yet penetrated. Here, then was an opportunity of ranging over those dangerous and interesting regions under the safeguard of a powerful escort; for the Commissioner, in virtue of his office, could claim the service of this newly-raised corps of riflemen, and the country they were to explore was destined for the settlement of some of the migrating tribes connected with his mission.

Our plan was promptly formed and put into execution. A couple of Creek Indians were sent off express, by the commander of Fort Gibson, to overtake the rangers and bring them to a halt until the Commissioner and his party should be able to join them. As we should have a march of three or four days through a wild country, before we could overtake the company of rangers, an escort of fourteen mounted riflemen, under the command of a lieutenant, was assigned us.

We sent word to the young Count and Mr. L. at the Osage Agency, of our new plan and prospects, and invited them to accompany us. The Count, however, could not forego the delights he had promised himself in mingling with absolutely savage life. In reply, he agreed to keep with us until we should come upon the trail of the Osage hunters, when it was his fixed resolve to strike off into the wilderness in pursuit of them; and his faithful Mentor, though he grieved at the madness of the scheme, was too stanch a friend to desert him. A general rendezvous of our party and escort was appointed, for the following morning, at the Agency.

We now made all arrangements for prompt departure. Our baggage had hitherto been transported on a light wagon, but we were now to break our way through an untravelled country, cut up by rivers, ravines, and thickets, where a vehicle of the kind would be a complete impediment. We were to travel on horseback, in hunters' style, and with as little encumbrance as possible. Our baggage, therefore, underwent a rigid and most abstemious reduction. A pair of saddlebags, and those by no means crammed, sufficed for each man's scanty wardrobe, and, with his great coat, were to be carried upon the steed he rode. The rest of the baggage was placed on pack-horses. Each one had a bear-skin and a couple of blankets for bedding, and there was a tent to shelter us in case of sickness or bad weather. We took care to provide ourselves with flour, coffee, and sugar, together with a small supply of salt pork for emergencies; for our main subsistence we were to depend upon the chase.

Such of our horses as had not been tired out in our recent journey, were taken with us as pack-horses, or supernumeraries; but as we were going on a long and rough tour, where there would be occasional hunting, and where, in case of meeting with hostile savages, the safety of the rider might depend upon the goodness of his steed, we took care to be well mounted. I procured a stout silver-gray; somewhat rough, but stanch and powerful; and retained a hardy pony which I had hitherto ridden, and which, being somewhat jaded, was suffered to ramble along with the pack-horses, to be mounted only in case of emergency.

All these arrangements being made, we left Fort Gibson, on the morning of the tenth of October, and crossing the river in the front of it, set off for the rendezvous at the Agency. A ride of a few miles brought us to the ford of the Verdigris, a wild rocky scene overhung with forest trees. We descended to the bank of the river and crossed in straggling file, the horses stepping cautiously from rock to rock, and in a manner feeling about for a foothold beneath the rushing and brawling stream.

Our little Frenchman, Tonish, brought up the rear with the pack-horses. He was in high glee, having experienced a kind of promotion. In our journey hitherto he had driven the wagon, which he seemed to consider a very inferior employ; now he was master of the horse.

He sat perched like a monkey behind the pack on one of the horses; he sang, he shouted, he yelped like an Indian, and ever and anon blasphemed the loitering pack-horses in his jargon of mingled French, English and Osage, which not one of them could understand.

As we were crossing the ford we saw on the opposite shore a Creek Indian on horseback. He had paused to reconnoitre us from the brow of a rock, and formed a picturesque object, in unison with the wild scenery around him. He wore a bright blue hunting-shirt trimmed with scarlet fringe; a gayly-colored handkerchief was bound round his head something like a turban, with one end hanging down beside his ear; he held a long rifle in his hand, and looked like a wild Arab on the prowl. Our loquacious and ever-meddling little Frenchman called out to him in his Babylonish jargon, but the savage having satisfied his curiosity tossed his hand in the air, turned the head of his steed, and galloping along the shore soon disappeared among the trees.

CHAPTER III.

AN INDIAN AGENCY.—RIFLEMEN.—OSAGES, CREEKS, TRAPPERS, DOGS, HORSES, HALF-BREEDS.—BEATTE, THE HUNTSMAN.

Having crossed the ford, we soon reached the Osage Agency, where Col. Choteau has his offices and magazines, for the dispatch of Indian affairs, and the distribution of presents and supplies. It consisted of a few log houses on the banks of the river, and presented a motley frontier scene. Here was our escort awaiting our arrival; some were on horseback, some on foot, some seated on the trunks of fallen trees, some shooting at a mark. They were a heterogeneous crew; some in frock-coats made of green blankets; others in leathern hunting-shirts, but the most part in marvellously ill-cut garments, much the worse for wear, and evidently put on for rugged service.

Near by these was a group of Osages: stately fellows; stern and simple in garb and aspect. They wore no ornaments; their dress consisted merely of blankets, leggins, and moccasons. Their heads were bare; their hair was cropped close, excepting a bristling ridge on the top, like the crest of a helmet, with a long scalp lock hanging behind. They had fine Roman countenances, and broad deep chests; and, as they generally wore their blankets wrapped round their loins, so as to leave the bust and arms bare, they looked like so many noble bronze figures. The Osages are the finest looking Indians I have ever seen in the West. They have not yielded sufficiently, as yet, to the influence of civilization to lay by their simple Indian garb, or to lose the habits of the hunter and the warrior; and their poverty prevents their indulging in much luxury of apparel.

In contrast to these was a gayly-dressed party of Creeks. There is something, at the first glance, quite oriental in the appearance of this tribe. They dress in calico hunting shirts, of various brilliant colors, decorated with bright fringes, and belted with broad girdles, embroidered with beads: they have leggins of dressed deer skins, or of green or scarlet cloth, with embroidered knee-bands and tassels: their moccasons are fancifully wrought and ornamented, and they wear gaudy handkerchiefs tastefully bound round their heads.

Beside these, there was a sprinkling of trappers, hunters, half-breeds, creoles, negroes of every hue; and all that other rabble rout of nondescript beings that keep about the frontiers, between civilized and savage life, as those equivocal birds, the bats, hover about the confines of light and darkness.

The little hamlet of the Agency was in a complete bustle; the blacksmith's shed, in particular, was a scene of preparation; a strapping negro was shoeing a horse; two half-breeds were fabricating iron spoons in which to melt lead for bullets. An old trapper, in leathern hunting frock and moccasons, had placed his rifle against a work-bench, while he superintended the operation, and gossiped about his hunting exploits; several large dogs were lounging in and out of the shop, or sleeping in the sunshine, while a little cur, with head cocked on one side, and one ear erect, was watching, with that curiosity common to little dogs, the process of shoeing the horse, as if studying the art, or waiting for his turn to be shod.

We found the Count and his companion, the Virtuoso, ready for the march. As they intended to overtake the Osages, and pass some time in hunting the buffalo and the wild horse, they had provided themselves accordingly; having, in addition to the steeds which they used for travelling, others of prime quality, which were to be led when on the march, and only to be mounted for the chase.

They had, moreover, engaged the services of a young man named Antoine, a half-breed of French and Osage origin. He was to be a kind of Jack-of-all-work; to cook, to hunt, and to take care of the horses; but he had a vehement propensity to do nothing, being one of the worthless brood engendered and brought up among the missions. He was, moreover, a little spoiled by being really a handsome young fellow, an Adonis of the frontier, and still worse by fancying himself highly connected, his sister being concubine to an opulent white trader!

For our own parts, the Commissioner and myself were desirous, before setting out, to procure another attendant well versed in wood craft, who might serve us as a hunter; for our little Frenchman would have his hands full when in camp, in cooking, and on the march, in taking care of the pack-horses. Such a one presented himself, or rather was recommended to us, in Pierre Beatte, a half-breed of French and Osage parentage. We were assured that he was acquainted with all parts of the country, having traversed it in all directions, both in hunting and war parties; that he would be of use both as guide and interpreter, and that he was a first-rate hunter.

I confess I did not like his looks when he was first presented to me. He was lounging about, in an old hunting frock and metasses or leggins, of deer skin, soiled and greased, and almost japanned by constant use. He was apparently about thirty-six years of age, square and strongly built. His features were not bad, being shaped not unlike those of Napoleon, but sharpened up, with high Indian cheek bones. Perhaps the dusky greenish hue of his complexion, aided his resemblance to an old bronze bust I had seen of the Emperor. He had, however, a sullen, saturnine expression, set off by a slouched woollen hat, and elf locks that hung about his ears.

Such was the appearance of the man, and his manners were equally unprepossessing. He was cold and laconic; made no promises or professions; stated the terms he required for the services of himself and his horse, which we thought rather high, but showed no disposition to abate them, nor any anxiety to secure our employ. He had altogether more of the red than the white man in his composition; and, as I had been taught to look upon all half-breeds with distrust, as an uncertain and faithless race, I would gladly have dispensed with the services of Pierre Beatte. We had no time, however, to look out for any one more to our taste, and had to make an arrangement with him on the spot. He then set about making his preparations for the journey, promising to join us at our evening's encampment.

One thing was yet wanting to fit me out for the Prairies—a thoroughly trustworthy steed: I was not yet mounted to my mind. The gray I had bought, though strong and serviceable, was rough. At the last moment I succeeded in getting an excellent animal; a dark bay; powerful, active, generous-spirited, and in capital condition. I mounted him with exultation, and transferred the silver gray to Tonish, who was in such ecstasies at finding himself so completely *en Cavalier*, that I feared he might realize the ancient and well-known proverb of "a beggar on horseback."

CHAPTER IV.

THE DEPARTURE.

The long-drawn notes of a bugle at length gave the signal for departure The rangers filed off in a straggling line of march through the woods: we were soon on horseback and following on, but were detained by the irregularity of the pack-horses. They were unaccustomed to keep the line, and straggled from side to side among the thickets, in spite of all the pesting and bedeviling of Tonish; who, mounted on his gallant gray, with a long rifle on his shoulder, worried after them, bestowing a superabundance of dry blows and curses.

We soon, therefore, lost sight of our escort, but managed to keep on their track, thridding lofty forests, and entangled thickets, and passing by Indian wigwams and negro huts, until towards dusk we arrived at a frontier farm-house, owned by a settler of the name of Berryhill. It was situated on a hill, below which the rangers had encamped in a circular grove, on the margin of a stream. The master of the house received us civilly, but could offer us no accommodation, for sickness prevailed in his family. He appeared himself to be in no very thriving condition, for though bulky in frame, he had a sallow, unhealthy complexion, and a whiffling double voice, shifting abruptly from a treble to a thorough-bass.

Finding his log house was a mere hospital, crowded with invalids, we ordered our tent to be pitched in the farm-yard.

We had not been long encamped, when our recently engaged attendant, Beatte, the Osage half-breed, made his appearance.

He came mounted on one horse and leading another, which seemed to be well packed with supplies for the expedition. Beatte was evidently an "old soldier," as to the art of taking care of himself and looking out for emergencies. Finding that he was in government employ, being engaged by the Commissioner, he had drawn rations of flour and bacon, and put them up so as to be weather-proof. In addition to the horse for the road, and for ordinary service, which was a rough, hardy animal, he had another for hunting. This was of a mixed breed like himself, being a cross of the domestic stock with the wild horse of the prairies; and a noble steed it was, of generous spirit, fine action, and admirable bottom. He had taken care to have his horses well shod at the Agency. He came prepared at all points for war or hunting: his rifle on his shoulder, his powder-horn and bullet-pouch at his side, his hunting-knife stuck in his belt, and coils of cordage at his saddle bow, which we were told were lariats, or noosed cords, used in catching the wild horse.

Thus equipped and provided, an Indian hunter on a prairie is like a cruiser on the ocean, perfectly independent of the world, and competent to self-protection and self-maintenance. He can cast himself loose from every one, shape his own course, and take care of his own fortunes. I thought Beatte seemed to feel his independence, and to consider himself superior to us all, now that we were launching into the wilderness. He maintained a half proud, half sullen look, and great taciturnity; and his first care was to unpack his horses and put them in safe quarters for the night. His whole demeanor was in perfect contrast to our vaporing, chattering, bustling little Frenchman. The latter, too, seemed jealous of this new-comer. He whispered to us that these half-breeds were a touchy, capricious people, little to be depended upon. That Beatte had evidently come prepared to take care of himself, and that, at any moment in the course of our tour, he would be liable to take some sudden disgust or affront, and abandon us at a moment's warning: having the means of shifting for himself, and being perfectly at home on the prairies.

CHAPTER V.

FRONTIER SCENES.—A LYCURGUS OF THE BORDER.—LYNCH'S LAW.—THE DANGER OF FINDING A HORSE.—THE YOUNG OSAGE.

On the following morning, (Oct. 11,) we were on the march by half-past seven o'clock, and rode through deep rich bottoms of alluvial soil, overgrown with redundant vegetation, and trees of an enormous size. Our route lay parallel to the west bank of the Arkansas, on the borders of which river, near the confluence of the Red Fork, we expected to overtake the main body of rangers. For some miles the country was sprinkled with Creek villages and farm-houses; the inhabitants of which appeared to have adopted, with considerable facility, the rudiments of civilization, and to have thriven in consequence. Their farms were well stocked, and their houses had a look of comfort and abundance.

We met with numbers of them returning from one of their grand games of ball, for which their nation is celebrated. Some were on foot, some on horseback; the latter, occasionally, with gayly-dressed females behind them They are a well-made race, muscular and closely knit, with well-turned thighs and legs. They have a Gipsy fondness for brilliant colors and gay decorations, and are bright and fanciful objects when seen at a distance on the prairies. One had a scarlet handkerchief bound round his head, surmounted with a tuft of black feathers like a cock's tail. Another had a white handkerchief, with red feathers; while a third, for want of a plume, had stuck in his turban a brilliant bunch of sumach.

On the verge of the wilderness we paused to inquire our way at a log house, owned by a white settler or squatter, a tall raw-boned old fellow, with red hair, a lank lantern visage, and an inveterate habit of winking with one eye, as if every thing he said was of knowing import. He was in a towering passion. One of his horses was missing; he was sure it had been stolen in the night by a straggling party of Osages encamped in a neighboring swamp; but he would have satisfaction! He would make an example of the villains. He had accordingly caught down his rifle from the wall, that invariable enforcer of right or wrong upon the frontiers, and, having saddled his steed, was about to sally forth on a foray into the swamp; while a brother squatter, with rifle in hand, stood ready to accompany him.

We endeavored to calm the old campaigner of the prairies, by suggesting that his horse might have strayed into the neighboring woods; but he had the frontier propensity to charge every thing to the Indians, and nothing could dissuade him from carrying fire and sword into the swamp.

After riding a few miles further we lost the trail of the main body of rangers, and became perplexed by a variety of tracks made by the Indians and settlers. At length coming to a log house, inhabited by a white man, the very last on the frontier, we found that we had wandered from our true course. Taking us back for some distance, he again brought us to the right trail;

putting ourselves upon which, we took our final departure, and launched into the broad wilderness.

The trail kept on like a straggling footpath, over hill and dale, through brush and brake, and tangled thicket, and open prairie. In traversing the wilds it is customary for a party either of horse or foot to follow each other in single file like the Indians; so that the leaders break the way for those who follow, and lessen their labor and fatigue. In this way, also, the number of a party is concealed, the whole leaving but one narrow well trampled track to mark their course.

We had not long regained the trail, when, on emerging from a forest, we beheld our raw-boned, hard-winking, hard-riding knight-errant of the frontier, descending the slope of a hill, followed by his companion in arms. As he drew near to us, the gauntness of his figure and ruefulness of his aspect reminded me of the description of the hero of La Mancha, and he was equally bent on affairs of doughty enterprise, being about to penetrate the thickets of the perilous swamp, within which the enemy lay ensconced.

While we were holding a parley with him on the slope of the hill, we descried an Osage on horseback issuing out of a skirt of wood about half a mile off, and leading a horse by a halter. The latter was immediately recognized by our hard-winking friend as the steed of which he was in quest. As the Osage drew near, I was struck with his appearance. He was about nineteen or twenty years of age, but well grown, with the fine Roman countenance common to his tribe, and as he rode with his blanket wrapped round his loins, his naked bust would have furnished a model for a statuary. He was mounted on a beautiful piebald horse, a mottled white and brown, of the wild breed of the prairies, decorated with a broad collar, from which hung in front a tuft of horse-hair dyed of a bright scarlet.

The youth rode slowly up to us with a frank open air, and signified by means of our interpreter Beatte, that the horse he was leading had wandered to their camp, and he was now on his way to conduct him back to his owner.

I had expected to witness an expression of gratitude on the part of our hard-favored cavalier, but to my surprise the old fellow broke out into a furious passion. He declared that the Indians had carried off his horse in the night, with the intention of bringing him home in the morning, and claiming a reward for finding him; a common practice, as he affirmed, among the Indians. He was, therefore, for tying the young Indian to a tree and giving him a sound lashing; and was quite surprised at the burst of indignation which this novel mode of requiting a service drew from us. Such, however, is too often the administration of law on the frontier, "Lynch's law," as it is technically termed, in which the plaintiff is apt to be witness, jury, judge, and executioner, and the defendant to be convicted and punished on mere presumption; and in this way, I am convinced, are occasioned many of those heart-burnings and resentments among the Indians, which lead to retaliation, and end in Indian wars. When I compared the open, noble countenance and frank demeanor of the young Osage, with the sinister visage and high-handed conduct of the frontiersman, I felt little doubt on whose back a lash would be most meritoriously bestowed.

Being thus obliged to content himself with the recovery of his horse, without the pleasure of flogging the finder into the bargain, the old Lycurgus, or rather Draco, of the frontier, set off growling on his return homeward, followed by his brother squatter

As for the youthful Osage, we were all prepossessed in his favor; the young Count especially, with the sympathies proper to his age and incident to his character, had taken quite a fancy to him. Nothing would suit but he must have the young Osage as a companion and squire in his expedition into the wilderness. The youth was easily tempted, and, with the prospect of a safe range over the buffalo prairies and the promise of a new blanket, he turned his bridle, left the swamp and the encampment of his friends behind him, and set off to follow the Count in his wanderings in quest of the Osage hunters.

Such is the glorious independence of man in a savage state. This youth, with his rifle, his blanket, and his horse, was ready at a moment's warning to rove the world; he carried all his worldly effects with him, and in the absence of artificial wants, possessed the great secret of personal freedom. We of society are slaves, not so much to others as to ourselves; our superfluities are the chains that bind us, impeding every movement of our bodies and thwarting every impulse of our souls. Such, at least, were my speculations at the time, though I am not sure but that they took their tone from the enthusiasm of the young Count, who seemed more enchanted than ever with the wild chivalry of the prairies, and talked of putting on the Indian dress and adopting the Indian habits during the time he hoped to pass with the Osages.

CHAPTER VI.

TRAIL OF THE OSAGE HUNTERS.—DEPARTURE OF THE COUNT AND HIS PARTY.—A DESERTED WAR CAMP.—A VAGRANT DOG.—THE ENCAMPMENT.

In the course of the morning the trail we were pursuing was crossed by another, which struck off through the forest to the west in a direct course for the Arkansas River. Beatte, our half-breed, after considering it for a moment, pronounced it the trail of the Osage hunters; and that it must lead to the place where they had forded the river on their way to the hunting grounds.

Here then the young Count and his companion came to a halt and prepared to take leave of us. The most experienced frontiersmen in the troop remonstrated on the hazard of the undertaking. They were about to throw themselves loose in the wilderness, with no other guides, guards, or attendants, than a young ignorant half-breed, and a still younger Indian. They were embarrassed by a pack-horse and two led horses, with which they would have to make their way through matted forests, and across rivers and morasses. The Osages and Pawnees were at war, and they might fall in with some warrior party of the latter, who are ferocious foes; besides, their small number, and their valuable horses would form a great temptation to some of the straggling bands of Osages loitering about the frontier, who might rob them of their horses in the night, and leave them destitute and on foot in the midst of the prairies.

Nothing, however, could restrain the romantic ardor of the

Count for a campaign of buffalo hunting with the Osages, and he had a game spirit that seemed always stimulated by the idea of danger. His travelling companion, of discreeter age and calmer temperament, was convinced of the rashness of the enterprise; but he could not control the impetuous zeal of his youthful friend and he was too loyal to leave him to pursue his hazardous scheme alone. To our great regret, therefore, we saw them abandon the protection of our escort, and strike off on their hap-hazard expedition. The old hunters of our party shook their heads, and our half-breed, Beatte, predicted all kinds of trouble to them; my only hope was, that they would soon meet with perplexities enough to cool the impetuosity of the young Count, and induce him to rejoin us. With this idea we travelled slowly, and made a considerable halt at noon. After resuming our march, we came in sight of the Arkansas. It presented a broad and rapid stream, bordered by a beach of fine sand, overgrown with willows and cotton-wood trees. Beyond the river, the eye wandered over a beautiful champaign country, of flowery plains and sloping up lands, diversified by groves and clumps of trees, and long screens of woodland; the whole wearing the aspect of complete, and even ornamental cultivation, instead of native wildness. Not far from the river, on an open eminence, we passed through the recently deserted camping place of an Osage war party. The frames of the tents or wigwams remained, consisting of poles bent into an arch, with each end stuck into the ground: these are intertwined with twigs and branches, and covered with bark and skins Those experienced in Indian lore, can ascertain the tribe, and whether on a hunting or a warlike expedition, by the shape and disposition of the wigwams. Beatte pointed out to us, in the present skeleton camp, the wigwam in which the chiefs had held their consultations round the council-fire; and an open area, well trampled down, on which the grand war-dance had been performed.

Pursuing our journey, as we were passing through a forest, we were met by a forlorn, half-famished dog, who came rambling along the trail, with inflamed eyes, and bewildered look. Though nearly trampled upon by the foremost rangers, he took notice of no one, but rambled heedlessly among the horses. The cry of 'mad dog" was immediately raised, and one of the rangers levelled his rifle, but was stayed by the ever-ready humanity of the Commissioner. "He is blind!" said he. "It is the dog of some poor Indian, following his master by the scent. It would be a shame to kill so faithful an animal." The ranger shouldered his rifle, the dog blundered blindly through the cavalcade unhurt, and keeping his nose to the ground, continued his course along the trail, affording a rare instance of a dog surviving a bad name.

About three o'clock, we came to a recent camping-place of the company of rangers: the brands of one of their fires were still smoking; so that, according to the opinion of Beatte, they could not have passed on above a day previously. As there was a fine stream of water close by, and plenty of pea-vines for the horses, we encamped here for the night.

We had not been here long, when we heard a halloo from a distance, and beheld the young Count and his party advancing through the forest. We welcomed them to the camp with heartfelt satisfaction; for their departure upon so hazardous an expedition had caused us great uneasiness. A short experiment had convinced them of the toil and difficulty of inexperienced travellers like themselves making their way through the wilderness with such a train of horses, and such slender attendance. Fortunately, they determined to rejoin us before nightfall; one night's camping out might have cost them their horses. The Count had prevailed upon his protegee and esquire, the young Osage, to continue with him, and still calculated upon achieving great exploits with his assistance, on the buffalo prairies

---

CHAPTER VII.

NEWS OF THE RANGERS.—THE COUNT AND HIS INDIAN SQUIRE.—HALT IN THE WOODS.—WOODLAND SCENE.—OSAGE VILLAGE.—OSAGE VISITORS AT OUR EVENING CAMP.

In the morning early, (Oct. 12,) the two Creeks who had been sent express by the commander of Fort Gibson, to stop the company of rangers, arrived at our encampment on their return. They had left the company encamped about fifty miles distant, in a fine place on the Arkansas, abounding in game, where they intended to await our arrival. This news spread animation throughout our party, and we set out on our march at sunrise, with renewed spirit.

In mounting our steeds, the young Osage attemped to throw a blanket upon his wild horse. The fine, sensitive animal took fright, reared and recoiled. The attitudes of the wild horse and the almost naked savage, would have formed studies for a painter or a statuary.

I often pleased myself in the course of our march, with noticing the appearance of the young Count and his newly-enlisted follower, as they rode before me. Never was preux chevalier better suited with an esquire. The Count was well mounted, and as I have before observed, was a bold and graceful rider. He was fond, too, of caracoling his horse, and dashing about in the buoyancy of youthful spirits. His dress was a gay Indian hunting frock of dressed deer skin, setting well to the shape, dyed of a beautiful purple, and fancifully embroidered with silks of various colors; as if it had been the work of some Indian beauty, to decorate a favorite chief. With this he wore leathern pantaloons and moccasons, a foraging cap, and a double-barrelled gun slung by a bandoleer athwart his back: so that he was quite a picturesque figure as he managed gracefully his spirited steed.

The young Osage would ride close behind him on his wild and beautifully mottled horse, which was decorated with crimson tufts of hair. He rode with his finely shaped head and bust naked; his blanket being girt round his waist. He carried his rifle in one hand, and managed his horse with the other, and seemed ready to dash off at a moment's warning, with his youthful leader, on any madcap foray or scamper. The Count, with the sanguine anticipations of youth, promised himself many hardy adventures and exploits in company with his youthful "brave," when we should get among the buffaloes, in the Pawnee hunting grounds.

After riding some distance, we crossed a narrow, deep stream, upon a solid bridge, the remains of an old beaver dam; the industrious community which had constructed it had all been destroyed. Above us, a streaming flight of wild geese, high in air, and making a vociferous noise, gave note of the waning year.

About half past ten o'clock we made a halt in a forest, where there was abundance of the pea-vine. Here we turned the horses loose to graze. A fire was made, water procured from an adjacent spring, and in a short time our little Frenchman, Tonish, had a pot of coffee prepared for our refreshment. While partaking of it, we were joined by an old Osage, one of a small hunting party who had recently passed this way. He was in search of his horse, which had wandered away, or been stolen. Our half-breed, Beatte, made a wry face on hearing of Osage hunters in this direction. "Until we pass those hunters," said he, "we shall see no buffaloes. They frighten away every thing like a prairie on fire."

The morning repast being over, the party amused themselves in various ways. Some shot with their rifles at a mark, others lay asleep half buried in the deep bed of foliage, with their heads resting on their saddles; others gossiped round the fire at the foot of a tree, which sent up wreaths of blue smoke among the branches. The horses banqueted luxuriously on the pea-vines, and some lay down and rolled amongst them.

We were overshadowed by lofty trees, with straight, smooth trunks, like stately columns; and as the glancing rays of the sun shone through the transparent leaves, tinted with the many-colored hues of autumn, I was reminded of the effect of sunshine among the stained windows and clustering columns of a Gothic cathedral. Indeed there is a grandeur and solemnity in our spacious forests of the West, that awaken in me the same feeling I have experienced in those vast and venerable piles, and the sound of the wind sweeping through them, supplies occasionally the deep breathings of the organ.

About noon the bugle sounded to horse, and we were again on the march, hoping to arrive at the encampment of the rangers before night; as the old Osage had assured us it was not above ten or twelve miles distant. In our course through a forest, we passed by a lonely pool, covered with the most magnificent water-lilies I had ever beheld; among which swam several wood-ducks, one of the most beautiful of water-fowl, remarkable for the gracefulness and brilliancy of its plumage.

After proceeding some distance farther, we came down upon the banks of the Arkansas, at a place where tracks of numerous horses, all entering the water, showed where a party of Osage hunters had recently crossed the river on their way to the buffalo range. After letting our horses drink in the river, we continued along its bank for a space, and then across prairies, where we saw a distant smoke, which we hoped might proceed from the encampment of the rangers. Following what we supposed to be their trail, we came to a meadow in which were a number of horses grazing: they were not, however, the horses of the troop. A little farther on, we reached a straggling Osage village, on the banks of the Arkansas. Our arrival created quite a sensation. A number of old men came forward and shook hands with us all severally; while the women and children huddled together in groups, staring at us wildly, chattering and laughing among themselves. We found that all the young men of the village had departed on a hunting expedition, leaving the women and children and old men behind. Here the Commissioner made a speech from on horseback; informing his hearers of the purport of his mission, to promote a general peace among the tribes of the West, and urging them to lay aside all warlike and bloodthirsty notions, and not to make any wanton attacks upon the Pawnees. This speech being interpreted by Beatte, seemed to have a most pacifying effect upon the multitude, who promised faithfully that, as far as in them lay, the peace should not be disturbed; and indeed their age and sex gave some reason to trust that they would keep their word.

Still hoping to reach the camp of the rangers before nightfall, we pushed on until twilight, when we were obliged to halt on the borders of a ravine. The rangers bivouacked under trees, at the bottom of the dell, while we pitched our tent on a rocky knoll near a running stream. The night came on dark and overcast, with flying clouds, and much appearance of rain. The fires of the rangers burnt brightly in the dell, and threw strong masses of light upon the robber-looking groups that were cooking, eating and drinking around them. To add to the wildness of the scene, several Osage Indians, visitors from the village we had passed, were mingled among the men. Three of them came and seated themselves by our fire. They watched every thing that was going on round them in silence, and looked like figures of monumental bronze. We gave them food, and, what they most relished, coffee; for the Indians partake in the universal fondness for this beverage, which pervades the West. When they had made their supper, they stretched themselves, side by side, before the fire, and began a low nasal chant, drumming with their hands upon their breasts, by way of accompaniment. Their chant seemed to consist of regular staves, every one terminating, not in a melodious cadence, but in the abrupt interjection huh! uttered almost like a hiccup. This chant, we were told by our interpreter, Beatte, related to ourselves, our appearance, our treatment of them, and all that they knew of our plans. In one part they spoke of the young Count, whose animated character and eagerness for Indian enterprise had struck their fancy, and they indulged in some waggery about him and the young Indian beauties, that produced great merriment among our half-breeds.

This mode of improvising is common throughout the savage tribes; and in this way, with a few simple inflections of the voice, they chant all their exploits in war and hunting, and occasionally indulge in a vein of comic humor and dry satire, to which the Indians appear to me much more prone than is generally imagined.

In fact, the Indians that I have had an opportunity of seeing in real life, are quite different from those described in poetry They are by no means the stoics that they are represented; taciturn, unbending, without a tear or a smile. Taciturn they are, it is true, when in company with white men, whose good-will they distrust, and whose language they do not understand; but the white man is equally taciturn under like circumstances. When the Indians are among themselves, however, there cannot be greater gossips. Half their time is taken up in talking over their adventures in war and hunting, and in telling whimsical stories. They are great mimics and buffoons, also, and entertain themselves excessively at the expense of the whites with whom they have associated, and who have supposed them impressed with profound respect for their grandeur and dignity. They are curious observers, noting every thing in silence, but with a keen and watchful eye; occasionally exchanging a glance or a grunt with each other, when any thing particularly strikes them: but reserving all comments until they are alone. Then it is that they give full scope to criticism, satire, mimicry, and mirth.

In the course of my journey along the frontier, I have had repeated opportunities of noticing their excitability and boisterous merriment at their games; and have occasionally noticed a group of Osages sitting round a fire until a late hour of the night, engaged in the most animated and lively conversation; and at times making the woods resound with peals of laughter As to tears, they have them in abundance, both real and affected; at times they make a merit of them. No one weeps more bitterly or profusely at the death of a relative or friend: and they have stated times when they repair to howl and lament at their graves. I have heard doleful wailings at daybreak, in the neighboring Indian villages, made by some of the inhabitants, who go out at that hour into the fields, to mourn and weep for the dead: at such times, I am told, the tears will stream down their cheeks in torrents.

As far as I can judge, the Indian of poetical fiction is like the shepherd of pastoral romance, a mere personification of imaginary attributes.

The nasal chant of our Osage guests gradually died away; they covered their heads with their blankets and fell fast asleep, and in a little while all was silent, excepting the pattering of scattered rain-drops upon our tent.

In the morning our Indian visitors breakfasted with us, but the young Osage who was to act as esquire to the Count in his knight-errantry on the prairies, was nowhere to be found. His wild horse, too, was missing, and, after many conjectures, we came to the conclusion that he had taken "Indian leave" of us in the night. We afterwards ascertained that he had been persuaded so to do by the Osages we had recently met with; who had represented to him the perils that would attend him in an expedition to the Pawnee hunting grounds, where he might fall into the hands of the implacable enemies of his tribe: and, what was scarcely less to be apprehended, the annoyances to which he would be subjected from the capricious and overbearing conduct of the white men; who, as I have witnessed in my own short experience, are prone to treat the poor Indians as little better than brute animals. Indeed, he had had a specimen of it himself in the narrow escape he made from the infliction of "Lynch's law," by the hard-winking worthy of the frontier, for the flagitious crime of finding a stray horse.

The disappearance of the youth was generally regretted by our party, for we had all taken a great fancy to him from his handsome, frank, and manly appearance, and the easy grace of his deportment. He was indeed a native-born gentleman. By none, however, was he so much lamented as by the young Count, who thus suddenly found himself deprived of his esquire. I regretted the departure of the Osage for his own sake, for we should have cherished him throughout the expedition, and I am convinced, from the munificent spirit of his patron, he would have returned to his tribe laden with wealth of beads and trinkets and Indian blankets.

CHAPTER VIII.

THE HONEY CAMP.

THE weather, which had been rainy in the night, having held up, we resumed our march at seven o'clock in the morning, in confident hope of soon arriving at the encampment of the rangers. We had not ridden above three or four miles when we came to a large tree which had recently been felled by an axe, for the wild honey contained in the hollow of its trunk, several broken flakes of which still remained. We now felt sure that the camp could not be far distant. About a couple of miles further some of the rangers set up a shout, and pointed to a number of horses grazing in a woody bottom. A few paces brought us to the brow of an elevated ridge, whence we looked down upon the encampment. It was a wild bandit, or Robin Hood, scene. In a beautiful open forest, traversed by a running stream, were booths of bark and branches, and tents of blankets, temporary shelters from the recent rain, for the rangers commonly bivouac in the open air. There were groups of rangers in every kind of uncouth garb. Some were cooking at large fires made at the feet of trees; some were stretching and dressing deer skins; some were shooting at a mark, and some lying about on the grass. Venison jerked, and hung on frames, was drying over the embers in one place; in another lay carcasses recently brought in by the hunters. Stacks of rifles were leaning against the trunks of the trees, and saddles, bridles, and powder-horns hanging above them, while the horses were grazing here and there among the thickets.

Our arrival was greeted with acclamation. The rangers crowded about their comrades to inquire the news from the fort: for our own part, we were received in frank simple hunter's style by Captain Bean, the commander of the company; a man about forty years of age, vigorous and active. His life had been chiefly passed on the frontier, occasionally in Indian warfare, so that he was a thorough woodsman, and a first-rate hunter. He was equipped in character; in leathern hunting shirt and leggins, and a leathern foraging cap.

While we were conversing with the Captain, a veteran huntsman approached, whose whole appearance struck me. He was of the middle size, but tough and weather-proved; a head partly bald and garnished with loose iron-gray locks, and a fine black eye, beaming with youthful spirit. His dress was similar to that of the Captain, a rifle shirt and leggins of dressed deer skin, that had evidently seen service; a powder-horn was slung by his side, a hunting knife stuck in his belt, and in his hand was an ancient and trusty rifle, doubtless as dear to him as a bosom friend. He asked permission to go hunting, which was readily granted. "That's old Ryan," said the Captain, when he had gone; "there's not a better hunter in the camp; he's sure to bring in game."

In a little while our pack-horses were unloaded and turned loose to revel among the pea-vines. Our tent was pitched; our fire made; the half of a deer had been sent to us from the Captain's lodge; Beatte brought in a couple of wild turkeys; the spits were laden, and the camp-kettle crammed with meat; and to crown our luxuries, a basin filled with great flakes of delicious honey, the spoils of a plundered bee-tree, was given us by one of the rangers.

Our little Frenchman, Tonish, was in an ecstasy, and tucking up his sleeves to the elbows, set to work to make a display of his culinary skill, on which he prided himself almost as much as upon his hunting, his riding, and his warlike prowess.

CHAPTER IX.

A BEE HUNT.

The beautiful forest in which we were encamped abounded in bee-trees; that is to say, trees in the decayed trunks of which wild bees had established their hives. It is surprising in what countless swarms the bees have overspread the Far West, within but a moderate number of years. The Indians consider them the harbinger of the white man, as the buffalo is of the red man; and say that, in proportion as the bee advances, the Indian and buffalo retire. We are always accustomed to associate the hum of the bee-hive with the farmhouse and flower-garden, and to consider those industrious little animals as connected with the busy haunts of man, and I am told that the wild bee is seldom to be met with at any great distance from the frontier. They have been the heralds of civilization, steadfastly preceding it as it advanced from the Atlantic borders, and some of the ancient settlers of the West pretend to give the very year when the honey-bee first crossed the Mississippi. The Indians with surprise found the mouldering trees of their forests suddenly teeming with ambrosial sweets, and nothing, I am told, can exceed the greedy relish with which they banquet for the first time upon this unbought luxury of the wilderness.

At present the honey-bee swarms in myriads, in the noble groves and forests which skirt and intersect the prairies, and extend along the alluvial bottoms of the rivers. It seems to me as if these beautiful regions answer literally to the description of the land of promise, "a land flowing with milk and honey;" for the rich pasturage of the prairies is calculated to sustain herds of cattle as countless as the sands upon the sea-shore, while the flowers with which they are enamelled render them a very paradise for the nectar-seeking bee.

We had not been long in the camp when a party set out in quest of a bee-tree; and, being curious to witness the sport, I gladly accepted an invitation to accompany them. The party was headed by a veteran bee-hunter, a tall lank fellow in homespun garb that hung loosely about his limbs, and a straw hat shaped not unlike a bee-hive; a comrade, equally uncouth in garb, and without a hat, straddled along at his heels, with a long rifle on his shoulder. To these succeeded half a dozen others, some with axes and some with rifles, for no one stirs far from the camp without his firearms, so as to be ready either for wild deer or wild Indian.

After proceeding some distance we came to an open glade on the skirts of the forest. Here our leader halted, and then advanced quietly to a low bush, on the top of which I perceived a piece of honey-comb. This I found was the bait or lure for the wild bees. Several were humming about it, and diving into its cells. When they had laden themselves with honey they would rise into the air, and dart off in a straight line, almost with the velocity of a bullet. The hunters watched attentively the course they took, and then set off in the same direction, stumbling along over twisted roots and fallen trees, with their eyes turned up to the sky. In this way they traced the honey-laden bees to their hive, in the hollow trunk of a blasted oak, where, after buzzing about for a moment, they entered a hole about sixty feet from the ground.

Two of the bee-hunters now plied their axes vigorously at the foot of the tree to level it with the ground. The mere spectators and amateurs, in the meantime, drew off to a cautious distance, to be out of the way of the falling of the tree and the vengeance of its inmates. The jarring blows of the axe seemed to have no effect in alarming or disturbing this most industrious community. They continued to ply at their usual occupations, some arriving full freighted into port, others sallying forth on new expeditions, like so many merchantmen in a money-making metropolis, little suspicious of impending bankruptcy and downfall. Even a loud crack which announced the disrupture of the trunk, failed to divert their attention from the intense pursuit of gain; at length down came the tree with a tremendous crash bursting open from end to end, and displaying all the hoarded treasures of the commonwealth.

One of the hunters immediately ran up with a whisp of lighted hay as a defence against the bees. The latter, however, made no attack and sought no revenge; they seemed stupefied by the catastrophe and unsuspicious of its cause, and remained crawling and buzzing about the ruins without offering us any molestation. Every one of the party now fell to, with spoon and hunting knife, to scoop out the flakes of honey-comb with which the hollow trunk was stored. Some of them were of old date and a deep brown color, others were beautifully white, and the honey in their cells was almost limpid. Such of the combs as were entire were placed in camp kettles to be conveyed to the encampment; those which had been shivered in the fall were devoured upon the spot. Every stark bee-hunter was to be seen with a rich morsel in his hand, dripping about his fingers, and disappearing as rapidly as a cream tart before the holiday appetite of a schoolboy.

Nor was it the bee-hunters alone that profited by the downfall of this industrious community; as if the bees would carry through the similitude of their habits with those of laborious and gainful man, I beheld numbers from rival hives, arriving on eager wing, to enrich themselves with the ruins of their neighbors. These busied themselves as eagerly and cheerfully as so many wreckers on an Indiaman that has been driven on shore; plunging into the cells of the broken honey-combs, banqueting greedily on the spoil, and then winging their way full freighted to their homes. As to the poor proprietors of the ruin, they seemed to have no heart to do any thing, not even to taste the nectar that flowed around them; but crawled backwards and forwards, in vacant desolation, as I have seen a poor fellow with his hands in his pockets, whistling vacantly and despondingly about the ruins of his house that had been burnt.

It is difficult to describe the bewilderment and confusion of the bees of the bankrupt hive who had been absent at the time of the catastrophe, and who arrived from time to time, with full cargoes from abroad. At first they wheeled about in the air, in the place where the fallen tree had once reared its head, astonished at finding it all a vacuum. At length, as if comprehending their disaster, they settled down in clusters on a dry branch of a neighboring tree, whence they seemed to contemplate the prostrate ruin, and to buzz forth doleful lamentations over the downfall of their republic. It was a scene on which the "melancholy Jacques" might have moralized by the hour.

We now abandoned the place, leaving much honey in the hollow of the tree. "It will all be cleared off by varmint," said one of the rangers. "What vermin?" asked I. "Oh, bears, and skunks, and racoons, and 'possums. The bears is the knowingest varmint for finding out a bee-tree in the world. They'll gnaw for days together at the trunk till they make a hole big enough to get in their paws, and then they'll haul out honey, bees and all."

CHAPTER X.

AMUSEMENTS IN THE CAMP.—CONSULTATIONS.—HUNTERS' FARE AND FEASTING.—EVENING SCENES.—CAMP MELODY.—THE FATE OF AN AMATEUR OWL.

On returning to the camp, we found it a scene of the greatest hilarity. Some of the rangers were shooting at a mark, others were leaping, wrestling, and playing at prison bars. They were mostly young men, on their first expedition, in high health and vigor, and buoyant with anticipations; and I can conceive nothing more likely to set the youthful blood into a flow, than a wild wood life of the kind, and the range of a magnificent wilderness, abounding with game, and fruitful of adventure. We send our youth abroad to grow luxurious and effeminate in Europe; it appears to me, that a previous tour on the prairies would be more likely to produce that manliness, simplicity, and self-dependence, most in unison with our political institutions.

While the young men were engaged in these boisterous amusements, a graver set, composed of the Captain, the Doctor, and other sages and leaders of the camp, were seated or stretched out on the grass, round a frontier map, holding a consultation about our position, and the course we were to pursue.

Our plan was to cross the Arkansas just above where the Red Fork falls into it, then to keep westerly, until we should pass through a grand belt of open forest, called the Cross Timber, which ranges nearly north and south from the Arkansas to Red River; after which, we were to keep a southerly course towards the latter river.

Our half-breed, Beatte, being an experienced Osage hunter, was called into the consultation. "Have you ever hunted in this direction?" said the Captain. "Yes," was the laconic reply.

"Perhaps, then, you can tell us in which direction lies the Red Fork?"

"If you keep along yonder, by the edge of the prairie, you will come to a bald hill, with a pile of stones upon it."

"I have noticed that hill as I was hunting," said the Captain.

"Well! those stones were set up by the Osages as a land-mark: from that spot you may have a sight of the Red Fork."

"In that case," cried the Captain, "we shall reach the Red Fork to-morrow; then cross the Arkansas above it, into the Pawnee country, and then in two days we shall crack buffalo bones!"

The idea of arriving at the adventurous hunting grounds of the Pawnees, and of coming upon the traces of the buffaloes, made every eye sparkle with animation. Our further conversation was interrupted by the sharp report of a rifle at no great distance from the camp.

"That's old Ryan's rifle," exclaimed the Captain; "there's a buck down, I'll warrant!" nor was he mistaken; for, before long, the veteran made his appearance, calling upon one of the younger rangers to return with him, and aid in bringing home the carcass.

The surrounding country, in fact, abounded with game, so that the camp was overstocked with provisions, and, as no less than twenty bee-trees had been cut down in the vicinity, every one revelled in luxury. With the wasteful prodigality of hunters, there was a continual feasting, and scarce any one put by provision for the morrow. The cooking was conducted in hunt ers' style: the meat was stuck upon tapering spits of dogwood, which were thrust perpendicularly into the ground, so as to sustain the joint before the fire, where it was roasted or broiled with all its juices retained in it in a manner that would have tickled the palate of the most experienced gourmand. As much could not be said in favor of the bread. It was little more than a paste made of flour and water, and fried like fritters, in lard; though some adopted a ruder style, twisting it round the ends of sticks, and thus roasting it before the fire. In either way, I have found it extremely palatable on the prairies. No one knows the true relish of food until he has a hunter's appetite.

Before sunset, we were summoned by little Tonish to a sumptuous repast. Blankets had been spread on the ground near to the fire, upon which we took our seats. A large dish, or bowl, made from the root of a maple tree, and which we had purchased at the Indian village, was placed on the ground before us, and into it were emptied the contents of one of the camp kettles, consisting of a wild turkey hashed, together with slices of bacon and lumps of dough. Beside it was placed another bowl of similar ware, containing an ample supply of fritters. After we had discussed the hash, two wooden spits, on which the ribs of a fat buck were broiling before the fire, were removed and planted in the ground before us, with a triumphant air, by little Tonish. Having no dishes, we had to proceed in hunters' style, cutting off strips and slices with our hunting-knives, and dipping them in salt and pepper. To do justice to Tonish's cookery, however, and to the keen sauce of the prairies, never have I tasted venison so delicious. With all this, our beverage was coffee, boiled in a camp kettle, sweetened with brown sugar, and drunk out of tin cups: and such was the style of our banqueting throughout this expedition, whenever provisions were plenty, and as long as flour and coffee and sugar held out.

As the twilight thickened into night, the sentinels were marched forth to their stations around the camp; an indispensable precaution in a country infested by Indians. The encampment now presented a picturesque appearance. Camp fires were blazing and smouldering here and there among the trees, with groups of rangers round them; some seated or lying on the ground, others standing in the ruddy glare of the flames, or in shadowy relief. At some of the fires there was much boisterous mirth, where peals of laughter were mingled with loud ribald jokes and uncouth exclamations; for the troop was evidently a raw, undisciplined band, levied among the wild youngsters of the frontier, who had enlisted, some for the sake of roving adventure, and some for the purpose of getting a knowledge of the country. Many of them were the neighbors of their officers, and accustomed to regard them with the familiarity of equals and companions. None of them had any idea of the restraint and decorum of a camp, or ambition to acquire a name for exactness in a profession in which they had no intention of continuing.

While this boisterous merriment prevailed at some of the fires, there suddenly rose a strain of nasal melody from another, at which a choir of "vocalists" were uniting their voices in a most lugubrious psalm tune. This was led by one of the lieutenants; a tall, spare man, who we were informed had officiated as schoolmaster, singing-master, and occasionally as Methodist preacher, in one of the villages of the frontier. The chant rose solemnly and sadly in the night air, and reminded me of the description of similar canticles in the camps of the Covenanters; and, indeed, the strange medley of figures and faces and uncouth garbs, congregated together in our troop, would not have disgraced the banners of Praise-God Barebones.

In one of the intervals of this nasal psalmody, an amateur owl, as if in competition, began his dreary hooting. Immediately there was a cry throughout the camp of "Charley's owl! Charley's owl!" It seems this "obscure bird" had visited the camp every night, and had been fired at by one of the sentinels, a half-witted lad, named Charley; who, on being called up for firing when on duty, excused himself by saying, that he understood that owls made uncommonly good soup.

One of the young rangers mimicked the cry of this bird of wisdom, who, with a simplicity little consonant with his character, came hovering within sight, and alighted on the naked branch of a tree, lit up by the blaze of our fire. The young Count immediately seized his fowling-piece, took fatal aim, and in a twinkling the poor bird of ill omen came fluttering to the ground. Charley was now called upon to make and eat his dish of owl-soup, but declined, as he had not shot the bird.

In the course of the evening, I paid a visit to the Captain's fire. It was composed of huge trunks of trees, and of sufficient magnitude to roast a buffalo whole. Here were a number of the prime hunters and leaders of the camp, some sitting, some standing, and others lying on skins or blankets before the fire, telling old frontier stories about hunting and Indian warfare.

As the night advanced, we perceived above the trees to the west, a ruddy glow flushing up the sky.

"That must be a prairie set on fire by the Osage hunters," said the Captain.

"It is at the Red Fork," said Beatte, regarding the sky. "It seems but three miles distant, yet it perhaps is twenty."

About half past eight o'clock, a beautiful pale light gradually sprang up in the east, a precursor of the rising moon. Drawing off from the Captain's lodge, I now prepared for the night's repose. I had determined to abandon the shelter of the tent, and henceforth to bivouac like the rangers. A bear-skin spread at the foot of a tree was my bed, with a pair of saddle-bags for a pillow. Wrapping myself in blankets, I stretched myself on this hunter's couch, and soon fell into a sound and sweet sleep, from which I did not awake until the bugle sounded at daybreak.

CHAPTER XI.

BREAKING UP OF THE ENCAMPMENT.—PICTURESQUE MARCH.—GAME.—CAMP SCENES.—TRIUMPH OF A YOUNG HUNTER.—ILL SUCCESS OF OLD HUNTERS.—FOUL MURDER OF A POLECAT.

(Oct. 14.) At the signal-note of the bugle, the sentinels and patrols marched in from their stations around the camp and were dismissed. The rangers were roused from their night's repose, and soon a bustling scene took place. While some cut wood, made fires, and prepared the morning's meal, others struck their foul-weather shelters of blankets, and made every preparation for departure; while others dashed about, through brush and brake, catching the horses and leading or driving them into camp.

During all this bustle the forest rang with whoops, and shouts, and peals of laughter; when all had breakfasted, packed up their effects and camp equipage, and loaded the pack-horses, the bugle sounded to saddle and mount. By eight o'clock the whole troop set off in a long straggling line, with whoop and halloo, intermingled with many an oath at the loitering pack-horses, and in a little while the forest, which for several days had been the scene of such unwonted bustle and uproar, relapsed into its primeval solitude and silence.

It was a bright sunny morning, with a pure transparent atmosphere that seemed to bathe the very heart with gladness. Our march continued parallel to the Arkansas, through a rich and varied country; sometimes we had to break our way through alluvial bottoms matted with redundant vegetation, where the gigantic trees were entangled with grape-vines, hanging like cordage from their branches; sometimes we coasted along sluggish brooks, whose feebly-trickling current just served to link together a succession of glassy pools, imbedded like mirrors in the quiet bosom of the forest, reflecting its autumnal foliage, and patches of the clear blue sky. Sometimes we scrambled up broken and rocky hills, from the summits of which we had wide views stretching on one side over distant prairies diversified by groves and forests, and on the other ranging along a line of blue and shadowy hills beyond the waters of the Arkansas.

The appearance of our troop was suited to the country; stretching along in a line of upwards of half a mile in length, winding among brakes and bushes, and up and down the defiles of the hills: the men in every kind of uncouth garb, with long rifles on their shoulders, and mounted on horses of every color. The pack-horses, too, would incessantly wander from the line of march, to crop the surrounding herbage, and were banged and beaten back by Tonish and his half-breed compeers, with volleys of mongrel oaths. Every now and then the notes of the bugle from the head of the column, would echo through the woodlands and along the hollow glens, summoning up stragglers, and announcing the line of march. The whole scene reminded me of the description given of bands of buccaneers penetrating the wilds of South America, on their plundering expeditions against the Spanish settlements.

At one time we passed through a luxuriant bottom of meadow bordered by thickets, where the tall grass was pressed down into numerous "deer beds," where those animals had couched the preceding night. Some oak trees also bore signs of having been clambered by bears, in quest of acorns, the marks of their claws being visible in the bark.

As we opened a glade of this sheltered meadow, we beheld several deer bounding away in wild affright, until, having gained some distance, they would stop and gaze back, with the curiosity common to this animal, at the strange intruders into their solitudes. There was immediately a sharp report of rifles in every direction, from the young huntsmen of the troop, but they were too eager to aim surely, and the deer, unharmed, bounded away into the depths of the forest.

In the course of our march we struck the Arkansas, but found ourselves still below the Red Fork, and, as the river made deep bends, we again left its banks and continued through the woods until nearly eight o'clock, when we encamped in a beautiful basin bordered by a fine stream, and shaded by clumps of lofty oaks.

The horses were now hobbled, that is to say, their fore legs were fettered with cords or leathern straps, so as to impede their movements, and prevent their wandering from the camp. They were then turned loose to graze. A number of rangers, prime hunters, started off in different directions in search of game. There was no whooping nor laughing about the camp as in the morning; all were either busy about the fires preparing the evening's repast, or reposing upon the grass. Shots were soon heard in various directions. After a time a huntsman rode into the camp with the carcass of a fine buck hanging across his horse. Shortly afterwards came in a couple of stripling hunters on foot, one of whom bore on his shoulders the body of a doe. He was evidently proud of his spoil, being probably one of his first achievements, though he and his companion were much bantered by their comrades, as young beginners who hunted in partnership.

Just as the night set in, there was a great shouting at one end of the camp, and immediately afterwards a body of young rangers came parading round the various fires, bearing one of their comrades in triumph on their shoulders. He had shot an elk for the first time in his life, and it was the first animal of the kind that had been killed on this expedition. The young huntsman, whose name was M'Lellan, was the hero of the camp for the night, and was the "father of the feast" into the bargain; for portions of his elk were seen roasting at every fire.

The other hunters returned without success. The captain had observed the tracks of a buffalo, which must have passed within a few days, and had tracked a bear for some distance until the foot-prints had disappeared. He had seen an elk too, on the banks of the Arkansas, which walked out on a sand-bar of the river, but before he could steal round through the bushes to get a shot, it had re-entered the woods.

Our own hunter, Beatte, returned silent and sulky, from an unsuccessful hunt. As yet he had brought us in nothing, and we had depended for our supplies of venison upon the Captain's mess. Beatte was evidently mortified, for he looked down with contempt upon the rangers, as raw and inexperienced woodsmen, but little skilled in hunting; they, on the other hand, regarded Beatte with no very complacent eye, as one of an evil breed, and always spoke of him as "the Indian."

Our little Frenchman Tonish also, by his incessant boasting and chattering, and gasconading, in his balderdashed dialect, had drawn upon himself the ridicule of many of the wags of the troop, who amused themselves at his expense in a kind of raillery by no means remarkable for its delicacy; but the little varlet was so completely fortified by vanity and self-conceit, that he was invulnerable to every joke. I must confess, however, that I felt a little mortified at the sorry figure our retainers were making among these moss-troopers of the frontier. Even our very equipments came in for a share of unpopularity, and I heard many sneers at the double-barrelled guns with which we were provided against smaller game; the lads of the West holding "shot-guns," as they call them, in great contempt, thinking grouse, partridges, and even wild turkeys as beneath their serious attention, and the rifle the only firearm worthy of a hunter.

I was awakened before daybreak the next morning, by the mournful howling of a wolf, who was skulking about the purlieus of the camp, attracted by the scent of venison. Scarcely had the first gray streak of dawn appeared, when a youngster at one of the distant lodges, shaking off his sleep, crowed in imitation of a cock, with a loud clear note and prolonged cadence, that would have done credit to the most veteran chanticleer. He was immediately answered from another quarter, as if from a rival rooster. The chant was echoed from lodge to lodge, and followed by the cackling of hens, quacking of ducks, gabbling of turkeys, and grunting of swine, until we seemed to have been transported into the midst of a farmyard, with all its inmates in full concert around us.

After riding a short distance this morning, we came upon a well-worn Indian track, and following it, scrambled to the summit of a hill, whence we had a wide prospect over a country diversified by rocky ridges and waving lines of upland, and enriched by groves and clumps of trees of varied tuft and foliage. At a distance to the west, to our great satisfaction, we beheld the Red Fork rolling its ruddy current to the Arkansas, and found that we were above the point of junction. We now descended and pushed forward, with much difficulty, through the rich alluvial bottom that borders the Arkansas. Here the trees were interwoven with grape-vines, forming a kind of cordage, from trunk to trunk and limb to limb; there was a thick undergrowth, also, of bush and bramble, and such an abundance of hops, fit for gathering, that it was difficult for our horses to force their way through.

The soil was imprinted in many places with the tracks of deer, and the claws of bears were to be traced on various trees. Every one was on the look-out in the hope of starting some game, when suddenly there was a bustle and a clamor in a distant part of the line. A bear! a bear! was the cry. We all pressed forward to be present at the sport, when to my infinite, though whimsical chagrin, I found it to be our two worthies, Beatte and Tonish, perpetrating a foul murder on a polecat, or skunk! The animal had ensconced itself beneath the trunk of a fallen tree, whence it kept up a vigorous defence in its peculiar style, until the surrounding forest was in a high state of fragrance.

Gibes and jokes now broke out on all sides at the expense of the Indian hunter, and he was advised to wear the scalp of the skunk as the only trophy of his prowess. When they found, however, that he and Tonish were absolutely bent upon bearing off the carcass as a peculiar dainty, there was a universal expression of disgust; and they were regarded as little better than cannibals.

Mortified at this ignominious debut of our two hunters, I insisted upon their abandoning their prize and resuming their march. Beatte complied with a dogged, discontented air, and lagged behind muttering to himself. Tonish, however, with his usual buoyancy, consoled himself by vociferous eulogies on the richness and delicacy of a roasted polecat, which he swore was considered the daintiest of dishes by all experienced Indian gourmands. It was with difficulty I could silence his loquacity by repeated and peremptory commands. A Frenchman's vivacity however, if repressed in one way, will break out in another, and Tonish now eased off his spleen by bestowing volleys of oaths and dry blows on the pack-horses. I was likely to be no gainer in the end, by my opposition to the humors of these varlets, for after a time, Beatte, who had lagged behind, rode up to the head of the line to resume his station as a guide, and I had the vexation to see the carcass of his prize, stripped of its skin, and looking like a fat sucking pig, dangling behind his saddle. I made a solemn vow, however, in secret, that our fire should not be dis graced by the cooking of that polecat

CHAPTER XII.

THE CROSSING OF THE ARKANSAS.

We had now arrived at the river, about a quarter of a mile above the junction of the Red Fork; but the banks were steep and crumbling, and the current was deep and rapid. It was impossible, therefore, to cross at this place; and we resumed our painful course through the forest, dispatching Beatte ahead, in search of a fording place. We had proceeded about a mile further, when he rejoined us, bringing intelligence of a place hard by, where the river, for a great part of its breadth, was rendered fordable by sand-bars, and the remainder might easily be swam by the horses.

Here, then, we made a halt. Some of the rangers set to work vigorously with their axes, felling trees on the edge of the river, wherewith to form rafts for the transportation of their baggage and camp equipage. Others patrolled the banks of the river farther up, in hopes of finding a better fording place; being unwilling to risk their horses in the deep channel.

It was now that our worthies, Beatte and Tonish, had an opportunity of displaying their Indian adroitness and resource. At the Osage village which we had passed a day or two before, they had procured a dry buffalo skin. This was now produced; cords were passed through a number of small eyelet holes with which it was bordered, and it was drawn up, until it formed a kind of deep trough. Sticks were then placed athwart it on the inside, to keep it in shape; our camp equipage and a part of our baggage were placed within, and the singular bark was carried down the bank and set afloat. A cord was attached to the prow, which Beatte took between his teeth, and throwing himself into the water, went ahead, towing the bark after him; while Tonish followed behind, to keep it steady and to propel it. Part of the way they had foothold, and were enabled to wade, but in the main current they were obliged to swim. The whole way, they whooped and yelled in the Indian style, until they landed safely on the opposite shore.

The Commissioner and myself were so well pleased with this Indian mode of ferriage, that we determined to trust ourselves in the buffalo hide. Our companions, the Count and Mr. L., had proceeded with the horses, along the river bank, in search of a ford which some of the rangers had discovered, about a mile and a half distant. While we were waiting for the return of our ferryman, I happened to cast my eyes upon a heap of luggage under a bush, and descried the sleek carcass of the polecat, snugly trussed up, and ready for roasting before the evening fire. I could not resist the temptation to plump it into the river, when it sunk to the bottom like a lump of lead; and thus our lodge was relieved from the bad odor which this savory viand had threatened to bring upon it.

Our men having recrossed with their cockle-shell bark, it was drawn on shore, half filled with saddles, saddlebags, and other luggage, amounting to a hundred weight; and being again placed in the water, I was invited to take my seat. It appeared to me pretty much like the embarkation of the wise men of Gotham, who went to sea in a bowl: I stepped in, however, without hesitation, though as cautiously as possible, and sat down on top of the luggage, the margin of the hide sinking to within a hand's breadth of the water's edge. Rifles, fowling-pieces, and other articles of small bulk, were then handed in, until I protested against receiving any more freight. We then launched forth upon the stream, the bark being towed as before.

It was with a sensation half serious, half comic, that I found myself thus afloat, on the skin of a buffalo, in the midst of a wild river, surrounded by wilderness, and towed along by a half savage, whooping and yelling like a devil incarnate. To please the vanity of little Tonish, I discharged the double-barrelled gun, to the right and left, when in the centre of the stream. The report echoed along the woody shores, and was answered by shouts from some of the rangers, to the great exultation of the little Frenchman, who took to himself the whole glory of this Indian mode of navigation.

Our voyage was accomplished happily; the Commissioner was ferried across with equal success, and all our effects were brought over in the same manner. Nothing could equal the vainglorious vaporing of little Tonish, as he strutted about the shore, and exulted in his superior skill and knowledge, to the rangers. Beatte, however, kept his proud, saturnine look, without a smile. He had a vast contempt for the ignorance of the rangers, and felt that he had been undervalued by them. His only observation was, "Dey now see de Indian good for someting, anyhow!"

The broad, sandy shore where we had landed, was intersected by innumerable tracks of elk, deer, bears, racoons, turkeys, and water-fowl. The river scenery at this place was beautifully diversified, presenting long, shining reaches, bordered by willows and cotton-wood trees; rich bottoms, with lofty forests; among which towered enormous plane trees, and the distance was closed in by high embowered promontories. The foliage had a yellow autumnal tint, which gave to the sunny landscape the golden tone of one of the landscapes of Claude Lorraine. There was animation given to the scene, by a raft of logs and branches, on which the Captain and his prime companion, the Doctor, were ferrying their effects across the stream; and by a long line of rangers on horseback, fording the river obliquely, along a series of sand-bars, about a mile and a half distant.

CHAPTER XIII.

THE CAMP OF THE GLEN.

CAMP GOSSIP.—PAWNEES AND THEIR HABITS.—A HUNTER'S ADVENTURE.—HORSES FOUND, AND MEN LOST.

Being joined by the Captain and some of the rangers, we struck into the woods for about half a mile, and then entered a wild, rocky dell, bordered by two lofty ridges of limestone, which narrowed as we advanced, until they met and united; making almost an angle. Here a fine spring of water rose among the rocks, and fed a silver rill that ran the whole length of the dell, freshening the grass with which it was carpeted.

In this rocky nook we encamped, among tall trees. The rangers gradually joined us, straggling through the forest singly or in groups; some on horseback, some on foot, driving their horses before them, heavily laden with baggage, some dripping wet, having fallen into the river; for they had experienced much fatigue and trouble from the length of the ford, and the depth and rapidity of the stream. They looked not unlike banditti returning with their plunder, and the wild dell was a retreat worthy to receive them. The effect was heightened after dark, when the light of the fires was cast upon rugged looking groups of men and horses; with baggage tumbled in heaps, rifles piled against the trees, and saddles, bridles, and powder-horns hanging about their trunks.

At the encampment we were joined by the young Count and his companion, and the young half-breed, Antoine, who had all passed successfully by the ford. To my annoyance, however, I discovered that both of my horses were missing. I had supposed them in the charge of Antoine: but he, with characteristic carelessness, had paid no heed to them, and they had probably wandered from the line on the opposite side of the river. It was arranged that Beatte and Antoine should recross the river at an early hour of the morning, in search of them.

A fat buck, and a number of wild turkeys being brought into the camp, we managed, with the addition of a cup of coffee, to make a comfortable supper; after which, I repaired to the Captain's lodge, which was a kind of council fire and gossiping place for the veterans of the camp.

As we were conversing together, we observed, as on former nights, a dusky, red glow in the west, above the summits of the surrounding cliffs. It was again attributed to Indian fires on the prairies; and supposed to be on the western side of the Arkansas. If so, it was thought they must be made by some party of Pawnees, as the Osage hunters seldom ventured in that quarter Our half-breeds, however, pronounced them Osage fires; and that they were on the opposite side of the Arkansas.

The conversation now turned upon the Pawnees, into whose hunting grounds we were about entering. There is always some wild untamed tribe of Indians, who form, for a time, the terror of a frontier, and about whom all kinds of fearful stories are told. Such, at present, was the case with the Pawnees, who rove the regions between the Arkansas and the Red River, and the prairies of Texas. They were represented as admirable horsemen, and always on horseback; mounted on fleet and hardy steeds, the wild race of the prairies. With these they roam the great plains that extend about the Arkansas, the Red River, and through Texas, to the Rocky Mountains; sometimes engaged in hunting the deer and buffalo, sometimes in warlike and predatory expeditions; for, like their counterparts, the sons of Ishmael, their hand is against every one, and every one's hand against them. Some of them have no fixed habitation, but dwell in tents of skins, easily packed up and transported, so that they are here to-day, and away, no one knows where, to-morrow.

One of the veteran hunters gave several anecdotes of their mode of fighting Luckless, according to his account, is the band of weary traders or hunters descried by them, in the midst of a prairie. Sometimes, they will steal upon them by stratagem, hanging with one leg over the saddle, and their bodies concealed; so that their troop at a distance has the appearance of a gang of wild horses. When they have thus gained sufficiently upon the enemy, they will suddenly raise themselves in their saddles, and come like a rushing blast, all fluttering with feathers, shaking their mantles, brandishing their weapons, and making hideous yells. In this way, they seek to strike a panic into the horses, and put them to the scamper, when they will pursue and carry them off in triumph.

The best mode of defence, according to this veteran woodsman, is to get into the covert of some wood, or thicket; or if there be none at hand, to dismount, tie the horses firmly head to head in a circle, so that they cannot break away and scatter, and resort to the shelter of a ravine, or make a hollow in the sand, where they may be screened from the shafts of the Pawnees. The latter chiefly use the bow and arrow, and are dexterous archers; circling round and round their enemy, and launching their arrows when at full speed. They are chiefly formidable on the prairies, where they have free career for their horses, and no trees to turn aside their arrows. They will rarely follow a flying enemy into the forest.

Several anecdotes, also, were given, of the secrecy and caution with which they will follow, and hang about the camp of an enemy, seeking a favorable moment for plunder or attack.

"We must now begin to keep a sharp look-out," said the Captain. "I must issue written orders, that no man shall hunt without leave, or fire off a gun, on pain of riding a wooden horse with a sharp back. I have a wild crew of young fellows, unaccustomed to frontier service. It will be difficult to teach them caution. We are now in the land of a silent, watchful, crafty people, who, when we least suspect it, may be around us, spying out all our movements, and ready to pounce upon all stragglers."

"How will you be able to keep your men from firing, if they see game while strolling round the camp?" asked one of the rangers.

"They must not take their guns with them unless they are on duty, or have permission."

"Ah, Captain!" cried the ranger, "that will never do for me. Where I go, my rifle goes. I never like to leave it behind; it's like a part of myself. There's no one will take such care of it as I, and there's nothing will take such care of me as my rifle."

"There's truth in all that," said the Captain, touched by a true hunter's sympathy. "I've had my rifle pretty nigh as long as I have had my wife, and a faithful friend it has been to me."

Here the Doctor, who is as keen a hunter as the Captain, joined in the conversation: "A neighbor of mine says, next to my rifle, I'd as leave lend you my wife."

"There's few," observed the Captain, "that take care of their rifles as they ought to be taken care of."

"Or of their wives either," replied the Doctor, with a wink.

"That's a fact," rejoined the Captain.

Word was now brought that a party of four rangers, headed by "Old Ryan," were missing. They had separated from the main body, on the opposite side of the river, when searching for a ford, and had straggled off, nobody knew whither. Many conjectures were made about them, and some apprehensions expressed for their safety.

"I should send to look after them," said the Captain, "but old Ryan is with them, and he knows how to take care of himself and of them too. If it were not for him, I would not give much for the rest; but he is as much at home in the woods or on a prairie, as he would be in his own farmyard. He's never lost, wherever he is. There's a good gang of them to stand by one another; four to watch and one to take care of the fire."

"It's a dismal thing to get lost at night in a strange and wild country," said one of the younger rangers.

"Not if you have one or two in company," said an older one. "For my part, I could feel as cheerful in this hollow as in my own home, if I had but one comrade to take turns to watch and keep the fire going. I could lie here for hours, and gaze up to that blazing star there, that seems to look down into the camp as if it were keeping guard over it."

"Aye, the stars are a kind of company to one, when you have to keep watch alone. That's a cheerful star, too, somehow; that's the evening star, the planet Venus they call it, I think."

"If that's the planet Venus," said one of the council, who, I believe, was the psalm-singing schoolmaster, "it bodes us no good; for I recollect reading in some book that the Pawnees worship that star, and sacrifice their prisoners to it. So I should not feel the better for the sight of that star in this part of the country."

"Well," said the sergeant, a thorough-bred woodsman, "star or no star, I have passed many a night alone in a wilder place than this, and slept sound too, I'll warrant you. Once, however, I had rather an uneasy time of it. I was belated in passing through a tract of wood, near the Tombigbee River; so I struck a light, made a fire, and turned my horse loose, while I stretched myself to sleep. By and by, I heard the wolves howl. My horse came crowding near me for protection, for he was terribly frightened. I drove him off, but he returned, and drew nearer and nearer, and stood looking at me and at the fire, and dozing, and nodding, and tottering on his fore feet, for he was powerful tired. After a while, I heard a strange dismal cry. I thought at first it might be an owl. I heard it again, and then I knew it was not an owl, but must be a panther. I felt rather awkward, for I had no weapon but a double-bladed penknife. I however prepared for defence in the best way I could, and piled up small brands from the fire, to pepper him with, should he come nigh The company of my horse now seemed a comfort to me; the poor creature laid down beside me and soon fell asleep, being so tired. I kept watch, and nodded and dozed, and started awake, and looked round, expecting to see the glaring eyes of the panther close upon me; but somehow or other, fatigue got the better of me, and I fell asleep outright. In the morning I found the tracks of a panther within sixty paces. They were as large as my two fists. He had evidently been walking backwards and forwards, trying to make up his mind to attack me; but luckily, he had not courage."

Oct. 16. I awoke before daybreak. The moon was shining feebly down into the glen, from among light drifting clouds; the camp fires were nearly burnt out, and the men lying about them, wrapped in blankets. With the first streak of day, our huntsman, Beatte, with Antoine, the young half-breed, set off to recross the river, in search of the stray horses, in company with several rangers who had left their rifles on the opposite shore. As the ford was deep, and they were obliged to cross in a diagonal line, against a rapid current, they had to be mounted on the tallest and strongest horses.

By eight o'clock, Beatte returned. He had found the horses, but had lost Antoine. The latter, he said, was a boy, a greenhorn, that knew nothing of the woods. He had wandered out of sight of him, and got lost. However, there were plenty more for him to fall in company with, as some of the rangers had gone astray also, and old Ryan and his party had not returned.

We waited until the morning was somewhat advanced, in nopes of being rejoined by the stragglers, but they did not make their appearance. The Captain observed, that the Indians on the opposite side of the river, were all well disposed to the whites; so that no serious apprehensions need be entertained for the safety of the missing. The greatest danger was, that their horses might be stolen in the night by straggling Osages. He determined, therefore, to proceed, leaving a rear-guard in the camp, to await their arrival.

I sat on a rock that overhung the spring at the upper part of the dell, and amused myself by watching the changing scene before me. First, the preparations for departure. Horses driven in from the purlieus of the camp; rangers riding about among rocks and bushes in quest of others that had strayed to a distance; the bustle of packing up camp equipage, and the clamor after kettles and frying-pans borrowed by one mess from another, mixed up with oaths and exclamations at restive horses, or others that had wandered away to graze after being packed: among which the voice of our little Frenchman, Tonish, was particularly to be distinguished.

The bugle sounded the signal to mount and march. The troop filed off in irregular line down the glen, and through the open forest, winding and gradually disappearing among the trees, though the clamor of voices and the notes of the bugle could be heard for some time afterwards. The rear-guard remained under the trees in the lower part of the dell, some on horseback, with their rifles on their shoulders; others seated by the fire or lying on the ground, gossiping in a low, lazy tone of voice their horses unsaddled, standing and dozing around: while one of the rangers, profiting by this interval of leisure, was shaving himself before a pocket mirror stuck against the trunk of a tree.

The clamor of voices and the notes of the bugle at length died away, and the glen relapsed into quiet and silence, broken occasionally by the low murmuring tone of the group around the fire, or the pensive whistle of some laggard among the trees; or the rustling of the yellow leaves, which the lightest breath of air brought down in wavering showers, a sign of the departing glories of the year.

CHAPTER XIV.

DEER-SHOOTING.—LIFE ON THE PRAIRIES.—BEAUTIFUL ENCAMPMENT —HUNTER'S LUCK.—ANECDOTES OF THE DELAWARES AND THEIR SUPERSTITIONS.

HAVING passed through the skirt of woodland bordering the river, we ascended the hills, taking a westerly course through an undulating country of "oak openings," where the eye stretched over wide tracts of hill and dale, diversified by forests, groves, and clumps of trees. As we were proceeding at a slow pace, those who were at the head of the line descried four deer grazing on a grassy slope about half a mile distant. They apparently had not perceived our approach, and continued to graze in perfect tranquillity. A young ranger obtained permission from the Captain to go in pursuit of them, and the troop halted in lengthened line, watching him in silence. Walking his horse slowly and cautiously, he made a circuit until a screen of wood intervened between him and the deer. Dismounting then, he left his horse among the trees, and creeping round a knoll, was hidden from our view. We now kept our eyes intently fixed on the deer, which continued grazing, unconscious of their danger. Presently there was the sharp report of a rifle; a fine buck made a convulsive bound and fell to the earth; his companions scampered off. Immediately our whole line of march was broken; there was a helter-skelter galloping of the youngsters of the troop, eager to get a shot at the fugitives; and one of the most conspicuous personages in the chase was our little Frenchman Tonish on his silver-gray; having abandoned his pack-horses at the first sight of the deer. It was some time before our scattered forces could be recalled by the bugle, and our march resumed.

Two or three times in the course of the day we were interrupted by hurry-scurry scenes of the kind. The young men of the troop were full of excitement on entering an unexplored country abounding in game, and they were too little accustomed to discipline or restraint to be kept in order. No one, however, was more unmanageable than Tonish. Having an intense conceit of his skill as a hunter, and an irrepressible passion for display, he was continually sallying forth, like an ill-broken hound, whenever any game was started, and had as often to be whipped back.

At length his curiosity got a salutary check. A fat doe came bounding along in full view of the whole line. Tonish dismounted, levelled his rifle, and had a fair shot. The doe kept on. He sprang upon his horse, stood up on the saddle like a posture-master, and continued gazing after the animal as if certain to see it fall. The doe, however, kept on its way rejoicing; a laugh broke out along the line, the little Frenchman slipped quietly into his saddle, began to belabor and blaspheme the wandering pack-horses, as if they had been to blame, and for some time we were relieved from his vaunting and vaporing.

In one place of our march we came to the remains of an old Indian encampment, on the banks of a fine stream, with the moss-grown skulls of deer lying here and there about it. As we were in the Pawnee country, it was supposed, of course, to have been a camp of those formidable rovers; the Doctor, however, after considering the shape and disposition of the lodges, pronounced it the camp of some bold Delawares, who had probably made a brief and dashing excursion into these dangerous hunting grounds.

Having proceeded some distance further, we observed a couple of figures on horseback, slowly moving parallel to us along the edge of a naked hill about two miles distant; and apparently reconnoitring us. There was a halt, and much gazing and conjecturing. Were they Indians? If Indians, were they Pawnees? There is something exciting to the imagination and stirring to the feelings, while traversing these hostile plains, in seeing a horseman prowling along the horizon. It is like descrying a sail at sea in time of war, when it may be either a privateer or a pirate. Our conjectures were soon set at rest by reconnoitring the two horsemen through a small spy-glass, when they proved to be two of the men we had left at the camp, who had set out to rejoin us, and had wandered from the track.

Our march this day was animating and delightful. We were in a region of adventure; breaking our way through a country hitherto untrodden by white men, excepting perchance by some solitary trapper. The weather was in its perfection, temperate, genial and enlivening; a deep blue sky with a few light feathery clouds, an atmosphere of perfect transparency, an air pure and bland, and a glorious country spreading out far and wide in the golden sunshine of an autumnal day; but all silent, lifeless, without a human habitation, and apparently without a human inhabitant! It was as if a ban hung over this fair but fated region. The very Indians dared not abide here, but made it a mere scene of perilous enterprise, to hunt for a few days, and then away.

After a march of about fifteen miles west we encamped in a beautiful peninsula, made by the windings and doublings of a deep, clear, and almost motionless brook, and covered by an open grove of lofty and magnificent trees. Several hunters immediately started forth in quest of game before the noise of the camp should frighten it from the vicinity. Our man, Beatte, also took his rifle and went forth alone, in a different course from the rest.

For my own part, I laid on the grass under the trees, and built castles in the clouds, and indulged in the very luxury of rural repose. Indeed I can scarcely conceive a kind of life more calculated to put both mind and body in a healthful tone. A morning's ride of several hours diversified by hunting incidents; an encampment in the afternoon under some noble grove on the borders of a stream; an evening banquet of venison, fresh killed, roasted, or broiled on the coals; turkeys just from the thickets and wild honey from the trees; and all relished with an appetite unknown to the gourmets of the cities. And at night—such sweet sleeping in the open air, or waking and gazing at the moon and stars, shining between the trees!

On the present occasion, however, we had not much reason to boast of our larder. But one deer had been killed during the day, and none of that had reached our lodge. We were fain, therefore, to stay our keen appetites by some scraps of turkey brought from the last encampment, eked out with a slice or two of salt pork. This scarcity, however, did not continue long. Before dark a young hunter returned well laden with spoil. He had shot a deer, cut it up in an artist-like style, and, putting the meat in a kind of sack made of the hide, had slung it across his shoulder and trudged with it to camp.

Not long after, Beatte made his appearance with a fat doe across his horse. It was the first game he had brought in, and I was glad to see him with a trophy that might efface the memory of the polecat. He laid the carcass down by our fire without saying a word, and then turned to unsaddle his horse; nor could any questions from us about his hunting draw from him more than laconic replies. If Beatte, however, observed this Indian taciturnity about what he had done, Tonish made up for it by boasting of what he meant to do. Now that we were in a good hunting country he meant to take the field. and, if we would take his word for it, our lodge would henceforth be overwhelmed with game. Luckily his talking did not prevent his working, the doe was skilfully dissected, several fat ribs roasted before the fire, the coffee kettle replenished, and in a little while we were enabled to indemnify ourselves luxuriously for our late meagre repast.

The Captain did not return until late, and he returned empty handed. He had been in pursuit of his usual game, the deer, when he came upon the tracks of a gang of about sixty elk. Having never killed an animal of the kind, and the elk being at this moment an object of ambition among all the veteran hunters of the camp, he abandoned his pursuit of the deer, and followed the newly-discovered track. After some time he came in sight of the elk, and had several fair chances of a shot, but was anxious to bring down a large buck which kept in the advance. Finding at length there was danger of the whole gang escaping him, he fired at a doe. The shot took effect, but the animal had sufficient strength to keep on for a time with its companions. From the tracks of blood he felt confident it was mortally wounded, but evening came on, he could not keep the trail, and had to give up the search until morning.

Old Ryan and his little band had not yet rejoined us, neither had our young half-breed Antoine made his appearance. It was determined, therefore, to remain at our encampment for the following day, to give time for all stragglers to arrive.

The conversation this evening, among the old huntsmen, turned upon the Delaware tribe, one of whose encampments we had passed in the course of the day; and anecdotes were given of their prowess in war and dexterity in hunting. They used to be deadly foes of the Osages, who stood in great awe of their desperate valor, though they were apt to attribute it to a whimsical cause. "Look at the Delawares," would they say, "dey got short leg—no can run—must stand and fight a great heap." In fact the Delawares are rather short legged, while the Osages are remarkable for length of limb.

The expeditions of the Delawares, whether of war or hunting, are wide and fearless; a small band of them will penetrate far into these dangerous and hostile wilds, and will push their encampments even to the Rocky Mountains. This daring temper may be in some measure encouraged by one of the superstitions of their creed. They believe that a guardian spirit, in the form of a great eagle, watches over them, hovering in the sky, far out of sight. Sometimes, when well pleased with them, he wheels down into the lower regions, and may be seen circling with wide-spread wings against the white clouds; at such times the seasons are propitious, the corn grows finely, and they have great success in hunting. Sometimes, however, he is angry, and then he vents his rage in the thunder, which is his voice, and the lightning, which is the flashing of his eye, and strikes dead the object of his displeasure.

The Delawares make sacrifices to this spirit, who occasionally lets drop a feather from his wing in token of satisfaction. These feathers render the wearer invisible, and invulnerable. Indeed, the Indians generally consider the feathers of the eagle possessed of occult and sovereign virtues.

At one time a party of the Delawares, in the course of a bold excursion into the Pawnee hunting grounds, were surrounded on one of the great plains, and nearly destroyed. The remnant took refuge on the summit of one of those isolated and conical hills which rise almost like artificial mounds, from the midst of the prairies. Here the chief warrior, driven almost to despair, sacrificed his horse to the tutelar spirit. Suddenly an enormous eagle, rushing down from the sky, bore off the victim in his talons, and mounting into the air, dropped a quill feather from his wing. The chief caught it up with joy, bound it to his forehead, and, leading his followers down the hill, cut his way through the enemy with great slaughter, and without any one of his party receiving a wound.

CHAPTER XV.

THE SEARCH FOR THE ELK.—PAWNEE STORIES.

With the morning dawn, the prime hunters of the camp were all on the alert, and set off in different directions, to beat up the country for game. The Captain's brother, Sergeant Bean, was among the first, and returned before breakfast with success, having killed a fat doe, almost within the purlieus of the camp.

When breakfast was over, the Captain mounted his horse, to

go in quest of the elk which he had wounded on the preceding evening; and which, he was persuaded, had received its death wound. I determined to join him in the search, and we accordingly sallied forth together, accompanied also by his brother, the sergeant, and a lieutenant. Two rangers followed on foot, to bring home the carcass of the doe which the sergeant had killed. We had not ridden far, when we came to where it lay, on the side of a hill, in the midst of a beautiful woodland scene. The two rangers immediately fell to work, with true hunters' skill to dismember it, and prepare it for transportation to the camp, while we continued on our course. We passed along sloping hill sides, among skirts of thicket and scattered forest trees, until we came to a place where the long herbage was pressed down with numerous elk beds. Here the Captain had first roused the gang of elks, and, after looking about diligently for a little while, he pointed out their "trail," the foot-prints of which were as large as those of horned cattle. He now put himself upon the track, and went quietly forward, the rest of us following him in Indian file. At length he halted at the place where the elk had been when shot at. Spots of blood on the surrounding herbage showed that the shot had been effective. The wounded animal had evidently kept for some distance with the rest of the herd, as could be seen by sprinklings of blood here and there, on the shrubs and weeds bordering the trail. These at length suddenly disappeared. "Somewhere hereabout," said the Captain, "the elk must have turned off from the gang. Whenever they feel themselves mortally wounded, they will turn aside, and seek some out-of-the-way place to die alone."

There was something in this picture of the last moments of a wounded deer, to touch the sympathies of one not hardened to the gentle disports of the chase; such sympathies, however, are but transient. Man is naturally an animal of prey; and, however changed by civilization, will readily relapse into his instinct for destruction. I found my ravenous and sanguinary propensities daily growing stronger upon the prairies.

After looking about for a little while, the Captain succeeded in finding the separate trail of the wounded elk, which turned off almost at right angles from that of the herd, and entered an open forest of scattered trees. The traces of blood became more faint and rare, and occurred at greater distances: at length they ceased altogether, and the ground was so hard, and the herbage so much parched and withered, that the foot-prints of the animal could no longer be perceived.

"The elk must lie somewhere in this neighborhood," said the Captain, "as you may know by those turkey-buzzards wheeling about in the air: for they always hover in that way above some carcass. However, the dead elk cannot get away, so let us follow the trail of the living ones: they may have halted at no great distance, and we may find them grazing, and get another crack at them."

We accordingly returned, and resumed the trail of the elks, which led us a straggling course over hill and dale, covered with scattered oaks. Every now and then we would catch a glimpse of a deer bounding away across some glade of the forest, but the Captain was not to be diverted from his elk hunt by such inferior game. A large flock of wild turkeys, too, were roused by the trampling of our horses; some scampered off as fast as their long legs could carry them; others fluttered up into the trees, where they remained with outstretched necks, gazing at us. The Captain would not allow a rifle to be discharged at them, lest it should alarm the elk, which he hoped to find in the vicinity. At length we came to where the forest ended in a steep bank, and the Red Fork wound its way below us, between broad sandy shores. The trail descended the bank, and we could trace it, with our eyes, across the level sands, until it terminated in the river, which, it was evident, the gang had forded on the preceding evening.

"It is needless to follow on any further," said the Captain. "The elk must have been much frightened, and, after crossing the river, may have kept on for twenty miles without stopping."

Our little party now divided, the lieutenant and sergeant making a circuit in quest of game, and the Captain and myself taking the direction of the camp. On our way, we came to a buffalo track, more than a year old. It was not wider than an ordinary footpath, and worn deep into the soil; for these animals follow each other in single file. Shortly afterwards, we met two rangers on foot, hunting. They had wounded an elk, but he had escaped; and in pursuing him, had found the one shot by the Captain on the preceding evening. They turned back, and conducted us to it. It was a noble animal, as large as a yearling heifer, and lay in an open part of the forest, about a mile and a half distant from the place where it had been shot. The turkey-buzzards, which we had previously noticed, were wheeling in the air above it. The observation of the Captain seemed verified. The poor animal, as life was ebbing away, had apparently abandoned its unhurt companions, and turned aside to die alone.

The Captain and the two rangers forthwith fell to work, with their hunting-knives, to flay and cut up the carcass. It was already tainted on the inside, but ample collops were cut from the ribs and haunches, and laid in a heap on the outstretched hide

Holes were then cut along the border of the hide, raw thongs were passed through them, and the whole drawn up like a sack, which was swung behind the Captain's saddle. All this while, the turkey-buzzards were soaring overhead, waiting for our departure, to swoop down and banquet on the carcass.

The wreck of the poor elk being thus dismantled, the Captain and myself mounted our horses, and jogged back to the camp, while the two rangers resumed their hunting.

On reaching the camp, I found there our young half-breed, Antoine. After separating from Beatte, in the search after the stray horses on the other side of the Arkansas, he had fallen upon a wrong track, which he followed for several miles, when he overtook old Ryan and his party, and found he had been following their traces.

They all forded the Arkansas about eight miles above our crossing place, and found their way to our late encampment in the glen, where the rear-guard we had left behind was waiting for them. Antoine, being well mounted, and somewhat impatient to rejoin us, had pushed on alone, following our trail, to our present encampment, and bringing the carcass of a young bear which he had killed.

Our camp, during the residue of the day, presented a mingled picture of bustle and repose. Some of the men were busy round the fires, jerking and roasting venison and bear's meat, to be packed up as a future supply. Some were stretching and dressing the skins of the animals they had killed; others were washing their clothes in the brook, and hanging them on the bushes to dry; while many were lying on the grass, and lazily gossiping in the shade. Every now and then a hunter would return, on horseback or on foot, laden with game, or empty handed. Those who brought home any spoil, deposited it at the Captain's fire, and then filed off to their respective messes, to relate their day's exploits to their companions. The game killed at this camp consisted of six deer, one elk, two bears, and six or eight turkeys.

During the last two or three days, since their wild Indian achievement in navigating the river, our retainers had risen in consequence among the rangers; and now I found Tonish making himself a complete oracle among some of the raw and inexperienced recruits, who had never been in the wilderness. He had continually a knot hanging about him, and listening to his extravagant tales about the Pawnees, with whom he pretended to have had fearful encounters. His representations, in fact, were calculated to inspire his hearers with an awful idea of the foe into whose lands they were intruding. According to his accounts, the rifle of the white man was no match for the bow and arrow of the Pawnee. When the rifle was once discharged, it took time and trouble to load it again, and in the mean time the enemy could keep on launching his shafts as fast as he could draw his bow. Then the Pawnee, according to Tonish, could shoot, with unerring aim, three hundred yards, and send his arrow clean through and through a buffalo; nay, he had known a Pawnee shaft pass through one buffalo and wound another. And then the way the Pawnees sheltered themselves from the shots of their enemy: they would hang with one leg over the saddle, crouching their bodies along the opposite side of their horse, and would shoot their arrows from under his neck, while at full speed!

If Tonish was to be believed, there was peril at every step in these debateable grounds of the Indian tribes. Pawnees lurked unseen among the thickets and ravines. They had their scouts and sentinels on the summit of the mounds which command a view over the prairies, where they lay crouched in the tall grass; only now and then raising their heads to watch the movements of any war or hunting party that might be passing in lengthened line below. At night, they would lurk round an encampment; crawling through the grass, and imitating the movements of a wolf, so as to deceive the sentinel on the outpost, until, having arrived sufficiently near, they would speed an arrow through his heart, and retreat undiscovered. In telling his stories, Tonish would appeal from time to time to Beatte, for the truth of what he said; the only reply would be a nod or shrug of the shoulders; the latter being divided in mind between a distaste for the gasconading spirit of his comrade, and a sovereign contempt for the inexperience of the young rangers in all that he considered true knowledge.

CHAPTER XVI.

A SICK CAMP.—THE MARCH.—THE DISABLED HORSE.—OLD RYAN AND THE STRAGGLERS.—SYMPTOMS OF CHANGE OF WEATHER, AND CHANGE OF HUMORS.

Oct. 18. We prepared to march at the usual hour, but word was brought to the Captain that three of the rangers, who had been attacked with the measles, were unable to proceed, and that another one was missing. The last was an old frontiersman, by the name of Sawyer, who had gained years without experience;

and having sallied forth to hunt, on the preceding day, had probably lost his way on the prairies. A guard of ten men was, therefore, left to take care of the sick, and wait for the straggler. If the former recovered sufficiently in the course of two or three days, they were to rejoin the main body, otherwise to be escorted back to the garrison.

Taking our leave of the sick camp, we shaped our course westward, along the heads of small streams, all wandering, in deep ravines, towards the Red Fork. The land was high and undulating, or "rolling," as it is termed in the West; with a poor hungry soil mingled with the sandstone, which is unusual in this part of the country, and checkered with harsh forests of post-oak and black-jack.

In the course of the morning, I received a lesson on the importance of being chary of one's steed on the prairies. The one I rode surpassed in action most horses of the troop, and was of great mettle and a generous spirit. In crossing the deep ravines, he would scramble up the steep banks like a cat, and was always for leaping the narrow runs of water. I was not aware of the imprudence of indulging him in such exertions, until, in leaping him across a small brook, I felt him immediately falter beneath me. He limped forward a short distance, but soon fell stark lame, having sprained his shoulder. What was to be done? He could not keep up with the troop, and was too valuable to be abandoned on the prairie. The only alternative was to send him back to join the invalids in the sick camp, and to share their fortunes. Nobody, however, seemed disposed to lead him back, although I offered a liberal reward. Either the stories of Tonish about the Pawnees had spread an apprehension of lurking foes, and imminent perils on the prairies; or there was a fear of missing the trail and getting lost. At length two young men stepped forward and agreed to go in company, so that, should they be benighted on the prairies, there might be one to watch while the other slept.

The horse was accordingly consigned to their care, and I looked after him with a rueful eye, as he limped off, for it seemed as if, with him, all strength and buoyancy had departed from me.

I looked round for a steed to supply his place, and fixed my eyes upon the gallant gray which I had transferred at the Agency to Tonish. The moment, however, that I hinted about his dismounting and taking up with the supernumerary pony, the little varlet broke out into vociferous remonstrances and lamentations, gasping and almost strangling, in his eagerness to give vent to them. I saw that to unhorse him would be to prostrate his spirit and cut his vanity to the quick. I had not the heart to inflict such a wound, or to bring down the poor devil from his transient vainglory; so I left him in possession of his gallant gray; and contented myself with shifting my saddle to the jaded pony.

I was now sensible of the complete reverse to which a horseman is exposed on the prairies. I felt how completely the spirit of the rider depended upon his steed. I had hitherto been able to make excursions at will from the line, and to gallop in pursuit of any object of interest or curiosity. I was now reduced to the tone of the jaded animal I bestrode, and doomed to plod on patiently and slowly after my file leader. Above all, I was made conscious how unwise it is, on expeditions of the kind, where a man's life may depend upon the strength, and speed, and freshness of his horse, to task the generous animal by any unnecessary exertion of his powers.

I have observed that the wary and experienced huntsman and traveller of the prairies is always sparing of his horse, when on a journey; never, except in emergency, putting him off of a walk. The regular journeyings of frontiersmen and Indians, when on a long march, seldom exceed above fifteen miles a day, and are generally about ten or twelve, and they never indulge in capricious galloping. Many of those, however, with whom I was travelling were young and inexperienced, and full of excitement at finding themselves in a country abounding with game. It was impossible to retain them in the sobriety of a march, or to keep them to the line. As we broke our way through the coverts and ravines, and the deer started up and scampered off to the right and left, the rifle balls would whiz after them, and our young hunters dash off in pursuit. At one time they made a grand burst after what they supposed to be a gang of bears, but soon pulled up on discovering them to be black wolves, prowling in company.

After a march of about twelve miles we encamped, a little after mid-day, on the borders of a brook which loitered through a deep ravine. In the course of the afternoon old Ryan, the Nestor of the camp, made his appearance, followed by his little band of stragglers. He was greeted with joyful acclamations, which showed the estimation in which he was held by his brother woodmen. The little band came laden with venison; a fine haunch of which the veteran hunter laid, as a present, by the Captain's fire.

Our men, Beatte and Tonish, both sallied forth, early in the afternoon, to hunt. Towards evening the former returned, with a fine buck across his horse. He laid it down, as usual, in silence, and proceeded to unsaddle and turn his horse loose.

Tonish came back without any game, but with much more glory; having made several capital shots, though unluckily the wounded deer had all escaped him.

There was an abundant supply of meat in the camp; for besides other game, three elk had been killed. The wary and veteran woodmen were all busy jerking meat, against a time of scarcity; the less experienced revelled in present abundance, leaving the morrow to provide for itself.

On the following morning, (Oct. 19,) I succeeded in changing my pony and a reasonable sum of money for a strong and active horse. It was a great satisfaction to find myself once more tolerably well mounted. I perceived, however, that there would be little difficulty in making a selection from among the troop, for the rangers had all that propensity for "swapping," or, as they term it, "trading," which pervades the West. In the course of our expedition, there was scarce a horse, rifle, powder-horn, or blanket, that did not change owners several times; and one keen "trader" boasted of having by dint of frequent bargains changed a bad horse into a good one, and put a hundred dollars in his pocket.

The morning was lowering and sultry, with low muttering of distant thunder. The change of weather had its effect upon the spirits of the troop. The camp was unusually sober and quiet; there was none of the accustomed farmyard melody of crowing and cackling at daybreak; none of the bursts of merriment, the loud jokes and banterings, that had commonly prevailed during the bustle of equipment. Now and then might be heard a short strain of a song, a faint laugh, or a solitary whistle; but, in general, every one went silently and doggedly about the duties of the camp, or the preparations for departure.

When the time arrived to saddle and mount, five horses were reported as missing; although all the woods and thickets had been beaten up for some distance round the camp. Several rangers were dispatched to "skir" the country round in quest of them. In the meantime, the thunder continued to growl, and we had a passing shower. The horses, like their riders, were affected by the change of weather. They stood here and there about the camp, some saddled and bridled, others loose, but all spiritless and dozing, with stooping head, one hind leg partly drawn up so as to rest on the point of the hoof, and the whole hide reeking with the rain, and sending up wreaths of vapor. The men, too, waited in listless groups the return of their comrades who had gone in quest of the horses; now and then turning up an anxious eye to the drifting clouds, which boded an approaching storm. Gloomy weather inspires gloomy thoughts. Some expressed fears that we were dogged by some party of Indians, who had stolen the horses in the night. The most prevalent apprehension, however, was, that they had returned on their traces to our last encampment, or had started off on a direct line for Fort Gibson. In this respect, the instinct of horses is said to resemble that of the pigeon. They will strike for home by a direct course, passing through tracts of wilderness which they have never before traversed.

After delaying until the morning was somewhat advanced, a lieutenant with a guard was appointed to await the return of the rangers, and we set off on our day's journey, considerably reduced in numbers; much, as I thought, to the discomposure of some of the troop, who intimated that we might prove too weak-handed, in case of an encounter with the Pawnees.

CHAPTER XVII.

THUNDER-STORM ON THE PRAIRIES.—THE STORM ENCAMPMENT.—NIGHT SCENE.—INDIAN STORIES.—A FRIGHTENED HORSE.

OUR march for a part of the day, lay a little to the south of west through straggling forests of the kind of low scrubbed trees already mentioned, called "post-oaks," and "black-jacks." The soil of these "oak barrens" is loose and unsound; being little better at times than a mere quicksand, in which, in rainy weather, the horse's hoof slips from side to side, and now and then sinks in a rotten, spongy turf, to the fetlock. Such was the case at present in consequence of successive thunder-showers, through which we draggled along in dogged silence. Several deer were roused by our approach, and scudded across the forest glades; but no one, as formerly, broke the line of march to pursue them. At one time, we passed the bones and horns of a buffalo, and at another time a buffalo track, not above three days old. These signs of the vicinity of this grand game of the prairies, had a reviving effect on the spirits of our huntsmen; but it was of transient duration.

In crossing a prairie of moderate extent, rendered little better than a slippery bog by the recent showers, we were overtaken by a violent thunder-gust. The rain came rattling upon us in torrents, and spattered up like steam along the ground; the whole landscape was suddenly wrapped in gloom that gave a vivid effect to the intense sheets of lightning, while the thunder seemed to burst over our very heads, and was reverberated by the groves and forests that checkered and skirted the prairie. Man and beast were so pelted, drenched, and confounded, that the line was thrown in complete confusion; some of the horses were so frightened as to be almost unmanageable, and our scattered cavalcade looked like a tempest-tossed fleet, driving hither and thither, at the mercy of wind and wave.

At length, at half past two o'clock, we came to a halt, and gathering together our forces, encamped in an open and lofty grove, with a prairie on one side and a stream on the other. The forest immediately rang with the sound of the axe, and the crash of falling trees. Huge fires were soon blazing; blankets were stretched before them, by way of tents; booths were hastily reared of bark and skins; every fire had its group drawn close round it, drying and warming themselves, or preparing a comforting meal. Some of the rangers were discharging and cleaning their rifles, which had been exposed to the rain; while the horses, relieved from their saddles and burdens, rolled in the wet grass.

The showers continued from time to time, until late in the evening. Before dark, our horses were gathered in and tethered about the skirts of the camp, within the outposts, through fear of Indian prowlers, who are apt to take advantage of stormy nights for their depredations and assaults. As the night thickened, the huge fires became more and more luminous; lighting up masses of the overhanging foliage, and leaving other parts of the grove in deep gloom. Every fire had its goblin group around it, while the tethered horses were dimly seen, like spectres, among the thickets; excepting that here and there a gray one stood out in bright relief.

The grove, thus fitfully lighted up by the ruddy glare of the fires. resembled a vast leafy dome, walled in by opaque darkness;

but every now and then two or three quivering flashes of lightning in quick succession, would suddenly reveal a vast champaign country, where fields and forests, and running streams, would start, as it were, into existence for a few brief seconds, and, before the eye could ascertain them, vanish again into gloom.

A thunder-storm on a prairie, as upon the ocean, derives grandeur and sublimity from the wild and boundless waste over which it rages and bellows. It is not surprising that these awful phenomena of nature should be objects of superstitious reverence to the poor savages, and that they should consider the thunder the angry voice of the Great Spirit. As our half-breeds sat gossiping round the fire, I drew from them some of the notions entertained on the subject by their Indian friends. The latter declare that extinguished thunderbolts are sometimes picked up by hunters on the prairies, who use them for the heads of arrows and lances, and that any warrior thus armed is invincible. Should a thunder-storm occur, however, during battle, he is liable to be carried away by the thunder, and never heard of more.

A warrior of the Konza tribe, hunting on a prairie, was overtaken by a storm, and struck down senseless by the thunder. On recovering, he beheld the thunderbolt lying on the ground, and a horse standing beside it. Snatching up the bolt, he sprang upon the horse, but found, too late, that he was astride of the lightning. In an instant he was whisked away over prairies and forests, and streams and deserts, until he was flung senseless at the foot of the Rocky Mountains; whence, on recovering, it took him several months to return to his own people.

This story reminded me of an Indian tradition, related by a traveller, of the fate of a warrior who saw the thunder lying upon the ground, with a beautifully wrought moccason on each side of it. Thinking he had found a prize, he put on the moccasons; but they bore him away to the land of spirits, whence he never returned.

These are simple and artless tales, but they had a wild and romantic interest heard from the lips of half-savage narrators, round a hunter's fire, in a stormy night, with a forest on one side, and a howling waste on the other; and where, peradventure, savage foes might be lurking in the outer darkness.

Our conversation was interrupted by a loud clap of thunder, followed immediately by the sound of a horse galloping off madly into the waste. Every one listened in mute silence. The hoofs resounded vigorously for a time, but grew fainter and fainter, until they died away in remote distance.

When the sound was no longer to be heard, the listeners turned to conjecture what could have caused this sudden scamper. Some thought the horse had been startled by the thunder; others, that some lurking Indian had galloped off with him. To this it was objected, that the usual mode with the Indians is to steal quietly upon the horse, take off his fetters, mount him gently, and walk him off as silently as possible, leading off others, without any unusual stir or noise to disturb the camp.

On the other hand, it was stated as a common practice with the Indians, to creep among a troop of horses when grazing at night, mount one quietly, and then start off suddenly at full speed. Nothing is so contagious among horses as a panic; one sudden break-away of this kind, will sometimes alarm the whole troop, and they will set off, helter-skelter, after the leader.

Every one who had a horse grazing on the skirts of the camp was uneasy, lest his should be the fugitive; but it was impossible to ascertain the fact until morning. Those who had tethered their horses felt more secure; though horses thus tied up, and limited to a short range at night, are apt to fall off in flesh and strength, during a long march; and many of the horses of the troop already gave signs of being wayworn.

After a gloomy and unruly night, the morning dawned bright and clear, and a glorious sunrise transformed the whole landscape, as if by magic. The late dreary wilderness brightened into a fine open country, with stately groves, and clumps of oaks of a gigantic size, some of which stood singly, as if planted for ornament and shade, in the midst of rich meadows; while our horses, scattered about, and grazing under them, gave to the whole the air of a noble park. It was difficult to realize the fact that we were so far in the wilds beyond the residence of man. Our encampment, alone, had a savage appearance; with its rude tents of skins and blankets, and its columns of blue smoke rising among the trees.

The first care in the morning, was to look after our horses. Some of them had wandered to a distance, but all were fortunately found; even the one whose clattering hoofs had caused such uneasiness in the night. He had come to a halt about a mile from the camp, and was found quietly grazing near a brook. The bugle sounded for departure about half past eight. As we were in greater risk of Indian molestation the farther we advanced, our line was formed with more precision than heretofore. Every one had his station assigned him, and was forbidden to leave it in pursuit of game, without special permission. The pack-horses were placed in the centre of the line, and a strong guard in the rear.

CHAPTER XVIII.

A GRAND PRAIRIE.—CLIFF CASTLE.—BUFFALO TRACKS.—DEER HUNTED BY WOLVES.—CROSS TIMBER.

After a toilsome march of some distance through a country cut up by ravines and brooks, and entangled by thickets, we emerged upon a grand prairie. Here one of the characteristic scenes of the Far West broke upon us. An immense extent of grassy, undulating, or, as it is termed, rolling country, with here and there a clump of trees, dimly seen in the distance like a ship at sea; the landscape deriving sublimity from its vastness and simplicity. To the southwest, on the summit of a hill, was a singular crest of broken rocks, resembling a ruined fortress. It reminded me of the ruin of some Moorish castle, crowning a height in the midst of a lonely Spanish landscape. To this hill we gave the name of Cliff Castle.

The prairies of these great hunting regions differed in the character of their vegetation from those through which I had hitherto passed. Instead of a profusion of tall flowering plants and long flaunting grasses, they were covered with a shorter growth of herbage called buffalo grass, somewhat coarse, but, at the proper seasons, affording excellent and abundant pasturage. At present it was growing wiry, and in many places was too much parched for grazing.

The weather was verging into that serene but somewhat arid season called the Indian Summer. There was a smoky haze in the atmosphere that tempered the brightness of the sunshine into a golden tint, softening the features of the landscape, and giving a vagueness to the outlines of distant objects. This haziness was daily increasing, and was attributed to the burning of distant prairies by the Indian hunting parties.

We had not gone far upon the prairie before we came to where deeply-worn footpaths were seen traversing the country; sometimes two or three would keep on parallel to each other, and but a few paces apart. These were pronounced to be traces of buffaloes, where large droves had passed. There were tracks also of horses, which were observed with some attention by our experienced hunters. They could not be the tracks of wild horses, as there were no prints of the hoofs of colts; all were full-grown. As the horses evidently were not shod, it was concluded they must belong to some hunting party of Pawnees. In the course of the morning, the tracks of a single horse, with shoes, were discovered. This might be the horse of a Cherokee hunter, or perhaps a horse stolen from the whites of the frontier. Thus, in traversing these perilous wastes, every footprint and dint of hoof becomes matter of cautious inspection and shrewd surmise; and the question continually is, whether it be the trace of friend or foe, whether of recent or ancient date, and whether the being that made it be out of reach, or liable to be encountered.

We were getting more and more into the game country: as we proceeded, we repeatedly saw deer to the right and left, bounding off for the coverts; but their appearance no longer excited the same eagerness to pursue. In passing along a slope of the prairie, between two rolling swells of land, we came in sight of a genuine natural hunting match. A pack of seven black wolves and one white one were in full chase of a buck, which they had nearly tired down. They crossed the line of our march without apparently perceiving us; we saw them have a fair run of nearly a mile, gaining upon the buck until they were leaping upon his haunches, when he plunged down a ravine. Some of our party galloped to a rising ground commanding a view of the ravine. The poor buck was completely beset, some on his flanks, some at his throat: he made two or three struggles and desperate bounds, but was dragged down, overpowered, and torn to pieces. The black wolves, in their ravenous hunger and fury, took no notice of the distant group of horsemen; but the white wolf, apparently less game, abandoned the prey, and scampered over hill and dale, rousing various deer that were crouched in the hollows, and which bounded off likewise in different directions. It was altogether a wild scene, worthy of the "hunting grounds."

We now came once more in sight of the Red Fork, winding its turbid course between well-wooded hills, and through a vast and magnificent landscape. The prairies bordering on the rivers are always varied in this way with woodland, so beautifully interspersed as to appear to have been laid out by the hand of taste; and they only want here and there a village spire, the battlements of a castle, or the turrets of an old family mansion rising from among the trees, to rival the most ornamented scenery of Europe.

About mid-day we reached the edge of that scattered belt of forest land, about forty miles in width, which stretches across the country from north to south, from the Arkansas to the Red River, separating the upper from the lower prairies, and commonly called the "Cross Timber." On the skirts of this forest land, just on the edge of a prairie, we found traces of a Pawnee encampment of between one and two hundred lodges, showing that the party must have been numerous. The skull of a buffalo lay near the camp, and the moss which had gathered on it proved that the encampment was at least a year old. About half a mile off we encamped in a beautiful grove, watered by a fine spring and rivulet. Our day's journey had been about fourteen miles.

In the course of the afternoon we were rejoined by two of Lieutenant King's party, which we had left behind a few days before, to look after stray horses. All the horses had been found, though some had wandered to the distance of several miles. The lieutenant, with seventeen of his companions, had remained at our last night's encampment to hunt, having come upon recent traces of buffalo. They had also seen a fine wild horse, which, however, had galloped off with a speed that defied pursuit.

Confident anticipations were now indulged, that on the following day we should meet with buffalo, and perhaps with wild horses, and every one was in spirits. We needed some excitement of the kind, for our young men were growing weary of marching and encamping under restraint, and provisions this day were scanty. The Captain and several of the rangers went out hunting, but brought home nothing but a small deer and a few turkeys. Our two men, Beatte and Tonish, likewise went out. The former returned with a deer athwart his horse, which, as usual, he laid down by our lodge, and said nothing. Tonish returned with no game, but with his customary budget of wonderful tales. Both he and the deer had done marvels. Not one had come within the lure of his rifle without being hit in a mortal part, yet, strange to say, every one had kept on his way without flinching. We all determined that, from the accuracy of his aim, Tonish must have shot with charmed balls, but that every deer had a charmed life. The most important intelligence brought by him, however, was, that he had seen the fresh tracks of several wild horses. He now considered himself upon the eve of great exploits, for there was nothing upon which he glorified himself more than his skill in horse-catching.

CHAPTER XIX.

HUNTERS' ANTICIPATIONS.—THE RUGGED FORD.—A WILD HORSE.

OCT. 21. This morning the camp was in a bustle at an early hour: the expectation of falling in with buffalo in the course of the day roused every one's spirit. There was a continual cracking of rifles, that they might be reloaded: the shot was drawn off from double-barrelled guns, and balls were substituted. Tonish, however, prepared chiefly for a campaign against wild horses. He took the field, with a coil of cordage hung at his saddle-bow, and a couple of white wands, something like fishing-rods, eight or ten feet in length, with forked ends. The coil of cordage thus used in hunting the wild horse, is called a lariat, and answers to the laso of South America. It is not flung, however, in the graceful and dexterous Spanish style. The hunter, after a hard chase, when he succeeds in getting almost head and head with the wild horse, hitches the running noose of the lariat over his head by means of the forked stick; then letting him have the full length of the cord, plays him like a fish, and chokes him into subjection.

All this Tonish promised to exemplify to our full satisfaction; we had not much confidence in his success, and feared he might knock up a good horse in a headlong gallop after a bad one: for, like all the French creoles, he was a merciless hard rider. It was determined, therefore, to keep a sharp eye upon him, and to check his sallying propensities.

We had not proceeded far on our morning's march, when we were checked by a deep stream, running along the bottom of a thickly-wooded ravine. After coasting it for a couple of miles we came to a fording place; but to get down to it was the difficulty, for the banks were steep and crumbling, and overgrown with forest trees, mingled with thickets, brambles, and grape-vines. At length the leading horseman broke his way through the thicket, and his horse, putting his feet together, slid down the black crumbling bank, to the narrow margin of the stream; then floundering across, with mud and water up to the saddle-girths, he scrambled up the opposite bank, and arrived safe on level ground. The whole line followed pell-mell after the leader, and pushing forward in close order, Indian file, they crowded each other down the bank and into the stream. Some of the horsemen missed the ford, and were soused over head and ears; one was unhorsed, and plumped head foremost into the middle of the stream: for my own part, while pressed forward, and hurried over the bank by those behind me, I was interrupted by a grape-vine, as thick as a cable, which hung in a festoon as low as the saddle-bow, and, dragging me from the saddle, threw me among the feet of the trampling horses. Fortunately, I escaped without injury, regained my steed, crossed the stream without further difficulty, and was enabled to join in the merriment occasioned by the ludicrous disasters of the fording.

It is at passes like this that occur the most dangerous ambuscades and sanguinary surprises of Indian warfare. A party of savages well placed among the thickets, might have made sad havoc among our men, while entangled in the ravine.

We now came out upon a vast and glorious prairie, spreading out beneath the golden beams of an autumnal sun. The deep and frequent traces of buffalo, showed it to be one of their favorite grazing grounds; yet none were to be seen. In the course of the morning, we were overtaken by the lieutenant and seventeen men, who had remained behind, and who came laden with the spoils of buffaloes; having killed three on the preceding day. One of the rangers, however, had little luck to boast of; his horse having taken fright at sight of the buffaloes, thrown his rider, and escaped into the woods.

The excitement of our hunters, both young and old, now rose almost to fever height; scarce any of them having ever encountered any of this far-famed game of the prairies. Accordingly, when in the course of the day the cry of buffalo! buffalo! rose from one part of the line, the whole troop were thrown in agitation. We were just then passing through a beautiful part of the prairie, finely diversified by hills and slopes, and woody dells, and high, stately groves. Those who had given the alarm, pointed out a large black-looking animal, slowly moving along the side of a rising ground, about two miles off. The ever-ready Tonish jumped up, and stood with his feet on the saddle, and his forked sticks in his hands, like a posture-master or scaramouch at a circus, just ready for a feat of horsemanship. After gazing at the animal for a moment, which he could have seen full as well without rising from his stirrups, he pronounced it a wild horse; and dropping again into his saddle, was about to dash off full tilt in pursuit, when, to his inexpressible chagrin, he was called back, and ordered to keep to his post, in rear of the baggage horses.

The Captain and two of his officers now set off to reconnoitre the game. It was the intention of the Captain, who was an admirable marksman, to endeavor to crease the horse; that is to say, to hit him with a rifle ball in the ridge of the neck. A wound of this kind paralyzes a horse for a moment; he falls to the ground, and may be secured before he recovers. It is a cruel expedient, however, for an ill-directed shot may kill or maim the noble animal.

As the Captain and his companions moved off laterally and slowly, in the direction of the horse, we continued our course forward; watching intently, however, the movements of the game. The horse moved quietly over the profile of the rising ground, and disappeared behind it. The Captain and his party were likewise soon hidden by an intervening hill.

After a time, the horse suddenly made his appearance to our right, just ahead of the line, emerging out of a small valley, on a brisk trot; having evidently taken the alarm. At sight of us, he stopped short, gazed at us for an instant with surprise, then tossing up his head, trotted off in fine style, glancing at us first over one shoulder, then over the other, his ample mane and tail streaming in the wind. Having dashed through a skirt of thicket, that looked like a hedge-row, he paused in the open field beyond, glanced back at us again, with a beautiful bend of the neck, snuffed the air, and then tossing his head again, broke into a gallop, and took refuge in a wood.

It was the first time I had ever seen a horse scouring his native wilderness in all the pride and freedom of his nature. How different from the poor, mutilated, harnessed, checked, reined-up victim of luxury, caprice, and avarice, in our cities!

After travelling about fifteen miles, we encamped about one o'clock, that our hunters might have time to procure a supply of provisions. Our encampment was in a spacious grove of lofty oaks and walnuts, free from under wood, on the border of a brook. While unloading the pack-horses, our little Frenchman was loud in his complaints at having been prevented from pursuing the wild horse, which he would certainly have taken. In the meantime, I saw our half-breed, Beatte, quietly saddle his best horse, a powerful steed of a half savage race, hang a lariat at the saddle-bow, take a rifle and forked stick in hand, and, mounting, depart from the camp without saying a word. It was evident he was going off in quest of the wild horse, but was disposed to hunt alone.

CHAPTER XX.

THE CAMP OF THE WILD HORSE.

HUNTERS' STORIES.—HABITS OF THE WILD HORSE.—THE HALF-BREED AND HIS PRIZE.—A HORSE CHASE.—A WILD SPIRIT TAMED.

We had encamped in a good neighborhood for game, as the reports of rifles in various directions speedily gave notice. One of our hunters soon returned with the meat of a doe, tied up in the skin, and slung across his shoulders. Another brought a fat buck across his horse. Two other deer were brought in, and a number of turkeys. All the game was thrown down in front of the Captain's fire, to be portioned out among the various messes. The spits and camp kettles were soon in full employ, and throughout the evening there was a scene of hunters' feasting and profusion.

We had been disappointed this day in our hopes of meeting with buffalo, but the sight of the wild horse had been a great novelty, and gave a turn to the conversation of the camp for the evening. There were several anecdotes told of a famous gray horse, which has ranged the prairies of this neighborhood for six or seven years, setting at naught every attempt of the hunters to capture him. They say he can pace and rack (or amble) faster than the fleetest horses can run. Equally marvellous accounts were given of a black horse on the Brassos, who grazed the prairies on that river's banks in the Texas. For years he outstripped all pursuit. His fame spread far and wide; offers were made for him to the amount of a thousand dollars; the boldest and most hard-riding hunters tried incessantly to make prize of him, but in vain. At length he fell a victim to his gallantry, being decoyed under a tree by a tame mare, and a noose dropped over his head by a boy perched among the branches.

The capture of the wild horse is one of the most favorite achievements of the prairie tribes; and, indeed, it is from this source that the Indian hunters chiefly supply themselves. The wild horses which range those vast grassy plains, extending from the Arkansas to the Spanish settlements, are of various forms and colors, betraying their various descents. Some resemble the common English stock, and are probably descended from horses which have escaped from our border settlements. Others are of a low but strong make, and are supposed to be of the Andalusian breed, brought out by the Spanish discoverers.

Some fanciful speculatists have seen in them descendants of the Arab stock, brought into Spain from Africa, and thence transferred to this country; and have pleased themselves with the idea, that their sires may have been of the pure coursers of the desert, that once bore Mahomet and his warlike disciples across the sandy plains of Arabia.

The habits of the Arab seem to have come with the steed. The introduction of the horse on the boundless prairies of the Far West, changed the whole mode of living of their inhabitants. It gave them that facility of rapid motion, and of sudden and distant change of place, so dear to the roving propensities of man. Instead of lurking in the depths of gloomy forests, and patiently threading the mazes of a tangled wilderness on foot, like his brethren of the north, the Indian of the West is a rover of the plain; he leads a brighter and more sunshiny life; almost always on horseback, on vast flowery prairies and under cloudless skies.

I was lying by the Captain's fire, late in the evening, listening to stories about those coursers of the prairies, and weaving speculations of my own, when there was a clamor of voices and a loud cheering at the other end of the camp; and word was passed that Beatte, the half-breed, had brought in a wild horse.

In an instant every fire was deserted; the whole camp crowded to see the Indian and his prize. It was a colt about two years old, well grown, finely limbed, with bright prominent eyes, and a spirited yet gentle demeanor. He gazed about him with an air of mingled stupefaction and surprise, at the men, the horses, and the camp-fires; while the Indian stood before him with folded arms, having hold of the other end of the cord which noosed his captive, and gazing on him with a most imperturbable aspect. Beatte, as I have before observed, has a greenish olive complexion, with a strongly marked countenance, not unlike the bronze casts of Napoleon; and as he stood before his captive horse, with folded arms and fixed aspect, he looked more like a statue than a man.

If the horse, however, manifested the least restiveness, Beatte would immediately worry him with the lariat, jerking him first on one side, then on the other, so as almost to throw him on the ground; when he had thus rendered him passive, he would resume his statue-like attitude and gaze at him in silence.

The whole scene was singularly wild; the tall grove, partially illumined by the flashing fires of the camp, the horses tethered here and there among the trees, the carcasses of deer hanging around, and in the midst of all, the wild huntsman and his wild horse, with an admiring throng of rangers, almost as wild.

In the eagerness of their excitement, several of the young rangers sought to get the horse by purchase or barter, and even offered extravagant terms; but Beatte declined all their offers. "You give great price now;" said he, "to-morrow you be sorry, and take back, and say d—d Indian!"

The young men importuned him with questions about the mode in which he took the horse, but his answers were dry and laconic; he evidently retained some pique at having been undervalued and sneered at by them; and at the same time looked down upon them with contempt as greenhorns, little versed in the noble science of woodcraft.

Afterwards, however, when he was seated by our fire, I readily drew from him an account of his exploit; for, though taciturn among strangers, and little prone to boast of his actions, yet his taciturnity, like that of all Indians, had its times of relaxation.

He informed me, that on leaving the camp, he had returned to the place where we had lost sight of the wild horse. Soon getting upon its track, he followed it to the banks of the river. Here, the prints being more distinct in the sand, he perceived that one of the hoofs was broken and defective, so he gave up the pursuit.

As he was returning to the camp, he came upon a gang of six horses, which immediately made for the river. He pursued them across the stream, left his rifle on the river bank, and putting his horse to full speed, soon came up with the fugitives. He attempted to noose one of them, but the lariat hitched on one of his ears, and he shook it off. The horses dashed up a hill, he followed hard at their heels, when, of a sudden, he saw their tails whisking in the air, and they plunging down a precipice. It was too late to stop. He shut his eyes, held in his breath, and went over with them—neck or nothing. The descent was between twenty and thirty feet, but they all came down safe upon a sandy bottom.

He now succeeded in throwing his noose round a fine young horse. As he galloped alongside of him, the two horses passed each side ot a sapling, and the end of the lariat was jerked out of his hand. He regained it, but an intervening tree obliged him again to let it go. Having once more caught it, and coming to a more open country, he was enabled to play the young horse with the line until he gradually checked and subdued him, so as to lead him to the place where he had left his rifle.

He had another formidable difficulty in getting him across the river, where both horses stuck for a time in the mire, and Beatte was nearly unseated from his saddle by the force of the current and the struggles of his captive. After much toil and trouble, however, he got across the stream, and brought his prize safe into camp.

For the remainder of the evening, the camp remained in a high state of excitement; nothing was talked of but the capture of wild horses; every youngster of the troop was for this harum-scarum kind of chase; every one promised himself to return from the campaign in triumph, bestriding one of these wild coursers of the prairies. Beatte had suddenly risen to great importance; he was the prime hunter, the hero of the day. Offers were made him by the best mounted rangers, to let him ride their horses in the chase, provided he would give them a share of the spoil. Beatte bore his honors in silence, and closed with none of the offers. Our stammering, chattering, gasconading little Frenchman, however, made up for his taciturnity, by vaunting as much upon the subject as if it were he that had caught the horse. Indeed he held forth so learnedly in the matter, and boasted so much of the many horses he had taken, that he began to be considered an oracle; and some of the youngsters were inclined to doubt whether he were not superior even to the taciturn Beatte.

The excitement kept the camp awake later than usual. The hum of voices, interrupted by occasional peals of laughter, was heard from the groups around the various fires, and the night was considerably advanced before all had sunk to sleep.

With the morning dawn the excitement revived, and Beatte and his wild horse were again the gaze and talk of the camp. The captive had been tied all night to a tree among the other horses. He was again led forth by Beatte, by a long halter or lariat, and, on his manifesting the least restiveness, was, as before, jerked and worried into passive submission. He appeared to be gentle and docile by nature, and had a beautifully mild expression of the eye. In his strange and forlorn situation, the poor animal seemed to seek protection and companionship in the very horse which had aided to capture him.

Seeing him thus gentle and tractable, Beatte, just as we were about to march, strapped a light pack upon his back, by way of giving him the first lesson in servitude. The native pride and independence of the animal took fire at this indignity. He reared, and plunged, and kicked, and tried in every way to get rid of the degrading burden. The Indian was too potent for him. At every paroxysm he renewed the discipline of the halter, until the poor animal, driven to despair, threw himself prostrate on the ground, and lay motionless, as if acknowledging himself vanquished. A stage hero, representing the despair of a captive prince, could not have played his part more dramatically. There was absolutely a moral grandeur in it.

The imperturbable Beatte folded his arms, and stood for a time, looking down in silence upon his captive; until seeing him perfectly subdued, he nodded his head slowly, screwed his mouth into a sardonic smile of triumph, and, with a jerk of the halter, ordered him to rise. He obeyed, and from that time forward offered no resistance. During that day he bore his pack patiently, and was led by the halter; but in two days he followed voluntarily at large among the supernumerary horses of the troop.

I could not but look with compassion upon this fine young animal, whose whole course of existence had been so suddenly reversed. From being a denizen of these vast pastures, ranging at will from plain to plain and mead to mead, cropping of every herb and flower, and drinking of every stream, he was suddenly reduced to perpetual and painful servitude, to pass his life under the harness and the curb, amid, perhaps, the din and dust and drudgery of cities. The transition in his lot was such as sometimes takes place in human affairs, and in the fortunes of towering individuals:—one day, a prince of the prairies—the next day, a pack-horse!

CHAPTER XXI.

THE FORDING OF THE RED FORK.—THE DREARY FORESTS OF THE "CROSS TIMBER."—BUFFALO!

We left the camp of the wild horse about a quarter before eight, and, after steering nearly south for three or four miles, arrived on the banks of the Red Fork, about seventy-five miles, as we supposed, above its mouth. The river was about three hundred yards wide, wandering among sand-bars and shoals. Its shores, and the long sandy banks that stretched out into the stream, were printed, as usual, with the traces of various animals that had come down to cross it, or to drink its waters.

Here we came to a halt, and there was much consultation about the possibility of fording the river with safety, as there was an apprehension of quicksands. Beatte, who had been somewhat in the rear, came up while we were debating. He was mounted on his horse of the half-wild breed, and leading his captive by the bridle. He gave the latter in charge to Tonish, and without saying a word, urged his horse into the stream, and crossed it in safety. Every thing was done by this man in a similar way, promptly, resolutely, and silently, without a previous promise or an after vaunt.

The troop now followed the lead of Beatte, and reached the opposite shore without any mishap, though one of the pack-horses wandering a little from the track, came near being swallowed up in a quicksand, and was with difficulty dragged to land.

After crossing the river, we had to force our way, for nearly a mile, through a thick canebrake, which, at first sight, appeared an impervious mass of reeds and brambles. It was a hard struggle; our horses were often to the saddle-girths in mire and water, and both horse and horseman harassed and torn by bush and brier. Falling, however, upon a buffalo track, we at length extricated ourselves from this morass, and ascended a ridge of land, where we beheld a beautiful open country before us; while to our right, the belt of forest land, called "The Cross Timber," continued stretching away to the southward, as far as the eye could reach. We soon abandoned the open country, and struck into the forest land. It was the intention of the Captain to keep on southwest by south, and traverse the Cross Timber diagonally, so as to come out upon the edge of the great western prairie. By thus maintaining something of a southerly direction, he trusted, while he crossed the belt of the forest, he would at the same time approach the Red River.

The plan of the Captain was judicious; but he erred from not being informed of the nature of the country. Had he kept directly west, a couple of days would have carried us through the forest land, and we might then have had an easy course along the skirts of the upper prairies, to Red River; by going diagonally, we were kept for many weary days toiling through a dismal series of rugged forests.

The Cross Timber is about forty miles in breadth, and stretches over a rough country of rolling hills, covered with scattered tracts of post-oak and black-jack; with some intervening valleys, which, at proper seasons, would afford good pasturage. It is very much cut up by deep ravines, which, in the rainy seasons, are the beds of temporary streams, tributary to the main rivers, and these are called "branches." The whole tract may present a pleasant aspect in the fresh time of the year, when the ground is covered with herbage; when the trees are in their green leaf, and the glens are enlivened by running streams. Unfortunately, we entered it too late in the season. The herbage was parched; the foliage of the scrubby forests was withered; the whole woodland prospect, as far as the eye could reach, had a brown and arid hue. The fires made on the prairies by the Indian hunters, had frequently penetrated these forests, sweeping in light transient flames along the dry grass, scorching and calcining the lower twigs and branches of the trees, and leaving them black and hard, so as to tear the flesh of man and horse that had to scramble through them. I shall not easily forget the mortal toil, and the vexations of flesh and spirit, that we underwent occasionally, in our wanderings through the Cross Timber. It was like struggling through forests of cast iron.

After a tedious ride of several miles, we came out upon an open tract of hill and dale, interspersed with woodland. Here we were roused by the cry of buffalo! buffalo! The effect was something like that of the cry of a sail! a sail! at sea. It was not a false alarm. Three or four of those enormous animals were visible to our sight grazing on the slope of a distant hill.

There was a general movement to set off in pursuit, and it was with some difficulty that the vivacity of the younger men of the troop could be restrained. Leaving orders that the line of march should be preserved, the Captain and two of his officers departed at a quiet pace, accompanied by Beatte, and by the ever-forward Tonish; for it was impossible any longer to keep the little Frenchman in check, being half crazy to prove his skill and prowess in hunting the buffalo.

The intervening hills soon hid from us both the game and the huntsmen. We kept on our course in quest of a camping place, which was difficult to be found; almost all the channels of the streams being dry, and the country being destitute of fountain heads.

After proceeding some distance, there was again a cry of buffalo, and two were pointed out on a hill to the left. The Captain being absent, it was no longer possible to restrain the ardor of the young hunters. Away several of them dashed, full speed, and soon disappeared among the ravines: the rest kept on, anxious to find a proper place for encampment.

Indeed we now began to experience the disadvantages of the season. The pasturage of the prairies was scanty and parched, the pea-vines which grew in the woody bottoms were withered, and most of the "branches" or streams were dried up. While wandering in this perplexity, we were overtaken by the Captain and all his party, except Tonish. They had pursued the buffalo for some distance without getting within shot, and had given up the chase, being fearful of fatiguing their horses, or being led off too far from camp. The little Frenchman, however, had galloped after them at headlong speed, and the last they saw of him, he was engaged, as it were, yard-arm and yard-arm, with a great buffalo bull, firing broadsides into him. "I tink dat little man crazy—somehow," observed Beatte, dryly.

CHAPTER XXII.

THE ALARM CAMP.

We now came to a halt, and had to content ourselves with an indifferent encampment. It was in a grove of scrub-oaks, on the borders of a deep ravine, at the bottom of which were a few scanty pools of water. We were just at the foot of a gradually-sloping hill, covered with half-withered grass, that afforded meagre pasturage. In the spot where we had encamped, the grass was high and parched. The view around us was circumscribed and much shut in by gently-swelling hills.

Just as we were encamping, Tonish arrived, all glorious, from his hunting match; his white horse hung all round with buffalo meat. According to his own account, he had laid low two mighty bulls. As usual, we deducted one half from his boastings; but, now that he had something real to vaunt about, there was no restraining the valor of his tongue.

After having in some measure appeased his vanity by boasting of his exploit, he informed us that he had observed the fresh track of horses, which, from various circumstances, he suspected to have been made by some roving band of Pawnees. This caused some little uneasiness. The young men who had left the line of march in pursuit of the two buffaloes, had not yet rejóined us: apprehensions were expressed that they might be waylaid and attacked. Our veteran hunter, old Ryan, also, immediately on our halting to encamp, had gone off on foot, in company with a young disciple. "Dat old man will have his brains knocked out by de Pawnees yet," said Beatte. "He tink he know every ting, but he don't know Pawnees, anyhow."

Taking his rifle, the Captain repaired on foot to reconnoitre the country from the naked summit of one of the neighboring hills. In the meantime, the horses were hobbled and turned loose to graze; and wood was cut, and fires made, to prepare the evening's repast.

Suddenly there was an alarm of fire in the camp! The flame from one of the kindling fires had caught to the tall dry grass: a breeze was blowing; there was danger that the camp would soon be wrapped in a light blaze. "Look to the horses!" cried one; "drag away the baggage!" cried another. "Take care of the rifles and powder-horns!" cried a third. All was hurry-scurry and uproar. The horses dashed wildly about: some of the men snatched away rifles and powder-horns, others dragged off saddles and saddle-bags. Meantime, no one thought of quelling the fire, nor indeed knew how to quell it. Beatte, however, and his comrades attacked it in the Indian mode, beating down the edges ot the fire with blankets and horse-cloths, and endeavoring to prevent its spreading among the grass; the rangers followed their example, and in a little while the flames were happily quelled.

The fires were now properly kindled on places from which the dry grass had been cleared away. The horses were scattered about a small valley, and on the sloping hill-side, cropping the scanty herbage. Tonish was preparing a sumptuous evening's meal from his buffalo meat, promising us a rich soup and a prime piece of roast beef: but we were doomed to experience another and more serious alarm.

There was an indistinct cry from some rangers on the summit of the hill, of which we could only distinguish the words, "The horses! the horses! get in the horses!"

Immediately a clamor of voices arose; shouts, questions,

replies, were all mingled together, so that nothing could be clearly understood, and every one drew his own inference.

"The Captain has started buffaloes," cried one, "and wants horses for the chase." Immediately a number of rangers seized their rifles, and scampered for the hill-top. "The prairie is on fire beyond the hill," cried another; "I see the smoke—the Captain means we shall drive the horses beyond the brook."

By this time a ranger from the hill had reached the skirts of the camp. He was almost breathless, and could only say that the Captain had seen Indians at a distance.

"Pawnees! Pawnees!" was now the cry among our wild-headed youngsters. "Drive the horses into the camp!" cried one. "Saddle the horses!" cried another. "Form the line!" cried a third. There was now a scene of clamor and confusion that baffles all description. The rangers were scampering about the adjacent field in pursuit of their horses. One might be seen tugging his steed along by a halter; another without a hat, riding bare-backed; another driving a hobbled horse before him, that made awkward leaps like a kangaroo.

The alarm increased. Word was brought from the lower end of the camp that there was a band of Pawnees in a neighboring valley. They had shot old Ryan through the head, and were chasing his companion "No, it was not old Ryan that was killed—it was one of the hunters that had been after the two buffaloes." "There are three hundred Pawnees just beyond the hill," cried one voice. "More, more!" cried another.

Our situation, shut in among hills, prevented our seeing to any distance, and left us a prey to all these rumors. A cruel enemy was supposed to be at hand, and an immediate attack apprehended. The horses by this time were driven into the camp, and were dashing about among the fires, and trampling upon the baggage. Every one endeavored to prepare for action; but here was the perplexity. During the late alarm of fire, the saddles, bridles, rifles, powder-horns, and other equipments, had been snatched out of their places, and thrown helter-skelter among the trees.

"Where is my saddle?" cried one. "Has any one seen my rifle?" cried another. "Who will lend me a ball?" cried a third, who was loading his piece. "I have lost my bullet pouch." "For God's sake help me to girth this horse!" cried another; "he's so restive I can do nothing with him." In his hurry and worry, he had put on the saddle the hind part before!

Some affected to swagger and talk bold; others said nothing, but went on steadily, preparing their horses and weapons, and on these I felt the most reliance. Some were evidently excited and elated with the idea of an encounter with Indians; and none more so than my young Swiss fellow traveller, who had a passion for wild adventure. Our man, Beatte, led his horses in the rear of the camp, placed his rifle against a tree, then seated himself by the fire in perfect silence. On the other hand, little Tonish, who was busy cooking, stopped every moment from his work to play the fanfaron, singing, swearing, and affecting an unusual hilarity, which made me strongly suspect that there was some little fright at bottom, to cause all this effervescence.

About a dozen of the rangers, as soon as they could saddle their horses, dashed off in the direction in which the Pawnees were said to have attacked the hunters. It was now determined, in case our camp should be assailed, to put our horses in the ravine in rear, where they would be out of danger from arrow or rifle ball, and to take our stand within the edge of the ravine.

This would serve as a trench, and the trees and thickets with which it was bordered, would be sufficient to turn aside any shaft of the enemy. The Pawnees, beside, are wary of attacking any covert of the kind; their warfare, as I have already observed, lies in the open prairie, where, mounted upon their fleet horses, they can swoop like hawks upon their enemy, or wheel about him and discharge their arrows. Still I could not but perceive, that, in case of being attacked by such a number of these well-mounted and warlike savages as were said to be at hand, we should be exposed to considerable risk from the inexperience and want of discipline of our newly-raised rangers, and from the very courage of many of the younger ones who seemed bent on adventure and exploit.

By this time the Captain reached the camp, and every one crowded round him for information. He informed us, that he had proceeded some distance on his reconnoitring expedition, and was slowly returning towards the camp, along the brow of a naked hill, when he saw something on the edge of a parallel hill, that looked like a man. He paused, and watched it; but it remained so perfectly motionless, that he supposed it a bush, or the top of some tree beyond the hill. He resumed his course, when it likewise began to move in a parallel direction. Another form now rose beside it, of some one who had either been lying down, or had just ascended the other side of the hill. The Captain stopped and regarded them; they likewise stopped. He then lay down upon the grass, and they began to walk. On his rising, they again stopped, as if watching him. Knowing that the Indians are apt to have their spies and sentinels thus posted on the summit of naked hills, commanding extensive prospects, his doubts were increased by the suspicious movements of these men. He now put his foraging cap on the end of his rifle, and waved it in the air. They took no notice of the signal. He then walked on, until he entered the edge of a wood, which concealed him from their view. Stopping out of sight for a moment, he again looked forth, when he saw the two men passing swiftly forward. As the hill on which they were walking made a curve toward that on which he stood, it seemed as if they were endeavoring to head him before he should reach the camp. Doubting whether they might not belong to some large party of Indians, either in ambush or moving along the valley beyond the hill, the Captain hastened his steps homeward, and, descrying some rangers on an eminence between him and the camp, he called out to them to pass the word to have the horses driven in, as these are generally the first objects of Indian depredation.

Such was the origin of the alarm which had thrown the camp in commotion. Some of those who heard the Captain's narration, had no doubt that the men on the hill were Pawnee scouts, belonging to the band that had waylaid the hunters. Distant shots were heard at intervals, which were supposed to be fired by those who had sallied out to rescue their comrades. Several more rangers, having completed their equipments, now rode forth in the direction of the firing; others looked anxious and uneasy

"If they are as numerous as they are said to be," said one, "and as well mounted as they generally are, we shall be a bad match for them with our jaded horses."

"Well," replied the Captain, "we have a strong encampment, and can stand a siege."

"Ay, but they may set fire to the prairie in the night, and burn us out of our encampment."

"We will then set up a counter-fire!"

The word was now passed that a man on horseback approached the camp.

"It is one of the hunters! It is Clements! He brings buffalo meat!" was announced by several voices as the horseman drew near.

It was, in fact, one of the rangers who had set off in the morning in pursuit of the two buffaloes. He rode into the camp, with the spoils of the chase hanging round his horse, and followed by his companions, all sound and unharmed, and equally well laden. They proceeded to give an account of a grand gallop they had had after the two buffaloes, and how many shots it had cost them to bring one to the ground.

"Well, but the Pawnees—the Pawnees—where are the Pawnees?"

"What Pawnees?"

"The Pawnees that attacked you."

"No one attacked us."

"But have you seen no Indians on your way?"

"Oh yes, two of us got to the top of a hill to look out for the camp, and saw a fellow on an opposite hill cutting queer antics, who seemed to be an Indian."

"Pshaw! that was I!" said the Captain.

Here the bubble burst. The whole alarm had risen from this mutual mistake of the Captain and the two rangers. As to the report of the three hundred Pawnees and their attack on the hunters, it proved to be a wanton fabrication, of which no further notice was taken; though the author deserved to have been sought out, and severely punished.

There being no longer any prospect of fighting, every one now thought of eating; and here the stomachs throughout the camp were in unison. Tonish served up to us his promised regale of buffalo soup and buffalo beef. The soup was peppered most horribly, and the roast beef proved the bull to have been one of the patriarchs of the prairies; never did I have to deal with a tougher morsel. However, it was our first repast on buffalo meat, so we ate it with a lively faith; nor would our little Frenchman allow us any rest, until he had extorted from us an acknowledgment of the excellence of his cookery; though the pepper gave us the lie in our throats.

The night closed in without the return of old Ryan and his companion. We had become accustomed, however, to the aberrations of this old cock of the woods, and no further solicitude was expressed on his account.

After the fatigues and agitations of the day, the camp soon sunk into a profound sleep, excepting those on guard, who were more than usually on the alert; for the traces recently seen of Pawnees, and the certainty that we were in the midst of their hunting grounds, excited to constant vigilance. About half past ten o'clock we were all startled from sleep, by a new alarm. A sentinel had fired off his rifle and run into camp, crying that there were Indians at hand.

Every one was on his legs in an instant. Some seized their rifles; some were about to saddle their horses; some hastened to the Captain's lodge, but were ordered back to their respective fires. The sentinel was examined. He declared he had seen an Indian approach, crawling along the ground; whereupon he had fired upon him, and run into camp. The Captain gave it as his opinion, that the supposed Indian was a wolf; he reprimanded the sentinel for deserting his post, and obliged him to return to it. Many seemed inclined to give credit to the story of the sentinel; for the events of the day had predisposed them to apprehend lurking foes and sudden assaults during the darkness of the night. For a long time they sat round their fires, with rifle in hand, carrying on low, murmuring conversations, and listening for some new alarm. Nothing further, however, occurred; the voices gradually died away; the gossipers nodded and dozed, and sunk to rest; and, by degrees, silence and sleep once more stole over the camp.

CHAPTER XXIII.

BEAVER DAM.—BUFFALO AND HORSE TRACKS.—A PAWNEE TRAIL.—WILD HORSES.—THE YOUNG HUNTER AND THE BEAR.—CHANGE OF ROUTE.

On mustering our forces in the morning, (Oct. 23,) old Ryan and his comrade were still missing; but, the Captain had such perfect reliance on the skill and resources of the veteran woodsman, that he did not think it necessary to take any measures with respect to him.

Our march this day lay through the same kind of rough rolling country; checkered by brown dreary forests of post-oak, and cut up by deep dry ravines. The distant fires were evidently increasing on the prairies. The wind had been at northwest for several days; and the atmosphere had become so smoky, as in the height of Indian summer, that it was difficult to distinguish objects at any distance.

In the course of the morning, we crossed a deep stream with a complete beaver dam, above three feet high, making a large pond, and doubtless containing several families of that industrious animal, though not one showed his nose above water. The Captain would not permit this amphibious commonwealth to be disturbed.

We were now continually coming upon the tracks of buffaloes and wild horses; those of the former, tended invariably to the south, as we could perceive by the direction of the trampled grass. It was evident, we were on the great highway of these migratory herds, but that they had chiefly passed to the southward.

Beatte, who generally kept a parallel course several hundred yards distant from our line of march, to be on the look-out for game, and who regarded every track with the knowing eye of an Indian, reported that he had come upon a very suspicious trail. There were the tracks of men who wore Pawnee moccasons. He had scented the smoke of mingled sumach and tobacco, such as the Indians use. He had observed tracks of horses, mingled with those of a dog; and a mark in the dust where a cord had been trailed along; probably the long bridle, one end of which the Indian horsemen suffer to trail on the ground. It was evident, they were not the tracks of wild horses. My anxiety began to revive about the safety of our veteran hunter Ryan, for I had taken a great fancy to this real old Leatherstocking; every one expressed a confidence, however, that wherever Ryan was, he was safe, and knew how to take care of himself.

We had accomplished the greater part of a weary day's march, and were passing through a glade of the oak openings, when we came in sight of six wild horses, among which I especially noticed two very handsome ones, a gray and a roan. They pranced about, with heads erect, and long flaunting tails, offering a proud contrast to our poor, spiritless, travel-tired steeds. Having reconnoitred us for a moment, they set off at a gallop, passed through a woody dingle, and in a little while emerged once more to view, trotting up a slope about a mile distant.

The sight of these horses was again a sore trial to the vaporing Tonish, who had his lariat and forked stick ready, and was on the point of launching forth in pursuit, on his jaded horse, when he was again ordered back to the pack-horses.

After a day's journey of fourteen miles in a southwest direction, we encamped on the banks of a small clear stream, on the northern border of the Cross Timbers; and on the edge of those vast prairies, that extend away to the foot of the Rocky Mountains. In turning loose the horses to graze, their bells were stuffed with grass to prevent their tinkling, lest it might be heard by some wandering horde of Pawnees.

Our hunters now went out in different directions, but without much success, as but one deer was brought into the camp. A young ranger had a long story to tell of his adventures. In skirting the thickets of a deep ravine he had wounded a buck, which he plainly heard to fall among the bushes. He stopped to fix the lock of his rifle, which was out of order, and to reload it: then advancing to the edge of the thicket, in quest of his game, he heard a low growling. Putting the branches aside, and stealing silently forward, he looked down into the ravine and beheld a huge bear dragging the carcass of the deer along the dry channel of a brook, and growling and snarling at four or five officious wolves, who seemed to have dropped in to take supper with him.

The ranger fired at the bear, but missed him. Bruin maintained his ground and his prize, and seemed disposed to make battle. The wolves, too, who were evidently sharp set, drew off to but a small distance. As night was coming on, the young hunter felt dismayed at the wildness and darkness of the place, and the strange company he had fallen in with; so he quietly withdrew, and returned empty handed to the camp, where, having told his story, he was heartily bantered by his more experienced comrades.

In the course of the evening, old Ryan came straggling into the camp, followed by his disciple, and as usual was received with hearty gratulations. He had lost himself yesterday, when hunting, and camped out all night, but had found our trail in the morning, and followed it up. He had passed some time at the beaver dam, admiring the skill and solidity with which it had been constructed. "These beavers," said he, "are industrious little fellows. They are the knowingest varment as I know; and I'll warrant the pond was stocked with them."

"Aye," said the Captain, "I have no doubt most of the small rivers we have passed are full of beaver. I would like to come and trap on these waters all winter."

"But would you not run the chance of being attacked by Indians?" asked one of the company.

"Oh, as to that, it would be safe enough here, in the winter time. There would be no Indians here until spring. I should want no more than two companions. Three persons are safer than a large number for trapping beaver. They can keep quiet, and need seldom fire a gun. A bear would serve them for food, for two months, taking care to turn every part of it to advantage."

A consultation was now held as to our future progress. We had thus far pursued a western course; and, having traversed the Cross Timber, were on the skirts of the Great Western Prairie We were still, however, in a very rough country, where food was scarce. The season was so far advanced that the grass was withered, and the prairies yielded no pasturage. The pea-vines of the bottoms, also, which had sustained our horses for some part of the journey, were nearly gone, and for several days past the poor animals had fallen off wofully both in flesh and spirit. The Indian fires on the prairies were approaching us from north and south, and west; they might spread also from the east, and leave a scorched desert between us and the frontier, in which our horses might be famished.

It was determined, therefore, to advance no further to the westward, but to shape our course more to the east, so as to strike the north fork of the Canadian, as soon as possible, where we hoped to find abundance of young cane; which, at this season of the year, affords the most nutritious pasturage for the horses; and, at the same time, attracts immense quantities of game. Here then we fixed the limits of our tour to the Far West, being within little more than a day's march of the boundary line of Texas.

CHAPTER XXIV

SCARCITY OF BREAD.—RENCONTRE WITH BUFFALOES.—WILD TURKEYS.—FALL OF A BUFFALO BULL.

THE morning broke bright and clear, but the camp had nothing of its usual gayety. The concert of the farmyard was at an end; not a cock crew, nor dog barked; nor was there either singing or laughing; every one pursued his avocations quietly and gravely. The novelty of the expedition was wearing off.

Some of the young men were getting as way-worn as their horses; and most of them, unaccustomed to the hunter's life, began to repine at its privations. What they most felt was the want of bread, their rations of flour having been exhausted for several days. The old hunters, who had often experienced this want, made light of it; and Beatte, accustomed when among the Indians to live for months without it, considered it a mere article of luxury. "Bread," he would say scornfully, "is only fit for a child."

About a quarter before eight o'clock, we turned our backs upon the Far West, and set off in a southeast course, along a gentle valley. After riding a few miles, Beatte, who kept parallel with us, along the ridge of a naked hill to our right, called out and made signals, as if something were coming round the hill to intercept us. Some who were near me cried out that it was a party of Pawnees. A skirt of thickets hid the approach of the supposed enemy from our view. We heard a trampling among the brushwood. My horse looked toward the place, snorted and pricked up his ears, when presently a couple of large huge buffalo bulls, who had been alarmed by Beatte, came crashing through the brake, and making directly towards us. At sight of us they wheeled round, and scuttled along a narrow defile of the hill. In an instant half a score of rifles cracked off; there was a universal whoop and halloo, and away went half the troop, helter-skelter in pursuit, and myself among the number. The most of us soon pulled up, and gave over a chase which led through birch and brier, and break-neck ravines. Some few of the rangers persisted for a time; but eventually joined the line, slowly lagging one after another. One of them returned on foot; he had been thrown while in full chase; his rifle had been broken in the fall, and his horse, retaining the spirit of the rider, had kept on after the buffalo. It was a melancholy predicament to be reduced to, without horse or weapon in the midst of the Pawnee hunting grounds.

For my own part, I had been fortunate enough recently, by a further exchange, to get possession of the best horse in the troop; a full-blooded sorrel of excellent bottom, beautiful form, and most generous qualities.

In such a situation, it almost seems as if a man changes his nature with his horse. I felt quite like another being, now that I had an animal under me, spirited yet gentle, docile to a remarkable degree, and easy, elastic, and rapid in all his movements. In a few days he became almost as much attached to me as a dog; would follow me when I dismounted, would come to me in the morning to be noticed and caressed; and would put his muzzle between me and my book, as I sat reading at the foot of a tree. The feeling I had for this my dumb companion of the prairies, gave me some faint idea of that attachment the Arab is said to entertain for the horse that has borne him about the deserts.

After riding a few miles further, we came to a fine meadow with a broad clear stream winding through it, on the banks of which there was excellent pasturage. Here we at once came to a halt, in a beautiful grove of elms, on the site of an old Osage encampment. Scarcely had we dismounted, when a universal firing of rifles took place upon a large flock of turkeys, scattered about the grove, which proved to be a favorite roosting-place for these simple birds. They flew to the trees, and sat perched upon their branches, stretching out their long necks, and gazing in stupid astonishment, until eighteen of them were shot down.

In the height of the carnage, word was brought that there

were four buffaloes in a neighboring meadow. The turkeys were now abandoned for nobler game. The tired horses were again mounted, and urged to the chase. In a little while we came in sight of the buffaloes, looking like brown hillocks among the long green herbage. Beatte endeavored to get ahead of them and turn them towards us, that the inexperienced hunters might have a chance. They ran round the base of a rocky hill, that hid us from the sight. Some of us endeavored to cut across the hill, but became entrapped in a thick wood, matted with grape-vines. My horse, who, under his former rider had hunted the buffalo, seemed as much excited as myself, and endeavored to force his way through the bushes. At length we extricated ourselves, and galloping over the hill, I found our little Frenchman Tonish, curvetting on horseback round a great buffalo which he had wounded too severely to fly, and which he was keeping employed until we should come up. There was a mixture of the grand and the comic, in beholding this tremendous animal and his fantastic assailant. The buffalo stood with his shagged front always presented to his foe; his mouth open, his tongue parched, his eyes like coals of fire, and his tail erect with rage; every now and then he would make a faint rush upon his foe, who easily evaded his attack, capering and cutting all kinds of antics before him.

We now made repeated shots at the buffalo, but they glanced into his mountain of flesh without proving mortal. He made a slow and grand retreat into the shallow river, turning upon his assailants whenever they pressed upon him; and when in the water, took his stand there as if prepared to sustain a siege. A rifle ball, however, more fatally lodged, sent a tremor through his frame. He turned and attempted to wade across the stream, but after tottering a few paces, slowly fell upon his side and expired. It was the fall of a hero, and we felt somewhat ashamed of the butchery that had effected it; but, after the first shot or two, we had reconciled it to our feelings, by the old plea of putting the poor animal out of his misery.

Two other buffaloes were killed this evening, but they were all bulls, the flesh of which is meagre and hard, at this season of the year. A fat buck yielded us more savory meat for our evening's repast.

CHAPTER XXV.

RINGING THE WILD HORSE.

We left the buffalo camp about eight o'clock, and had a toilsome and harassing march of two hours, over ridges of hills, covered with a ragged meagre forest of scrub-oaks, and broken by deep gullies. Among the oaks I observed many of the most diminutive size; some not above a foot high, yet bearing abundance of small acorns. The whole of the Cross Timber, in fact, abounds with mast. There is a pine-oak which produces an acorn pleasant to the taste, and ripening early in the season.

About ten o'clock in the morning, we came to where this line of rugged hills swept down into a valley, through which flowed the north fork of the Red River. A beautiful meadow about half a mile wide, enamelled with yellow autumnal flowers, stretched for two or three miles along the foot of the hills, bordered on the opposite side by the river, whose banks were fringed with cotton-wood trees, the bright foliage of which refreshed and delighted the eye, after being wearied by the contemplation of monotonous wastes of brown forest.

The meadow was finely diversified by groves and clumps of trees, so happily dispersed, that they seemed as if set out by the hand of art. As we cast our eyes over this fresh and delightful valley, we beheld a troop of wild horses, quietly grazing on a green lawn, about a mile distant to our right, while to our left, at nearly the same distance, were several buffaloes; some feeding, others reposing and ruminating among the high rich herbage, under the shade of a clump of cotton-wood trees. The whole had the appearance of a broad beautiful tract of pasture land, on the highly ornamented estate of some gentleman farmer, with his cattle grazing about the lawns and meadows.

A council of war was now held, and it was determined to profit by the present favorable opportunity, and try our hand at the grand hunting manœuvre, which is called ringing the wild horse. This requires a large party of horsemen, well mounted. They extend themselves in each direction, singly, at certain distances apart, and gradually form a ring of two or three miles in circumference, so as to surround the game. This has to be done with extreme care, for the wild horse is the most readily alarmed inhabitant of the prairie, and can scent a hunter at a great distance, if to windward.

The ring being formed, two or three ride towards the horses, who start off in an opposite direction. Whenever they approach the bounds of the ring, however, a huntsman presents himself and turns them from their course. In this way, they are checked and driven back at every point; and kept galloping round and round this magic circle, until, being completely tired down, it is easy for the hunters to ride up beside them, and throw the lariat over their heads. The prime horses of most speed, courage, and bottom, however, are apt to break through and escape, so that, in general, it is the second-rate horses that are taken.

Preparations were now made for a hunt of the kind. The pack-horses were taken into the woods and firmly tied to trees, lest, in a rush of the wild horses, they should break away with them. Twenty-five men were then sent under the command of a lieutenant, to steal along the edge of the valley within the strip of wood that skirted the hills. They were to station themselves about fifty yards apart, within the edge of the woods, and not advance or show themselves until the horses dashed in that direction. Twenty-five men were sent across the valley, to steal in like manner along the river bank that bordered the opposite side, and to station themselves among the trees. A third party, of about the same number, was to form a line, stretching across the lower part of the valley, so as to connect the two wings. Beatte and our other half-breed Antoine, together with the ever-officious Tonish, were to make a circuit through the woods, so as to get to the upper part of the valley, in the rear of the horses, and to drive them forward into the kind of sack that we had formed, while the two wings should join behind them and make a complete circle.

The flanking parties were quietly extending themselves, out of sight, on each side of the valley, and the residue were stretching themselves, like the links of a chain, across it, when the wild horses gave signs that they scented an enemy; snuffing the air, snorting, and looking about. At length they pranced off slowly toward the river, and disappeared behind a green bank. Here, had the regulations of the chase been observed, they would have been quietly checked and turned back by the advance of a hunter from among the trees; unluckily, however, we had our wildfire Jack-o'-lantern little Frenchman to deal with. Instead of keeping quietly up the right side of the valley, to get above the horses, the moment he saw them move toward the river, he broke out of the covert of woods, and dashed furiously across the plain in pursuit of them, being mounted on one of the led horses belonging to the Count. This put an end to all system. The half-breeds and half a score of rangers joined in the chase. Away they all went over the green bank; in a moment or two the wild horses reappeared, and came thundering down the valley, with Frenchman, half-breeds, and rangers galloping and yelling like devils behind them. It was in vain that the line drawn across the valley attempted to check and turn back the fugitives. They were too hotly pressed by their pursuers; in their panic they dashed through the line, and clattered down the plain. The whole troop joined in the headlong chase, some of the rangers without hats or caps, their hair flying about their ears, others with handkerchiefs tied round their heads. The buffaloes, who had been calmly ruminating among the herbage, heaved up their huge forms, gazed for a moment with astonishment at the tempest that came scouring down the meadow, then turned and took to heavy-rolling flight. They were soon overtaken: the promiscuous throng were pressed together by the contracting sides of the valley, and away they went, pell-mell, hurry-scurry, wild buffalo, wild horse, wild huntsman, with clang and clatter, and whoop and halloo, that made the forests ring.

At length the buffaloes turned into a green brake on the river bank, while the horses dashed up a narrow defile of the hills, with their pursuers close at their heels. Beatte passed several of them, having fixed his eye upon a fine Pawnee horse, that had his ears slit, and saddle marks upon his back. He pressed him gallantly, but lost him in the woods. Among the wild horses was a fine black mare, far gone with foal. In scrambling up the defile, she tripped and fell. A young ranger sprang from his horse, and seized her by the mane and muzzle. Another ranger dismounted, and came to his assistance. The mare struggled fiercely, kicking and biting, and striking with her fore feet, but a noose was slipped over her head, and her struggles were in vain. It was some time, however, before she gave over rearing and plunging, and lashing out with her feet on every side. The two rangers then led her along the valley by two long lariats, which enabled them to keep at a sufficient distance on each side to be out of the reach of her hoofs, and whenever she struck out in one direction, she was jerked in the other. In this way her spirit was gradually subdued.

As to little Scaramouch Tonish, who had marred the whole scene by his precipitancy, he had been more successful than he deserved, having managed to catch a beautiful cream-colored colt, about seven months old, which had not strength to keep up with its companions. The mercurial little Frenchman was beside himself with exultation. It was amusing to see him with his prize. The colt would rear and kick, and struggle to get free, when Tonish would take him about the neck, wrestle with him, jump on his back, and cut as many antics as a monkey with a kitten. Nothing surprised me more, however, than to witness how soon these poor animals, thus taken from the unbounded freedom of the prairie, yielded to the dominion of man. In the course of two or three days the mare and colt went with the led horses, and became quite docile.

CHAPTER XXVI.

FORDING OF THE NORTH FORK.—DREARY SCENERY OF THE CROSS TIMBER.—SCAMPER OF HORSES IN THE NIGHT.—OSAGE WAR PARTY.—EFFECTS OF A PEACE HARANGUE.—BUFFALO.—WILD HORSE.

Resuming our march, we forded the North Fork, a rapid stream, and of a purity seldom to be found in the rivers of the prairies. It evidently had its sources in high land, well supplied with springs. After crossing the river, we again ascended among hills, from one of which we had an extensive view over this belt of cross timber, and a cheerless prospect it was; hill beyond hill, forest beyond forest, all of one sad russet hue—excepting that here and there a line of green cotton-wood trees, sycamores, and willows, marked the course of some streamlet through a valley. A procession of buffaloes, moving slowly up the profile of one of those distant hills, formed a characteristic object in the savage scene. To the left, the eye stretched beyond this rugged wilderness of hills, and ravines, and ragged forests, to a prairie about ten miles off, extending in a clear blue line along the horizon. It was like looking from among rocks and breakers upon a distant tract of tranquil ocean. Unluckily, our route did not lie in that direction; we still had to traverse many a weary mile of the "cross timber."

We encamped towards evening in a valley, beside a scanty pool, under a scattered grove of elms, the upper branches of which were fringed with tufts of the mystic mistletoe. In the course of the night, the wild colt whinnied repeatedly; and about two hours before day, there was a sudden *stampede*, or rush of horses, along the purlieus of the camp, with a snorting and neighing, and clattering of hoofs, that startled most of the rangers from their sleep, who listened in silence, until the sound died away like the rushing of a blast. As usual, the noise was at first attributed to some party of marauding Indians: but as the day dawned, a couple of wild horses were seen in a neighboring meadow, which scoured off on being approached. It was now supposed that a gang of them had dashed through our camp in the night. A general mustering of our horses took place, many were found scattered to a considerable distance, and several were not to be found. The prints of their hoofs, however, appeared deeply dinted in the soil, leading off at full speed into the waste, and their owners, putting themselves on the trail, set off in weary search of them.

We had a ruddy daybreak, but the morning gathered up gray and lowering, with indications of an autumnal storm. We resumed our march silently and seriously, through a rough and cheerless country, from the highest points of which we could descry large prairies, stretching indefinitely westward. After travelling for two or three hours, as we were traversing a withered prairie, resembling a great brown heath, we beheld seven Osage warriors approaching at a distance. The sight of any human being in this lonely wilderness was interesting; it was like speaking a ship at sea. One of the Indians took the lead of his companions, and advanced towards us with head erect, chest thrown forward, and a free and noble mien. He was a fine-looking fellow, dressed in scarlet frock and fringed leggins of deer skin. His head was decorated with a white tuft, and he stepped forward with something of a martial air, swaying his bow and arrows in one hand.

We held some conversation with him through our interpreter, Beatte, and found that he and his companions had been with the main part of their tribe hunting the buffalo, and had met with great success; and he informed us, that in the course of another day's march, we would reach the prairies on the banks of the Grand Canadian, and find plenty of game. He added, that as their hunt was over, and the hunters on their return homeward, he and his comrades had set out on a war party, to waylay and hover about some Pawnee camp, in hopes of carrying off scalps or horses.

By this time his companions, who at first stood aloof, joined him. Three of them had indifferent fowling-pieces; the rest were armed with bows and arrows. I could not but admire the finely shaped heads and busts of these savages, and their graceful attitudes and expressive gestures, as they stood conversing with our interpreter, and surrounded by a cavalcade of rangers. We endeavored to get one of them to join us, as we were desirous of seeing him hunt the buffalo with his bow and arrow. He seemed at first inclined to do so, but was dissuaded by his companions.

The worthy Commissioner now remembered his mission as pacificator, and made a speech, exhorting them to abstain from all offensive acts against the Pawnees; informing them of the plan of their father at Washington, to put an end to all war among his red children; and assuring them that he was sent to the frontier to establish a universal peace. He told them, therefore, to return quietly to their homes, with the certainty that the Pawnees would no longer molest them, but would soon regard them as brothers.

The Indians listened to the speech with their customary

silence and decorum; after which, exchanging a few words among themselves, they bade us farewell, and pursued their way across the prairie.

Fancying that I saw a lurking smile in the countenance of our interpreter, Beatte, I privately inquired what the Indians had said to each other after hearing the speech. The leader, he said, had observed to his companions, that, as their great father intended so soon to put an end to all warfare, it behooved them to make the most of the little time that was left them. So they had departed, with redoubled zeal, to pursue their project of horse stealing!

We had not long parted from the Indians before we discovered three buffaloes among the thickets of a marshy valley to our left. I set off with the Captain and several rangers, in pursuit of them. Stealing through a straggling grove, the Captain, who took the lead, got within rifle shot, and wounded one of them in the flank. They all three made off in headlong panic, through thickets and brushwood, and swamp and mire, bearing down every obstacle by their immense weight. The Captain and rangers soon gave up a chase which threatened to knock up their horses; I had got upon the traces of the wounded bull, however, and was in hopes of getting near enough to use my pistols, the only weapons with which I was provided; but before I could effect it, he reached the foot of a rocky hill, covered with post-oak and brambles, and plunged forward, dashing and crashing along, with neck or nothing fury, where it would have been madness to have followed him.

The chase had led me so far on one side, that it was some time before I regained the trail of our troop. As I was slowly ascending a hill, a fine black mare came prancing round the summit, and was close to me before she was aware. At sight of me she started back, then turning, swept at full speed down into the valley, and up the opposite hill, with flowing mane and tail, and action free as air. I gazed after her as long as she was in sight, and breathed a wish that so glorious an animal might never come under the degrading thraldom of whip and curb, but remain a free rover of the prairies.

CHAPTER XXVII.

FOUL WEATHER ENCAMPMENT.—ANECDOTES OF BEAR HUNTING.—INDIAN NOTIONS ABOUT OMENS.—SCRUPLES RESPECTING THE DEAD.

On overtaking the troop, I found it encamping in a rich bottom of woodland, traversed by a small stream, running between deep crumbling banks. A sharp cracking off of rifles was kept up for some time in various directions, upon a numerous flock of turkeys, scampering among the thickets, or perched upon the trees. We had not been long at a halt, when a drizzling rain ushered in the autumnal storm that had been brewing. Preparations were immediately made to weather it; our tent was pitched, and our saddles, saddlebags, packages of coffee, sugar, salt, and every thing else that could be damaged by the rain, were gathered under its shelter. Our men, Beatte, Tonish, and Antoine, drove stakes with forked ends into the ground, laid poles across them for rafters, and thus made a shed or pent-house, covered with bark and skins, sloping towards the wind, and open towards the fire. The rangers formed similar shelters of bark and skins, or of blankets stretched on poles, supported by forked stakes, with great fires in front.

These precautions were well timed. The rain set in sullenly and steadily, and kept on, with slight intermissions, for two days. The brook which flowed peaceably on our arrival, swelled into a turbid and boiling torrent, and the forest became little better than a mere swamp. The men gathered under their shelters of skins and blankets, or sat cowering round their fires; while columns of smoke curling up among the trees, and diffusing themselves in the air, spread a blue haze through the woodland. Our poor, way-worn horses, reduced by weary travel and scanty pasturage, lost all remaining spirit, and stood, with drooping heads, flagging ears, and half closed eyes, dozing and steaming in the rain: while the yellow autumnal leaves, at every shaking of the breeze, came wavering down around them.

Notwithstanding the bad weather, however, our hunters were not idle, but during the intervals of the rain, sallied forth on horseback to prowl through the woodland. Every now and then the sharp report of a distant rifle boded the death of a deer. Venison in abundance was brought in. Some busied themselves under the sheds, flaying and cutting up the carcasses, or round the fires with spits and camp kettles, and a rude kind of feasting, or rather gormandizing, prevailed throughout the camp. The axe was continually at work, and wearied the forest with its echoes. Crash! some mighty tree would come down; in a few minutes its limbs would be blazing and crackling on the huge camp fires, with some luckless deer roasting before it, that had once sported beneath its shade.

The change of weather had taken sharp hold of our little

Frenchman. His meagre frame, composed of bones and whipcord, was racked with rheumatic pains and twinges. He had the toothache—the earache—his face was tied up—he had shooting pains in every limb: yet all seemed but to increase his restless activity, and he was in an incessant fidget about the fire, roasting, and stewing, and groaning, and scolding, and swearing.

Our man Beatte returned grim and mortified, from hunting. He had come upon a bear of formidable dimensions, and wounded him with a rifle shot. The bear took to the brook, which was swollen and rapid. Beatte dashed in after him and assailed him in the rear with his hunting knife. At every blow the bear turned furiously upon him, with a terrific display of white teeth. Beatte, having a foothold in the brook, was enabled to push him off with his rifle, and, when he turned to swim, would flounder after, and attempt to hamstring him. The bear, however, succeeded in scrambling off among the thickets, and Beatte had to give up the chase.

This adventure, if it produced no game, brought up at least several anecdotes, round the evening fire, relative to bear hunting, in which the grizzly bear figured conspicuously. This powerful and ferocious animal, is a favorite theme of hunter's story, both among red and white men; and his enormous claws are worn round the neck of an Indian brave, as a trophy more honorable than a human scalp. He is now scarcely seen below the upper prairies, and the skirts of the Rocky Mountains. Other bears are formidable when wounded and provoked, but seldom make battle when allowed to escape. The grizzly bear, alone, of all the animals of our western wilds, is prone to unprovoked hostility. His prodigious size and strength, make him a formidable opponent; and his great tenacity of life often baffles the skill of the hunter, notwithstanding repeated shots of the rifle and wounds of the hunting knife.

One of the anecdotes related on this occasion, gave a picture of the accidents and hard shifts, to which our frontier rovers are inured. A hunter, while in pursuit of a deer, fell into one of those deep funnel-shaped pits, formed on the prairies by the settling of the waters after heavy rains, and known by the name of sink-holes. To his great horror, he came in contact, at the bottom, with a huge grizzly bear. The monster grappled him; a deadly contest ensued, in which the poor hunter was severely torn and bitten, and had a leg and an arm broken, but succeeded in killing his rugged foe. For several days he remained at the bottom of the pit, too much crippled to move, and subsisting on the raw flesh of the bear, during which time he kept his wounds open, that they might heal gradually and effectually. He was at length enabled to scramble to the top of the pit, and so out upon the open prairie. With great difficulty he crawled to a ravine, formed by a stream, then nearly dry. Here he took a delicious draught of water, which infused new life into him; then dragging himself along from pool to pool, he supported himself by small fish and frogs.

One day he saw a wolf hunt down and kill a deer in the neighboring prairie. He immediately crawled forth from the ravine, drove off the wolf, and, lying down beside the carcass of the deer, remained there until he made several hearty meals, by which his strength was much recruited.

Returning to the ravine, he pursued the course of the brook, until it grew to be a considerable stream. Down this he floated, until he came to where it emptied into the Mississippi. Just at the mouth of the stream, he found a forked tree, which he launched with some difficulty, and, getting astride of it, committed himself to the current of the mighty river. In this way he floated along, until he arrived opposite the fort at Council Bluffs. Fortunately he arrived there in the daytime, otherwise he might have floated unnoticed, past this solitary post, and perished in the idle waste of waters. Being descried from the fort, a canoe was sent to his relief, and he was brought to shore more dead than alive, where he soon recovered from his wounds, but remained maimed for life.

Our man Beatte had come out of his contest with the bear, very much worsted and discomfited. His drenching in the brook, together with the recent change of weather, had brought on rheumatic pains in his limbs, to which he is subject. Though ordinarily a fellow of undaunted spirit, and above all hardship, yet he now sat down by the fire, gloomy and dejected, and for once gave way to repining. Though in the prime of life, and of a robust frame, and apparently iron constitution, yet, by his own account he was little better than a mere wreck. He was, in fact, a living monument of the hardships of wild frontier life. Baring his left arm, he showed it warped and contracted by a former attack of rheumatism; a malady with which the Indians are often afflicted; for their exposure to the vicissitudes of the elements, does not produce that perfect hardihood and insensibility to the changes of the seasons that many are apt to imagine. He bore the scars of various maims and bruises; some received in hunting, some in Indian warfare. His right arm had been broken by a fall from his horse; at another time his steed had fallen with him, and crushed his left leg.

"I am all broke to pieces and good for nothing;" said he, "I no care now what happen to me any more." "However," added he, after a moment's pause, "for all that, it would take a pretty strong man to put me down, anyhow."

I drew from him various particulars concerning himself, which served to raise him in my estimation. His residence was on the Neosho, in an Osage hamlet or neighborhood, under the superintendence of a worthy missionary from the banks of the Hudson, by the name of Requa, who was endeavoring to instruct the savages in the art of agriculture, and to make husbandmen and herdsmen of them. I had visited this agricultural mission of Requa in the course of my recent tour along the frontier, and had considered it more likely to produce solid advantages to the poor Indians, than any of the mere praying and preaching missions along the border.

In this neighborhood, Pierre Beatte had his little farm, his Indian wife, and his half-breed children; and aided Mr. Requa in his endeavors to civilize the habits, and meliorate the condition of the Osage tribe. Beatte had been brought up a Catholic, and was inflexible in his religious faith; he could not pray with Mr. Requa, he said, but he could work with him, and he evinced a zeal for the good of his savage relations and neighbors. Indeed, though his father had been French, and he himself had been brought up in communion with the whites, he evidently was more of an Indian in his tastes, and his heart yearned towards his mother's nation. When he talked to me of the wrongs and insults that the poor Indians suffered in their intercourse with the rough settlers on the frontiers; when he described the precarious and degraded state of the Osage tribe, diminished in numbers, broken in spirit, and almost living on sufferance in the land where they once figured so heroically, I could see his veins swell, and his nostrils distend with indignation; but he would check the feeling with a strong exertion of Indian self-command, and, in a manner, drive it back into his bosom.

He did not hesitate to relate an instance wherein he had joined his kindred Osages, in pursuing and avenging themselves on a party of white men who had committed a flagrant outrage upon them; and I found, in the encounter that took place, Beatte had shown himself the complete Indian.

He had more than once accompanied his Osage relations in their wars with the Pawnees, and related a skirmish which took place on the borders of these very hunting grounds, in which several Pawnees were killed. We should pass near the place, he said, in the course of our tour, and the unburied bones and skulls of the slain were still to be seen there. The surgeon of the troop, who was present at our conversation, pricked up his ears at this intelligence. He was something of a phrenologist, and offered Beatte a handsome reward if he would procure him one of the skulls.

Beatte regarded him for a moment with a look of stern surprise.

"No!" said he at length, "dat too bad! I have heart strong enough—I no care kill, but *let the dead alone!*"

He added, that once in travelling with a party of white men, he had slept in the same tent with a doctor, and found that he had a Pawnee skull among his baggage: he at once renounced the doctor's tent, and his fellowship. "He try to coax me," said Beatte, "but I say no, we must part—I no keep such company."

In the temporary depression of his sprits, Beatte gave way to those superstitious forebodings to which Indians are prone. He had sat for some time, with his cheek upon his hand, gazing into the fire. I found his thoughts were wandering back to his humble home, on the banks of the Neosho; he was sure, he said, that he should find some one of his family ill, or dead, on his return: his left eye had twitched and twinkled for two days past; an omen which always boded some misfortune of the kind.

Such are the trivial circumstances which, when magnified into omens, will shake the souls of these men of iron. The least sign of mystic and sinister portent, is sufficient to turn a hunter or a warrior from his course, or to fill his mind with apprehensions of impending evil. It is this superstitious propensity, common to the solitary and savage rovers of the wilderness, that gives such powerful influence to the prophet and the dreamer.

The Osages, with whom Beatte had passed much of his life, retain these superstitious fancies and rites in much of their original force. They all believe in the existence of the soul after its separation from the body, and that it carries with it all its mortal tastes and habitudes. At an Osage village in the neighborhood of Beatte, one of the chief warriors lost an only child, a beautiful girl, of a very tender age. All her playthings were buried with her. Her favorite little horse, also, was killed, and laid in the grave beside her, that she might have it to ride in the land of spirits.

I will here add a little story, which I picked up in the course of my tour through Beatte's country, and which illustrates the superstitions of his Osage kindred. A large party of Osages had been encamped for some time on the borders of a fine stream called the Nickanansa. Among them was a young hunter, one of the bravest and most graceful of the tribe, who was to be married to an Osage girl, who, for her beauty, was called the Flower of the Prairies. The young hunter left her for a time among her relatives in the encampment, and went to St. Louis, to dispose of the products of his hunting, and purchase ornaments for his bride. After an absence of some weeks, he returned to the banks of the Nickanansa, but the camp was no longer there; the bare frames of the lodges and the brands of extinguished fires alone marked the place. At a distance he beheld a female seated, as if weeping, by the side of the stream. It was his affianced bride. He ran to embrace her, but she turned mournfully away. He dreaded lest some evil had befallen the camp.

"Where are our people?" cried he.

"They are gone to the banks of the Wagrushka."

"And what art thou doing here alone?"

"Waiting for thee."

"Then let us hasten to join our people on the banks of the Wagrushka."

He gave her his pack to carry, and walked ahead, according to the Indian custom.

They came to where the smoke of the distant camp was seen rising from the woody margin of the stream. The girl seated herself at the foot of a tree. "It is not proper for us to return together," said she; "I will wait here."

The young hunter proceeded to the camp alone, and was received by his relations with gloomy countenances.

"What evil has happened," said he, "that ye are all so sad?"

No one replied.

He turned to his favorite sister, and bade her go forth, seek his bride, and conduct her to the camp.

"Alas!" cried she, "how shall I seek her? She died a few days since."

The relations of the young girl now surrounded him, weeping and wailing; but he refused to believe the dismal tidings. "But a few moments since," cried he, "I left her alone and in health: come with me, and I will conduct you to her."

He led the way to the tree where she had seated herself, but the was no longer there, and his pack lay on the ground. The fatal truth struck him to the heart; he fell to the ground dead.

I give this simple little story almost in the words in which it was related to me, as I lay by the fire in an evening encampment on the banks of the haunted stream where it is said to have happened.

CHAPTER XXVIII.

A SECRET EXPEDITION.—DEER BLEATING.—MAGIC BALLS.

On the following morning we were rejoined by the rangers who had remained at the last encampment, to seek for the stray horses They had tracked them for a considerable distance through bush and brake, and across streams, until they found them cropping the herbage on the edge of a prairie. Their heads were in the direction of the fort, and they were evidently grazing their way homeward, heedless of the unbounded freedom of the prairie so suddenly laid open to them.

About noon the weather held up, and I observed a mysterious consultation going on between our half-breeds and Tonish; it ended in a request that we would dispense with the services of the latter for a few hours, and permit him to join his comrades in a grand foray. We objected that Tonish was too much disabled by aches and pains for such an undertaking; but he was wild with eagerness for the mysterious enterprise, and, when permission was given him, seemed to forget all his ailments in an instant.

In a short time the trio were equipped and on horseback; with rifles on their shoulders and handkerchiefs twisted round their heads, evidently bound for a grand scamper. As they passed by the different lodges of the camp, the vainglorious little Frenchman could not help boasting to the right and left of the great things he was about to achieve; though the taciturn Beatte, who rode in advance, would every now and then check his horse, and look back at him with an air of stern rebuke. It was hard, however, to make the loquacious Tonish play "Indian."

Several of the hunters, likewise, sallied forth, and the prime old woodman, Ryan, came back early in the afternoon, with ample spoil, having killed a buck and two fat does. I drew near to a group of rangers that had gathered round him as he stood by the spoil, and found they were discussing the merits of a stratagem sometimes used in deer hunting. This consists in imitating, with a small instrument called a bleat, the cry of the fawn, so as to lure the doe within reach of the rifle. There are bleats of various kinds, suited to calm or windy weather, and to the age of the fawn. The poor animal, deluded by them, in its anxiety about its young, will sometimes advance close up to the hunter. "I once bleated a doe," said a young hunter, "until it came within twenty yards of me, and presented a sure mark. I levelled my rifle three times, but had not the heart to shoot, for the poor doe looked so wistfully, that it in a manner made my heart yearn. I thought of my own mother, and how anxious she used to be about me when I was a child; so to put an end to the matter, I gave a halloo, and started the doe out of rifle shot in a moment."

"And you did right," cried honest old Ryan. "For my part, I never could bring myself to bleating deer. I've been with hunters who had bleats, and have made them throw them away. It is a rascally trick to take advantage of a mother's love for her young."

Towards evening, our three worthies returned from their mysterious foray. The tongue of Tonish gave notice of their approach, long before they came in sight; for he was vociferating at the top of his lungs, and rousing the attention of the whole camp. The lagging gait and reeking flanks of their horses, gave evidence of hard riding; and, on nearer approach, we found them hung round with meat, like a butcher's shambles. In fact they had been scouring an immense prairie that extended beyond the forest, and which was covered with herds of buffalo. Of this prairie, and the animals upon it, Beatte had received intelligence a few days before, in his conversation with the Osages: but had kept the information a secret from the rangers, that he and his comrades might have the first dash at the game. They had contented themselves with killing four; though, if Tonish might be believed, they might have slain them by scores.

These tidings, and the buffalo meat brought home in evidence, spread exultation through the camp, and every one looked forward with joy to a buffalo hunt on the prairies. Tonish was again the oracle of the camp, and held forth by the hour to a knot of listeners, crouched round the fire, with their shoulders up to their ears. He was now more boastful than ever of his skill as a marksman. All his want of success in the early part of our march, he attributed to being "out of luck," if not "spellbound;" and finding himself listened to with apparent credulity, gave an instance of the kind, which he declared had happened to himself, but which was evidently a tale picked up among his relations, the Osages.

According to this account, when about fourteen years of age, as he was one day hunting, he saw a white deer come out from a ravine. Crawling near to get a shot, he beheld another and another come forth, until there were seven, all as white as snow. Having crept sufficiently near, he singled one out and fired, but without effect; the deer remained unfrightened. He loaded and fired again, and again he missed. Thus he continued firing and missing until all his ammunition was expended, and the deer remained without a wound. He returned home despairing of his skill as a marksman, but was consoled by an old Osage hunter. These white deer, said he, have a charmed life, and can only be killed by bullets of a particular kind.

The old Indian cast several balls for Tonish, but would not suffer him to be present on the occasion, nor inform him of the ingredients and mystic ceremonials.

Provided with these balls, Tonish again set out in quest of the white deer, and succeeded in finding them. He tried at first with ordinary balls, but missed as before. A magic ball, however, immediately brought a fine buck to the ground. Whereupon the rest of the herd immediately disappeared and were never seen again.

Oct. 29. The morning opened gloomy and lowering; but towards eight o'clock the sun struggled forth and lighted up the forest, and the notes of the bugle gave signal to prepare for marching. Now began a scene of bustle, and clamor, and gayety. Some were scampering and brawling after their horses, some were riding in bare-backed, and driving in the horses of their comrades. Some were stripping the poles of the wet blankets that had served for shelters ; others packing up with all possible dispatch, and loading the baggage horses as they arrived, while others were cracking off their damp rifles and charging them afresh, to be ready for the sport.

About ten o'clock we began our march. I loitered in the rear of the troop as it forded the turbid brook and defiled through the labyrinths of the forest. I always felt disposed to linger until the last straggler disappeared among the trees and the distant note of the bugle died upon the ear, that I might behold the wilderness relapsing into silence and solitude. In the present instance, the deserted scene of our late bustling encampment had a forlorn and desolate appearance. The surrounding forest had been in many places trampled into a quagmire. Trees felled and partly hewn in pieces, and scattered in huge fragments ; tent-poles stripped of their covering ; smouldering fires, with great morsels of roasted venison and buffalo meat, standing in wooden spits before them, hacked and slashed by the knives of hungry hunters ; while around were strewed the hides, the horns, the antlers and bones of buffaloes and deer, with uncooked joints, and unplucked turkeys, left behind with that reckless improvidence and wastefulness which young hunters are apt to indulge when in a neighborhood where game abounds. In the meantime a score or two of turkey-buzzards, or vultures, were already on the wing, wheeling their magnificent flight high in the air, and preparing for a descent upon the camp as soon as it should be abandoned.

CHAPTER XXIX.

THE GRAND PRAIRIE.—A BUFFALO HUNT.

After proceeding about two hours in a southerly direction, we emerged towards mid-day from the dreary belt of the Cross Timber, and to our infinite delight beheld "the great Prairie," stretching to the right and left before us. We could distinctly trace the meandering course of the Main Canadian, and various smaller streams, by the strips of green forest that bordered them. The landscape was vast and beautiful. There is always an expansion of feeling in looking upon these boundless and fertile wastes; but I was doubly conscious of it after emerging from our "close dungeon of innumerous boughs."

From a rising ground Beatte pointed out the place where he and his comrades had killed the buffaloes; and we beheld several black objects moving in the distance, which he said were part of the herd. The Captain determined to shape his course to a woody bottom about a mile distant, and to encamp there for a day or two, by way of having a regular buffalo hunt, and getting a supply of provisions. As the troop defiled along the slope of the hill towards the camping ground, Beatte proposed to my messmates and myself, that we should put ourselves under his guidance, promising to take us where we should have plenty of sport. Leaving the line of march, therefore, we diverged towards the prairie; traversing a small valley, and ascending a gentle swell of land. As we reached the summit, we beheld a gang of wild horses about a mile off. Beatte was immediately on the alert, and no longer thought of buffalo hunting. He was mounted on his powerful half-wild horse, with a lariat coiled at the saddle-bow, and set off in pursuit; while we remained on a rising ground watching his manœuvres with great solicitude. Taking advantage of a strip of woodland, he stole quietly along, so as to get close to them before he was perceived. The moment they caught sight of him a grand scamper took place. We watched him skirting along the horizon like a privateer in full chase of a merchantman; at length he passed over the brow of a ridge, and down into a shallow valley; in a few moments he was on the opposite hill, and close upon one of the horses. He was soon head and head, and appeared to be trying to noose his prey; but they both disappeared again below the hill, and we saw no more of them. It turned out afterwards, that he had noosed a powerful horse, but could not hold him, and had lost his lariat in the attempt.

While we were waiting for his return, we perceived two buffalo bulls descending a slope, towards a stream, which wound through a ravine fringed with trees. The young Count and myself endeavored to get near them under covert of the trees. They discovered us while we were yet three or four hundred yards off, and turning about, retreated up the rising ground. We urged our horses across the ravine, and gave chase. The immense weight of head and shoulders causes the buffalo to labor heavily up hill; but it accelerates his descent. We had the advantage, therefore, and gained rapidly upon the fugitives, though it was difficult to get our horses to approach them, their very scent inspiring them with terror. The Count, who had a double-barrelled gun loaded with ball, fired, but it missed. The bulls now altered their course, and galloped down hill with headlong rapidity. As they ran in different directions, we each singled one and separated. I was provided with a brace of veteran brass-barrelled pistols, which I had borrowed at Fort Gibson, and which had evidently seen some service. Pistols are very effective in buffalo hunting, as the hunter can ride up close to the animal, and fire at it while at full speed; whereas the long heavy rifles used on the frontier, cannot be easily managed, nor discharged with accurate aim from horseback. My object, therefore, was to get within pistol shot of the buffalo. This was no very easy matter. I was well mounted on a horse of excellent speed and bottom, that seemed eager for the chase, and soon overtook the game; but the moment he came nearly parallel, he would keep sheering off, with ears forked and pricked forward, and every symptom of aversion and alarm. It was no wonder. Of all animals, a buffalo, when close pressed by the hunter, has an aspect the most diabolical. His two short black horns, curve out of a huge frontlet of shaggy hair; his eyes glow like coals; his mouth is open, his tongue parched and drawn up into a half crescent; his tail is erect, and tufted and whisking about in the air, he is a perfect picture of mingled rage and terror.

It was with difficulty I urged my horse sufficiently near, when, taking aim, to my chagrin, both pistols missed fire. Unfortunately the locks of these veteran weapons were so much worn, that in the gallop, the priming had been shaken out of the pans. At the snapping of the last pistol I was close upon the buffalo, when, in his despair, he turned round with a sudden snort and rushed upon me. My horse wheeled about as if on a pivot, made a convulsive spring, and, as I had been leaning on one side with pistol extended, I came near being thrown at the feet of the buffalo.

Three or four bounds of the horse carried us out of the reach of the enemy; who, having merely turned in desperate self-defence, quickly resumed his flight. As soon as I could gather in my panic-stricken horse, and prime the pistols afresh, I again spurred in pursuit of the buffalo, who had slackened his speed to take breath. On my approach he again set off full tilt, heaving himself forward with a heavy rolling gallop, dashing with headlong precipitation through brakes and ravines, while several deer and wolves, startled from their coverts by his thundering career, ran helter-skelter to right and left across the waste.

A gallop across the prairies in pursuit of game, is by no means so smooth a career as those may imagine, who have only the idea of an open level plain. It is true, the prairies of the hunting ground are not so much entangled with flowering plants and long herbage as the lower prairies, and are principally covered with short buffalo grass; but they are diversified by hill and dale, and where most level, are apt to be cut up by deep rifts and ravines, made by torrents after rains; and which, yawning from an even surface, are almost like pitfalls in the way of the hunter, checking him suddenly, when in full career, or subjecting him to the risk of limb and life. The plains, too, are beset by burrowing holes of small animals, in which the horse is apt to sink to the fetlock, and throw both himself and his rider. The late rain had covered some parts of the prairie, where the ground was hard, with a thin sheet of water, through which the horse had to splash his way. In other parts there were innumerable shallow hollows, eight or ten feet in diameter, made by the buffaloes, who wallow in sand and mud like swine. These being filled with water, shone like mirrors, so that the horse was continually leaping over them or springing on one side. We had reached, too, a rough part of the prairie, very much broken and cut up; the buffalo, who was running for life, took no heed to his course, plunging down break-neck ravines, where it was necessary to skirt the borders in search of a safer descent. At length we came to where a winter stream had torn a deep chasm across the whole prairie, leaving open jagged rocks, and forming a long glen bordered by steep crumbling cliffs of mingled stone and clay. Down one of these the buffalo flung himself, half tumbling, half leaping, and then scuttled along the bottom; while I, seeing all further pursuit useless, pulled up, and gazed quietly after him from the border of the cliff, until he disappeared amidst the windings of the ravine.

Nothing now remained but to turn my steed and rejoin my companions. Here at first was some little difficulty. The ardor of the chase had betrayed me into a long, heedless gallop. I now found myself in the midst of a lonely waste, in which the prospect was bounded by undulating swells of land, naked and uniform, where, from the deficiency of landmarks and distinct features, an inexperienced man may become bewildered, and lose his way as readily as in the wastes of the ocean. The day, too, was overcast, so that I could not guide myself by the sun; my only mode was to retrace the track my horse had made in coming, though this I would often lose sight of, where the ground was covered with parched herbage.

To one unaccustomed to it, there is something inexpressibly lonely in the solitude of a prairie. The loneliness of a forest seems nothing to it. There the view is shut in by trees, and the imagination is left free to picture some livelier scene beyond. But here we have an immense extent of landscape without a sign of human existence. We have the consciousness of being far, far beyond the bounds of human habitation; we feel as if moving in the midst of a desert world. As my horse lagged slowly back over the scenes of our late scamper, and the delirium of the chase had passed away, I was peculiarly sensible to these circumstances. The silence of the waste was now and then broken by the cry of a distant flock of pelicans, stalking like spectres about a shallow pool; sometimes by the sinister croaking of a raven in the air, while occasionally a scoundrel wolf would scour off from before me; and, having attained a safe distance, would sit down and howl and whine with tones that gave a dreariness to the surrounding solitude.

After pursuing my way for some time, I descried a horseman on the edge of a distant hill, and soon recognized him to be the Count. He had been equally unsuccessful with myself; we were shortly after rejoined by our worthy comrade, the Virtuoso, who, with spectacles on nose, had made two or three ineffectual shots from horseback.

We determined not to seek the camp until we had made one more effort. Casting our eyes about the surrounding waste, we descried a herd of buffalo about two miles distant, scattered apart, and quietly grazing near a small strip of trees and bushes. It required but little stretch of fancy to picture them so many cattle grazing on the edge of a common, and that the grove might shelter some lowly farmhouse.

We now formed our plan to circumvent the herd, and by getting on the other side of them, to hunt them in the direction where we knew our camp to be situated: otherwise, the pursuit might take us to such a distance as to render it impossible to find our way back before nightfall. Taking a wide circuit therefore, we moved slowly and cautiously, pausing occasionally, when we saw any of the herd desist from grazing. The wind fortunately set from them, otherwise they might have scented us and have taken the alarm. In this way, we succeeded in getting round the herd without disturbing it. It consisted of about forty head, bulls, cows and calves. Separating to some distance from each other, we now approached slowly in a parallel line, hoping by degrees to steal near without exciting attention. They began, however, to move off quietly, stopping at every step or two to graze, when suddenly a bull that, unobserved by us, had been taking his siesta under a clump of trees to our left, roused himself from his lair, and hastened to join his companions. We were still at a considerable distance, but the game had taken the alarm. We quickened our pace, they broke into a gallop, and now commenced a full chase.

As the ground was level, they shouldered along with great speed, following each other in a line; two or three bulls bringing up the rear, the last of whom, from his enormous size and venerable frontlet, and beard of sunburnt hair, looked like the patriarch of the herd; and as if he might long have reigned the monarch of the prairie.

There is a mixture of the awful and the comic in the look of these huge animals, as they bear their great bulk forwards, with an up and down motion of the unwieldy head and shoulders; their tail cocked up like the cue of Pantaloon in a pantomime, the end whisking about in a fierce yet whimsical style, and their eyes glaring venomously with an expression of fright and fury.

For some time I kept parallel with the line, without being able to force my horse within pistol shot, so much had he been alarmed by the assault of the buffalo in the preceding chase. At length I succeeded, but was again balked by my pistols missing fire. My companions, whose horses were less fleet, and more way-worn, could not overtake the herd; at length Mr. L., who was in the rear of the line, and losing ground, levelled his double-barrelled gun, and fired a long raking shot. It struck a buffalo just above the loins, broke its back-bone, and brought it to the ground. He stopped and alighted to dispatch his prey, when borrowing his gun, which had yet a charge remaining in it, I put my horse to his speed, again overtook the herd which was thundering along, pursued by the Count. With my present weapon there was no need of urging my horse to such close quarters; galloping along parallel, therefore, I singled out a buffalo, and by a fortunate shot brought it down on the spot. The ball had struck a vital part; it could not move from the place where it fell, but lay there struggling in mortal agony, while the rest of the herd kept on their headlong career across the prairie.

Dismounting, I now fettered my horse to prevent his straying, and advanced to contemplate my victim. I am nothing of a sportsman; I had been prompted to this unwonted exploit by the magnitude of the game, and the excitement of an adventurous chase. Now that the excitement was over, I could not but look with commiseration upon the poor animal that lay struggling and bleeding at my feet. His very size and importance, which had before inspired me with eagerness, now increased my compunction. It seemed as if I had inflicted pain in proportion to the bulk of my victim, and as if there were a hundred-fold greater waste of life than there would have been in the destruction of an animal of inferior size.

To add to these after-qualms of conscience, the poor animal lingered in his agony. He had evidently received a mortal wound, but death might be long in coming. It would not do to leave him here to be torn piecemeal, while yet alive, by the wolves that had already snuffed his blood, and were skulking and howling at a distance, and waiting for my departure; and by the ravens that were flapping about, croaking dismally in the air. It became now an act of mercy to give him his quictus, and put him out of his misery. I primed one of the pistols, therefore, and advanced close up to the buffalo. To inflict a wound thus in cold blood, I found a totally different thing from firing in the heat of the chase. Taking aim, however, just behind the fore-shoulder, my pistol for once proved true; the ball must have passed through the heart, for the animal gave one convulsive throe and expired.

While I stood meditating and moralizing over the wreck I had so wantonly produced, with my horse grazing near me, I was rejoined by my fellow-sportsman, the Virtuoso; who, being a man of universal adroitness, and withal, more experienced and hardened in the gentle art of "venerie," soon managed to carve out the tongue of the buffalo, and delivered it to me to bear back to the camp as a trophy.

CHAPTER XXX.

A COMRADE LOST.—A SEARCH FOR THE CAMP.—THE COMMISSIONER, THE WILD HORSE, AND THE BUFFALO.—A WOLF SERENADE.

Our solicitude was now awakened for the young Count. With his usual eagerness and impetuosity he had persisted in urging his jaded horse in pursuit of the herd, unwilling to return without having likewise killed a buffalo. In this way he had kept on following them, hither and thither, and occasionally firing an ineffectual shot, until by degrees horseman and herd became indistinct in the distance, and at length swelling ground and strips of trees and thickets hid them entirely from sight.

By the time my friend, the amateur, joined me, the young Count had been long lost to view. We held a consultation on the matter. Evening was drawing on. Were we to pursue him, it would be dark before we should overtake him, granting we did not entirely lose trace of him in the gloom. We should then be too much bewildered to find our way back to the encampment; even now, our return would be difficult. We determined, therefore, to hasten to the camp as speedily as possible, and send out our half-breeds, and some of the veteran hunters, skilled in cruising about the prairies, to search for our companion.

We accordingly set forward in what we supposed to be the direction of the camp. Our weary horses could hardly be urged beyond a walk. The twilight thickened upon us; the landscape grew gradually indistinct; we tried in vain to recognize various landmarks which we had noted in the morning. The features of the prairies are so similar as to baffle the eye of any but an

Indian, or a practised woodman. At length night closed in. We hoped to see the distant glare of camp fires; we listened to catch the sound of the bells about the necks of the grazing horses. Once or twice we thought we distinguished them; we were mistaken. Nothing was to be heard but a monotonous concert of insects, with now and then the dismal howl of wolves mingling with the night breeze. We began to think of halting for the night, and bivouacking under the lee of some thicket. We had implements to strike a light: there was plenty of fire-wood at hand, and the tongues of our buffaloes would furnish us with a repast.

Just as we were preparing to dismount, we heard the report of a rifle, and shortly after, the notes of the bugle, calling up the night guard. Pushing forward in that direction, the camp fires soon broke on our sight, gleaming at a distance from among the thick groves of an alluvial bottom.

As we entered the camp, we found it a scene of rude hunters' revelry and wassail. There had been a grand day's sport, in which all had taken a part. Eight buffaloes had been killed; roaring fires were blazing on every side; all hands were feasting upon roasted joints, broiled marrow-bones, and the juicy hump, far-famed among the epicures of the prairies. Right glad were we to dismount and partake of the sturdy cheer, for we had been on our weary horses since morning without tasting food.

As to our worthy friend, the Commissioner, with whom we had parted company at the outset of this eventful day, we found him lying in a corner of the tent, much the worse for wear, in the course of a successful hunting match.

It seems that our man, Beatte, in his zeal to give the Commissioner an opportunity of distinguishing himself, and gratifying his hunting propensities, had mounted him upon his half-wild horse, and started him in pursuit of a huge buffalo bull, that had already been frightened by the hunters. The horse, which was fearless as his owner, and, like him, had a considerable spice of devil in his composition, and who, beside, had been made familiar with the game, no sooner came in sight and scent of the buffalo than he set off full speed, bearing the involuntary hunter hither and thither, and whither he would not—up hill and down hill—leaping pools and brooks—dashing through glens and gullies, until he came up with the game. Instead of sheering off, he crowded upon the buffalo. The Commissioner, almost in self-defence, discharged both barrels of a double-barrelled gun into the enemy. The broadside took effect, but was not mortal. The buffalo turned furiously upon his pursuer: the horse, as he had been taught by his owner, wheeled off. The buffalo plunged after him. The worthy Commissioner, in great extremity, drew his sole pistol from his holster, fired it off as a stern-chaser, shot the buffalo full in the breast, and brought him lumbering forward to the earth.

The Commissioner returned to camp, lauded on all sides for his signal exploit; but grievously battered and way-worn. He had been a hard rider per force, and a victor in spite of himself. He turned a deaf ear to all compliments and congratulations; had but little stomach for the hunter's fare placed before him, and soon retreated to stretch his limbs in the tent, declaring that nothing should tempt him again to mount that half devil Indian horse, and that he had enough of buffalo hunting for the rest of his life.

It was too dark now to send any one in search of the young Count. Guns, however, were fired, and the bugle sounded from time to time, to guide him to the camp, if by chance he should straggle within hearing; but the night advanced without his making his appearance. There was not a star visible to guide him, and we concluded that wherever he was, he would give up wandering in the dark, and bivouack until daybreak.

It was a raw, overcast night. The carcasses of the buffaloes killed in the vicinity of the camp, had drawn about it an unusual number of wolves, who kept up the most forlorn concert of whining yells, prolonged into dismal cadences and inflexions, literally converting the surrounding waste into a howling wilderness. Nothing is more melancholy than the midnight howl of a wolf on a prairie. What rendered the gloom and wildness of the night and the savage concert of the neighboring waste the more dreary to us, was the idea of the lonely and exposed situation of our young and inexperienced comrade. We trusted, however, that on the return of daylight, he would find his way back to the camp, and then all the events of the night would be remembered only as so many savory gratifications of his passion for adventure.

CHAPTER XXXI.

A HUNT FOR A LOST COMRADE.

The morning dawned, and an hour or two passed without any tidings of the Count. We began to feel uneasiness lest, having no compass to aid him, he might perplex himself and wander in some opposite direction. Stragglers are thus often lost for days; what made us the more anxious about him was, that he had no provisions with him, was totally unversed in "wood craft," and liable to fall into the hands of some lurking or straggling party of savages.

As soon as our people, therefore, had made their breakfast, we beat up for volunteers for a cruise in search of the Count. A dozen of the rangers, mounted on some of the best and freshest horses, and armed with rifles, were soon ready to start; our half-breeds Beatte and Antoine also, with our little mongrel Frenchman, were zealous in the cause; so Mr. L. and myself taking the lead, to show the way to the scene of our little hunt, where we had parted company with the Count, we all set out across the prairie. A ride of a couple of miles brought us to the carcasses of the two buffaloes we had killed. A legion of ravenous wolves were already gorging upon them. At our approach they reluctantly drew off, skulking with a caitiff look to the distance of a few hundred yards, and there awaiting our departure, that they might return to their banquet.

I conducted Beatte and Antoine to the spot whence the young Count had continued the chase alone. It was like putting hounds upon the scent. They immediately distinguished the track of his horse amidst the trampings of the buffaloes, and set off at a round pace, following with the eye in nearly a straight course, for upwards of a mile, when they came to where the herd had divided, and run hither and thither about a meadow. Here the track of the horse's hoofs wandered and doubled and often crossed each other; our half-breeds were like hounds at fault While we were at a halt, waiting until they should unravel the maze, Beatte suddenly gave a short Indian whoop, or rather yelp, and pointed to a distant hill. On regarding it attentively, we perceived a horseman on the summit. "It is the Count!" cried

Beatte, and set off at full gallop, followed by the whole company. In a few moments he checked his horse. Another figure on horseback had appeared on the brow of the hill. This completely altered the case. The Count had wandered off alone; no other person had been missing from the camp. If one of these horsemen were indeed the Count, the other must be an Indian. If an Indian, in all probability a Pawnee. Perhaps they were both Indians; scouts of some party lurking in the vicinity. While these and other suggestions were hastily discussed, the two horsemen glided down from the profile of the hile, and we lost sight of them. One of the rangers suggested that there might be a straggling party of Pawnees behind the hill, and that the Count might have fallen into their hands. The idea had an electric effect upon the little troop. In an instant every horse was at full speed, the half-breeds leading the way; the young rangers as they rode set up wild yelps of exultation at the thoughts of having a brush with the Indians. A neck or nothing gallop brought us to the skirts of the hill, and revealed our mistake. In a ravine we found the two horsemen standing by the carcass of a buffalo which they had killed. They proved to be two rangers, who, unperceived, had left the camp a little before us, and had come here in a direct line, while we had made a wide circuit about the prairie.

This episode being at an end, and the sudden excitement being over, we slowly and coolly retraced our steps to the meadow, but it was some time before our half-breeds could again get on the track of the Count. Having at length found it, they succeeded in following it through all its doublings, until they came to where it was no longer mingled with the tramp of buffaloes, but became single and separate, wandering here and there about the prairies, but always tending in a direction opposite to that of the camp. Here the Count had evidently given up the pursuit of the herd, and had endeavored to find his way to the encampment, but had become bewildered as the evening shades thickened around him, and had completely mistaken the points of the compass.

In all this quest our half-breeds displayed that quickness of eye, in following up a track, for which Indians are so noted. Beatte, especially, was as stanch as a veteran hound. Sometimes he would keep forward on an easy trot; his eyes fixed on the ground a little ahead of his horse, clearly distinguishing prints in the herbage which to me were invisible, excepting on the closest inspection. Sometimes he would pull up and walk his horse slowly, regarding the ground intensely, where to my eye nothing was apparent. Then he would dismount, lead his horse by the bridle, and advance cautiously step by step, with his face bent towards the earth, just catching, here and there, a casual indication of the vaguest kind to guide him onward. In some places where the soil was hard, and the grass withered, he would lose the track entirely, and wander backwards and forwards, and right and left, in search of it; returning occasionally to the place where he had lost sight of it, to take a new departure. If this failed he would examine the banks of the neighboring streams, or the sandy bottoms of the ravines, in hopes of finding tracks where the Count had crossed. When he again came upon the track, he would remount his horse, and resume his onward course. At length, after crossing a stream, in the crumbling banks of which the hoofs of the horse were deeply dented, we came upon a high dry pariria, where our half-breeds were completely baffled. Not a foot-print was to be discerned, though they searched in every direction ; and Beatte at length coming to a pause, shook his head despondingly.

Just then a small herd of deer, roused from a neighboring ravine, came bounding by us. Beatte sprang from his horse, levelled his rifle, and wounded one slightly, but without bringing it to the ground. The report of the rifle was almost immediately followed by a long halloo from a distance. We looked around but could see nothing. Another long halloo was heard, and at length a horseman was descried, emerging out of a skirt of forest. A single glance showed him to be the young Count ; there was a universal shout and scamper, every one setting off full gallop to greet him. It was a joyful meeting to both parties ; for, much anxiety had been felt by us all on account of his youth and inexperience, and for his part, with all his love of adventure, he seemed right glad to be once more among his friends.

As we supposed, he had completely mistaken his course on the preceding evening, and had wandered about until dark, when he thought of bivouacking. The night was cold, yet he feared to make a fire, lest it might betray him to some lurking party of Indians. Hobbling his horse with his pocket handkerchief, and leaving him to graze on the margin of the prairie, he clambered into a tree, fixed his saddle in the fork of the branches, and placing himself securely with his back against the trunk, prepared to pass a dreary and anxious night, regaled occasionally with the howlings of the wolves. He was agreeably disappointed. The fatigue of the day soon brought on a sound sleep ; he had delightful dreams about his home in Switzerland, nor did he wake until it was broad daylight.

He then descended from his roosting-place, mounted his horse, and rode to the naked summit of a hill, whence he beheld a trackless wilderness around him, but, at no great distance, the Grand Canadian, winding its way between borders of forest land The sight of this river consoled him with the idea that, should he fail in finding his way back to the camp, or, in being found by some party of his comrades, he might follow the course of the stream, which could not fail to conduct him to some frontier post, or Indian hamlet. So closed the events of our hap-hazard buffalo hunt.

CHAPTER XXXII.

A REPUBLIC OF PRAIRIE DOGS.

ON returning from our expedition in quest of the young Count, I learned that a burrow, or village, as it is termed, of prairie dogs had been discovered on the level summit of a hill, about a mile from the camp. Having heard much of the habits and peculiarities of these little animals, I determined to pay a visit to the community. The prairie dog is, in fact, one of the curiosities of the Far West, about which travellers delight to tell marvellous tales, endowing him at times with something of the politic and social habits of a rational being, and giving him systems of civil government and domestic economy, almost equal to what they used to bestow upon the beaver.

The prairie dog is an animal of the coney kind, and about the size of a rabbit. He is of a sprightly mercurial nature; quick, sensitive, and somewhat petulant. He is very gregarious, living in large communities, sometimes of several acres in extent, where innumerable little heaps of earth show the entrances to the subterranean cells of the inhabitants, and the well beaten tracks, like lanes and streets, show their mobility and restlessness. According to the accounts given of them, they would seem to be continually full of sport, business, and public affairs; whisking about hither and thither, as if on gossiping visits to each other's houses, or congregating in the cool of the evening, or after a shower, and gambolling together in the open air. Sometimes, especially when the moon shines, they pass half the night in revelry, barking or yelping with short, quick, yet weak tones, like those of very young puppies. While in the height of their playfulness and clamor, however, should there be the least alarm, they all vanish into their cells in an instant, and the village remains blank and silent. In case they are hard pressed by their pursuers, without any hope of escape, they will assume a pugnacious air, and a most whimsical look of impotent wrath and defiance.

The prairie dogs are not permitted to remain sole and undisturbed inhabitants of their own homes. Owls and rattlesnakes are said to take up their abodes with them; but whether as invited guests or unwelcome intruders, is a matter of controversy. The owls are of a peculiar kind, and would seem to partake of the character of the hawk; for they are taller and more erect on their legs, more alert in their looks and rapid in their flight than ordinary owls, and do not confine their excursions to the night, but sally forth in broad day.

Some say that they only inhabit cells which the prairie dogs have deserted, and suffered to go to ruin, in consequence of the death in them of some relative; for they would make out this ittle animal to be endowed with keen sensibilities, that will not permit it to remain in the dwelling where it has witnessed the death of a friend. Other fanciful speculators represent the owl as a kind of housekeeper to the prairie dog; and, from having a note very similar, insinuate that it acts, in a manner, as family preceptor, and teaches the young litter to bark.

As to the rattlesnake, nothing satisfactory has been ascertained of the part he plays in this most interesting household; though he is considered as little better than a sycophant and sharper, that winds himself into the concerns of the honest, credulous little dog, and takes him in most sadly. Certain it is, if he acts as toad-eater, he occasionally solaces himself with more than the usual perquisites of his order; as he is now and then detected with one of the younger members of the family in his maw.

Such are a few of the particulars that I could gather about the domestic economy of this little inhabitant of the prairies, who, with his pigmy republic, appears to be a subject of much whimsical speculation and burlesque remarks, among the hunters of the Far West.

It was towards evening that I set out with a companion, to visit the village in question. Unluckily, it had been invaded in the course of the day by some of the rangers, who had shot two or three of its inhabitants, and thrown the whole sensitive community in confusion. As we approached, we could perceive numbers of the inhabitants seated at the entrances of their cells, while sentinels seemed to have been posted on the outskirts, to keep a look-out. At sight of us, the picket guards scampered in and gave the alarm; whereupon every inhabitant gave a short yelp, or bark, and dived into his hole, his heels twinkling in the air as if he had thrown a somerset.

We traversed the whole village, or republic, which covered an area of about thirty acres; but not a whisker of an inhabitant was to be seen. We probed their cells as far as the ramrods of our rifles would reach, but could unearth neither dog, nor owl, nor rattlesnake. Moving quietly to a little distance, we lay down upon the ground, and watched for a long time, silent and motionless. By and by, a cautious old burgher would slowly put forth the end of his nose, but instantly draw it in again. Another, at a greater distance, would emerge entirely; but, catching a glance of us, would throw a somerset, and plunge back again into his hole. At length, some who resided on the opposite side of the village, taking courage from the continued stillness, would steal forth, and hurry off to a distant hole, the residence possibly of some family connection, or gossiping friend, about whose safety they were solicitous, or with whom they wished to compare notes about the late occurrences.

Others, still more bold, assembled in little knots, in the streets and public places, as if to discuss the recent outrages offered to the commonwealth, and the atrocious murders of their fellow-burghers.

We rose from the ground and moved forward, to take a nearer view of these public proceedings, when, yelp! yelp! yelp!—there was a shrill alarm passed from mouth to mouth; the meetings suddenly dispersed; feet twinkled in the air in every direction; and in an instant all had vanished into the earth.

The dusk of the evening put an end to our observations, but the train of whimsical comparisons produced in my brain by the moral attributes which I had heard given to these little politic animals, still continued after my return to camp; and late in the night, as I lay awake after all the camp was asleep, and heard in the stillness of the hour, a faint clamor of shrill voices from the distant village, I could not help picturing to myself the inhabitants gathered together in noisy assemblage, and windy debate. to devise plans for the public safety, and to vindicate the invaded rights and insulted dignity of the republic.

CHAPTER XXXIII.

A COUNCIL IN THE CAMP.—REASONS FOR FACING HOMEWARDS.—HORSES LOST.—DEPARTURE WITH A DETACHMENT ON THE HOMEWARD ROUTE.—SWAMP.—WILD HORSE.—CAMP SCENE BY NIGHT. THE OWL, HARBINGER OF DAWN.

WHILE breakfast was preparing, a council was held as to our future movements. Symptoms of discontent had appeared for a day or two past, among the rangers, most of whom, unaccustomed to the life of the prairies, had become impatient of its privations, as well as the restraints of the camp. The want of bread had been felt severely, and they were wearied with constant travel. In fact, the novelty and excitement of the expedition were at an end. They had hunted the deer, the bear, the elk, the buffalo, and the wild horse, and had no further object of leading interest to look forward to. A general inclination prevailed, therefore, to turn homewards.

Grave reasons disposed the Captain and his officers to adopt this resolution. Our horses were generally much jaded by the fatigues of travelling and hunting, and had fallen away sadly for want of good pasturage, and from being tethered at night, to protect them from Indian depredations. The late rains, too, seemed to have washed away the nourishment from the scanty herbage that remained; and since our encampment during the storm, our horses had lost flesh and strength rapidly. With every possible care, horses, accustomed to grain, and to the regular and plentiful nourishment of the stable and the farm, lose heart and condition in travelling on the prairies. In all expeditions of the kind we were engaged in, the hardy Indian horses, which are generally mustangs, or a cross of the wild breed, are to be preferred. They can stand all fatigues, hardships, and privations, and thrive on the grasses and wild herbage of the plains.

Our men, too, had acted with little forethought; galloping off whenever they had a chance, after the game that we encountered while on the march. In this way they had strained and wearied their horses, instead of husbanding their strength and spirits. On a tour of the kind, horses should as seldom as possible be put off of a quiet walk; and the average day's journey should not exceed ten miles.

We had hoped, by pushing forward, to reach the bottoms of the Red River, which abound with young cane, a most nourishing forage for cattle at this season of the year. It would now take us several days to arrive there, and in the meantime many of our horses would probably give out. It was the time, too, when the hunting parties of Indians set fire to the prairies; the herbage, throughout this part of the country, was in that parched state, favorable to combustion, and there was daily more and more risk, that the prairies between us and the fort would be set on fire by some of the return parties of Osages, and a scorched desert left for us to traverse. In a word, we had started too late in the season, or loitered too much in the early part of our march, to accomplish our originally-intended tour; and there was imminent hazard, if we continued on, that we should lose the greater part of our horses; and, besides suffering various other inconveniences, be obliged to return on foot. It was determined, therefore, to give up all further progress, and, turning our faces to the southeast, to make the best of our way back to Fort Gibson.

This resolution being taken, there was an immediate eagerness to put it into operation. Several horses, however, were missing, and among others those of the Captain and the Surgeon. Persons had gone in search of them, but the morning advanced without any tidings of them. Our party in the meantime, being all ready for a march, the Commissioner determined to set off in the advance, with his original escort of a lieutenant and fourteen rangers, leaving the Captain to come on at his convenience, with the main body. At ten o'clock, we accordingly started, under the guidance of Beatte, who had hunted over this part of the country, and knew the direct route to the garrison.

For some distance we skirted the prairie, keeping a southeast direction; and in the course of our ride we saw a variety of wild animals, deer, white and black wolves, baffaloes, and wild horses. To the latter, our half-breeds and Tonish gave ineffectual chase, only serving to add to the weariness of their already jaded steeds. Indeed it is rarely that any but the weaker and least fleet of the wild horses are taken in these hard racings; while the horse of the huntsman is prone to be knocked up The latter, in fact, risks a good horse to catch a bad one. On this occasion, Tonish, who was a perfect imp on horseback, and noted for ruining every animal he bestrode, succeeded in laming and almost disabling the powerful gray on which we had mounted him at the outset of our tour.

After proceeding a few miles, we left the prairie, and struck to the east, taking what Beatte pronounced an old Osage war-track. This led us through a rugged tract of country, overgrown with scrubbed forests and entangled thickets and intersected by deep ravines, and brisk-running streams, the sources of Little River. About three o'clock, we encamped by some pools of water in a small valley, having come about fourteen miles. We had brought on a supply of provisions from our last camp, and supped heartily upon stewed buffalo meat, roasted venison, beignets, or fritters of flour fried in bear's lard, and tea made of a species of the golden-rod, which we had found, throughout our whole route, almost as grateful a beverage as coffee. Indeed our coffee, which, as long as it held out, had been served up with every meal, according to the custom of the West, was by no means a beverage to boast of. It was roasted in a frying-pan, without much care, pounded in a leathern bag, with a round stone, and boiled in our prime and almost only kitchen utensil, the camp kettle, in "branch" or brook water; which, on the prairies, is deeply colored by the soil, of which it always holds abundant particles in a state of solution and suspension. In fact, in the course of our tour, we had tasted the quality of every variety of soil, and the draughts of water we had taken might vie in diversity of color, if not of flavor, with the tinctures of an apothecary's shop. Pure, limpid water is a rare luxury on the prairies, at least at this season of the year. Supper over, we placed sentinels about our scanty and diminished camp, spread our skins and blankets under the trees, now nearly destitute of foliage, and slept soundly until morning.

We had a beautiful daybreak. The camp again resounded with cheerful voices; every one was animated with the thoughts of soon being at the fort, and revelling on bread and vegetables.

Even our saturnine man, Beatte, seemed inspired on this occa sion; and as he drove up the horses for the march, I heard him singing, in nasal tones, a most forlorn Indian ditty. All this transient gayety, however, soon died away amidst the fatigues of our march, which lay through the same kind of rough, hilly, thicketed country as that of yesterday. In the course of the morning we arrived at the valley of the Little River, where it wound through a broad bottom of alluvial soil. At present it had overflowed its banks, and inundated a great part of the valley. The difficulty was to distinguish the stream from the broad sheets of water it had formed, and to find a place where it might be forded; for it was in general deep and miry, with abrupt crumbling banks. Under the pilotage of Beatte, therefore, we wandered for some time among the links made by this winding stream, in what appeared to us a trackless labyrinth of swamps, thickets, and standing pools. Sometimes our jaded horses dragged their limbs forward with the utmost difficulty, having to toil for a great distance, with the water up to the stirrups, and beset at the bottom with roots and creeping plants. Sometimes we had to force our way through dense thickets of brambles and grapevines, which almost pulled us out of our saddles. In one place, one of the pack-horses sunk in the mire and fell on his side, so as to be extricated with great difficulty. Wherever the soil was bare, or there was a sand-bank, we beheld innumerable tracks of bears, wolves, wild horses, turkeys, and water-fowl; showing the abundant sport this valley might afford to the huntsman. Our men, however, were sated with hunting, and too weary to be excited by these signs, which in the outset of our tour would have put them in a fever of anticipation. Their only desire at present, was to push on doggedly for the fortress.

At length we succeeded in finding a fording place, where we all crossed Little River, with the water and mire to the saddle-girths, and then halted for an hour and a half, to overhaul the wet baggage, and give the horses time to rest.

On resuming our march, we came to a pleasant little meadow, surrounded by groves of elms and cotton-wood trees, in the midst of which was a fine black horse grazing. Beatte, who was in the advance, beckoned us to halt, and, being mounted on a mare, approached the horse gently, step by step, imitating the whinny of the animal with admirable exactness. The noble courser of the prairie gazed for a time, snuffed the air, neighed, pricked up his ears, and pranced round and round the mare in gallant style; but kept at too great a distance for Beatte to throw the lariat. He was a magnificent object, in all the pride and glory of his nature. It was admirable to see the lofty and airy carriage of his head; the freedom of every movement; the elasticity with which he trod the meadow. Finding it impossible to get within noosing distance, and seeing that the horse was receding and growing alarmed, Beatte slid down from his saddle, levelled his rifle across the back of his mare, and took aim, with the evident intention of creasing him. I felt a throb of anxiety for the safety of the noble animal, and called out to Beatte to desist. It was too late; he pulled the trigger as I spoke; luckily he did not shoot with his usual accuracy, and I had the satisfaction to see the coal-black steed dash off unharmed into the forest.

On leaving this valley, we ascended among broken hills and rugged, ragged forests, equally harassing to horse and rider. The ravines, too, were of red clay, and often so steep, that in descending, the horses would put their feet together and fairly slide down, and then scramble up the opposite side like cats. Here and there among the thickets in the valleys, we met with sloes and persimmon, and the eagerness with which our men broke from the line of march, and ran to gather these poor fruits, showed how much they craved some vegetable condiment, after living so long exclusively on animal food.

About half past three we encamped near a brook in a meadow where there was some scanty herbage for our half-famished horses. As Beatte had killed a fat doe in the course of the day, and one of our company a fine turkey, we did not lack for provisions.

It was a splendid autumnal evening. The horizon, after sunset, was of a clear apple green, rising into a delicate lake which gradually lost itself in a deep purple blue. One narrow streak of cloud, of a mahogany color, edged with amber and gold, floated in the west, and just beneath it was the evening star, shining with the pure brilliancy of a diamond. In unison with this scene, there was an evening concert of insects of various kinds, all blended and harmonized into one sober and somewhat melancholy note, which I have always found to have a soothing effect upon the mind, disposing it to quiet musings.

The night that succeeded was calm and beautiful. There was a faint light from the moon, now in its second quarter, and after it had set, a fine starlight, with shooting meteors. The wearied rangers, after a little murmuring conversation round their fires, sank to rest at an early hour, and I seemed to have the whole scene to myself. It is delightful in thus bivouacking on the prairies, to lie awake and gaze at the stars; it is like watching them from the deck of a ship at sea, when at one view we have the whole cope of heaven. One realizes, in such lonely scenes, that companionship with these beautiful luminaries which made astronomers of the eastern shepherds, as they watched their flocks by night. How often, while contemplating their mild and benignant radiance, I have called to mind the exquisite text of Job. "Canst thou bind the secret influences of the Pleiades, or loose the bands of Orion?" I do not know why it was, but I felt this night unusually affected by the solemn magnificence of the firmament; and seemed, as I lay thus under the open vault of heaven, to inhale with the pure untainted air, an exhilarating buoyancy of spirit, and, as it were, an ecstasy of mind. I slept and waked alternately; and when I slept, my dreams partook of the happy tone of my waking reveries. Towards morning, one of the sentinels, the oldest man in the troop, came and took a seat near me: he was weary and sleepy, and impatient to be relieved. I found he had been gazing at the heavens also, but with different feelings.

"If the stars don't deceive me," said he, "it is near daybreak."

"There can be no doubt of that," said Beatte, who lay close by. "I heard an owl just now."

"Does the owl, then, hoot towards daybreak?" asked I.

"Aye, sir, just as the cock crows."

This was a useful habitude of the bird of wisdom, of which I was not aware. Neither the stars nor owl deceived their votaries. In a short time there was a faint streak of light in the east.

CHAPTER XXXIV.

OLD CREEK ENCAMPMENT.—SCARCITY OF PROVISIONS.—BAD WEATHER.—WEARY MARCHING.—A HUNTER'S BRIDGE.

The country through which we passed this morning (Nov. 2), was less rugged, and of more agreeable aspect than that we had lately traversed. At eleven o'clock, we came out upon an extensive prairie, and about six miles to our left beheld a long line of green forest, marking the course of the north fork of the Arkansas. On the edge of the prairie, and in a spacious grove of noble trees which overshadowed a small brook, were the traces of an old Creek hunting camp. On the bark of the trees were rude delineations of hunters and squaws, scrawled with charcoal; together with various signs and hieroglyphics, which our half-breeds interpreted as indicating that from this encampment the hunters had returned home.

In this beautiful camping ground we made our mid-day halt. While reposing under the trees, we heard a shouting at no great distance, and presently the Captain and the main body of rangers, whom we had left behind two days since, emerged from the thickets, and crossing the brook, were joyfully welcomed into the camp. The Captain and the Doctor had been unsuccessful in the search after their horses, and were obliged to march for the greater part of the time on foot; yet they had come on with more than ordinary speed.

We resumed our march about one o'clock, keeping easterly, and approaching the north fork obliquely; it was late before we found a good camping place; the beds of the streams were dry, the prairies, too, had been burnt in various places, by Indian hunting parties. At length we found water in a small alluvial bottom, where there was tolerable pasturage.

On the following morning, there were flashes of lightning in the east, with low, rumbling thunder, and clouds began to gather about the horizon. Beatte prognosticated rain, and that the wind would veer to the north. In the course of our march, a flock of brant were seen overhead, flying from the north. "There comes the wind!" said Beatte; and, in fact, it began to blow from that quarter almost immediately, with occasional flurries of rain. About half past nine o'clock, we forded the north fork of the Canadian, and encamped about one, that our hunters might have time to beat up the neighborhood for game; for a serious scarcity began to prevail in the camp. Most of the rangers were young, heedless, and inexperienced, and could not be prevailed upon, while provisions abounded, to provide for the future, by jerking meat, or carrying away any on their horses. On leaving an encampment, they would leave quantities of meat lying about, trusting to Providence and their rifles for a future supply. The consequence was, that any temporary scarcity of game, or ill luck in hunting, produced almost a famine in the camp. In the present instance, they had left loads of buffalo meat at the camp on the great prairie; and, having ever since been on a forced march, leaving no time for hunting, they were now destitute of supplies, and pinched with hunger. Some had not eaten any thing since the morning of the preceding day. Nothing would have persuaded them when revelling in the abundance of the buffalo encampment, that they would so soon be in such famishing plight.

The hunters returned with indifferent success. The game

had been frightened away from this part of the country, by Indian hunting parties, which had preceded us. Ten or a dozen wild turkeys were brought in, but not a deer had been seen. The rangers began to think turkeys and even prairie hens deserving of attention; game which they had hitherto considered unworthy of their rifles.

The night was cold and windy, with occasional sprinklings of rain; but we had roaring fires to keep us comfortable. In the night, a flight of wild geese passed over the camp, making a great cackling in the air; symptoms of approaching winter.

We set forward at an early hour the next morning, in a north-east course, and came upon the trace of a party of Creek Indians, which enabled our poor horses to travel with more ease. We entered upon a fine champaign country. From a rising ground we had a noble prospect, over extensive prairies, finely diversified by groves and tracts of woodland, and bounded by long lines of distant hills, all clothed with the rich mellow tints of autumn. Game, too, was more plenty. A fine buck sprang up from among the herbage on our right, and dashed off at full speed; but, a young ranger by the name of Childers, who was on foot, levelled his rifle, discharged a ball that broke the neck of the bounding deer, and sent him tumbling head over heels forward. Another buck and a doe, beside several turkeys were killed before we came to a halt, so that the hungry mouths of the troop were once more supplied.

About three o'clock we encamped in a grove after a forced march of twenty-five miles, that had proved a hard trial to the horses. For a long time after the head of the line had encamped, the rest kept straggling in, two and three at a time; one of our pack-horses had given out, about nine miles back, and a pony belonging to Beatte, shortly after. Many of the other horses looked so gaunt and feeble, that doubts were entertained of their being able to reach the fort. In the night, there was heavy rain, and the morning dawned cloudy and dismal. The camp resounded, however, with something of its former gayety. The rangers had supped well, and were renovated in spirits. anticipating a speedy arrival at the garrison. Before we set forward on our march, Beatte returned, and brought his pony to the camp with great difficulty. The pack-horse, however, was completely knocked up and had to be abandoned. The wild mare, too, had cast her foal, through exhaustion, and was not in a state to go forward. She and the pony, therefore, were left at this encampment, where there was water and good pasturage; and where there would be a chance of their reviving, and being afterwards sought out and brought to the garrison.

We set off about eight o'clock, and had a day of weary and harassing travel; part of the time over rough hills, and part over rolling prairies. The rain had rendered the soil slippery and plashy, so as to afford unsteady foothold. Some of the rangers dismounted, their horses having no longer strength to bear them. We made a halt in the course of the morning, but the horses were too tired to graze. Several of them laid down, and there was some difficulty in getting them on their feet again. Our troop presented a forlorn appearance, straggling slowly along, in a broken and scattered line, that extended over hill and dale, for three miles and upwards, in groups of three and four widely apart; some on horseback, some on foot, with a few laggards far in the rear. About four o'clock, we halted for the night in a spacious forest, beside a deep narrow river, called the Little North Fork, or Deep Creek. It was late before the main part of the troop straggled into the encampment, many of the horses having given out. As this stream was too deep to be forded, we waited until the next day to devise means to cross it; but our half-breeds swam the horses of our party to the other side in the evening, as they would have better pasturage, and the stream was evidently swelling. The night was cold and unruly; the wind sounding hoarsely through the forest and whirling about the dry leaves. We made long fires of great trunks of trees, which diffused something of consolation if not cheerfulness around.

The next morning there was general permission given to hunt until twelve o'clock; the camp being destitute of provisions. The rich woody bottom in which we were encamped, abounded with wild turkeys, of which a considerable number were killed. In the meantime, preparations were made for crossing the river, which had risen several feet during the night; and it was determined to fell trees for the purpose, to serve as bridges.

The Captain and Doctor, and one or two other leaders of the camp, versed in woodcraft, examined with learned eye the trees growing on the river bank, until they singled out a couple of the largest size, and most suitable inclinations. The axe was then vigorously applied to their roots, in such a way as to insure their falling directly across the stream. As they did not reach to the opposite bank, it was necessary for some of the men to swim across and fell trees on the other side, to meet them. They at length succeeded in making a precarious footway across the deep and rapid current, by which the baggage could be carried over: but it was necessary to grope our way, step by step, along the trunks and main branches of the trees, which for a part of the distance were completely submerged, so that we were to our waists in water. Most of the horses were then swam across, but some of them were too weak to brave the current, and evidently too much knocked up to bear any further travel. Twelve men, therefore, were left at the encampment to guard these horses, until by repose and good pasturage they should be sufficiently recovered to complete their journey; and the Captain engaged to send the men a supply of flour and other necessaries, as soon as we should arrive at the Fort.

CHAPTER XXXV.

A LOOK-OUT FOR LAND.—HARD TRAVELLING AND HUNGRY HALTING.—A FRONTIER FARMHOUSE.—ARRIVAL AT THE GARRISON.

It was a little after one o'clock when we again resumed our weary wayfaring. The residue of that day and the whole of the next were spent in toilsome travel. Part of the way was over stony hills, part across wide prairies, rendered spongy and miry by the recent rain, and cut up by brooks swollen into torrents. Our poor horses were so feeble, that it was with difficulty we could get them across the deep ravines and turbulent streams. In traversing the miry plains, they slipped and staggered at every step, and most of us were obliged to dismount and walk for the greater part of the way. Hunger prevailed throughout the troop; every one began to look anxious and haggard, and to feel the growing length of each additional mile. At one time, in crossing a hill, Beatte climbed a high tree, commanding a wide prospect, and took a look-out, like a mariner from the mast-head at sea. He came down with cheering tidings. To the left he had beheld a line of forest stretching across the country, which he knew to be the woody border of the Arkansas; and at a distance he had recognized certain landmarks, from which he concluded that we could not be above forty miles distant from the fort. It was like the welcome cry of land to tempest-tossed mariners.

In fact we soon after saw smoke rising from a woody glen at a distance. It was supposed to be made by a hunting-party of Creek or Osage Indians from the neighborhood of the fort, and was joyfully hailed as a harbinger of man. It was now confidently hoped that we would soon arrive among the frontier hamlets of Creek Indians, which are scattered along the skirts of the uninhabited wilderness; and our hungry rangers trudged forward with reviving spirit, regaling themselves with savory anticipations of farmhouse luxuries, and enumerating every article of good cheer, until their mouths fairly watered at the shadowy feasts thus conjured up.

A hungry night, however, closed in upon a toilsome day. We encamped on the border of one of the tributary streams of the Arkansas, amidst the ruins of a stately grove that had been riven by a hurricane. The blast had torn its way through the forest in a narrow column, and its course was marked by enormous trees shivered and splintered, and upturned, with their roots in the air: all lay in one direction, like so many brittle reeds broken and trodden down by the hunter.

Here was fuel in abundance, without the labor of the axe: we had soon immense fires blazing and sparkling in the frosty air, and lighting up the whole forest; but, alas! we had no meat to cook at them. The scarcity in the camp almost amounted to famine. Happy was he who had a morsel of jerked meat, or even the half-picked bones of a former repast

For our part, we were more lucky at our mess than our neighbors; one of our men having shot a turkey. We had no bread to eat with it, nor salt to season it withal. It was simply boiled in water; the latter was served up as soup, and we were fain to rub each morsel of the turkey on the empty salt-bag, in hopes some saline particle might remain to relieve its insipidity.

The night was biting cold; the brilliant moonlight sparkled on the frosty crystals which covered every object around us. The water froze beside the skins on which we bivouacked, and in the morning I found the blanket in which I was wrapped covered with a hoar frost; yet I had never slept more comfortably.

After a shadow of a breakfast, consisting of turkey bones and a cup of coffee without sugar, we decamped at an early hour; for hunger is a sharp quickener on a journey. The prairies were all gemmed with frost, that covered the tall weeds and glistened in the sun. We saw great flights of prairie hens, or grouse, that hovered from tree to tree, or sat in rows along the naked branches, waiting until the sun should melt the frost from the weeds and herbage. Our rangers no longer despised such humble game, but turned from the ranks in pursuit of a prairie hen as eagerly as they formerly would go in pursuit of a deer.

Every one now pushed forward, anxious to arrive at some human habitation before night. The poor horses were urged beyond their strength, in the thought of soon being able to indemnify them for present toil, by rest and ample provender. Still the distances seemed to stretch out more than ever, and the blue hills, pointed out as landmarks on the horizon, to recede as we advanced. Every step became a labor; every now and then a miserable horse would give out and lie down. His owner would raise him by main strength, force him forward to the margin of some stream, where there might be a scanty border of herbage, and then abandon him to his fate. Among those that were thus left on the way, was one of the led horses of the Count; a prime hunter, that had taken the lead of every thing in the chase of the wild horses. It was intended, however, as soon as we should arrive at the fort, to send out a party provided with corn, to bring in such of the horses as should survive.

In the course of the morning, we came upon Indian tracks, crossing each other in various directions, a proof that we must be in the neighborhood of human habitations. At length, on passing through a skirt of wood, we beheld two or three log houses, sheltered under lofty trees on the border of a prairie, the habitations of Creek Indians, who had small farms adjacent. Had they been sumptuous villas, abounding with the luxuries of civilization, they could not have been hailed with greater delight.

Some of the rangers rode up to them in quest of food: the greater part, however, pushed forward in search of the habitation of a white settler, which we were told was at no great distance. The troop soon disappeared among the trees, and I followed slowly in their track; for my once fleet and generous steed faltered under me, and was just able to drag one foot after the other, yet I was too weary and exhausted to spare him.

In this way we crept on, until, on turning a thick clump of trees, a frontier farmhouse suddenly presented itself to view. It was a low tenement of logs, overshadowed by great forest trees, but it seemed as if a very region of Cocaigne prevailed around it. Here was a stable and barn, and granaries teeming with abundance, while legions of grunting swine, gobbling turkeys, cackling hens and strutting roosters, swarmed about the farmyard.

My poor jaded and half-famished horse raised his head and

pricked up his ears at the well-known sights and sounds. He gave a chuckling inward sound, something like a dry laugh; whisked his tail, and made great leeway toward a corn-crib, filled with golden ears of maize, and it was with some difficulty that I could control his course, and steer him up to the door of the cabin. A single glance within was sufficient to raise every gastronomic faculty. There sat the Captain of the rangers and his officers, round a three-legged table, crowned by a broad and smoking dish of boiled beef and turnips. I sprang off my horse in an instant, cast him loose to make his way to the corn-crib, and entered this palace of plenty. A fat good-humored negress received me at the door. She was the mistress of the house, the spouse of the white man, who was absent. I hailed her as some swart fairy of the wild, that had suddenly conjured up a banquet in the desert; and a banquet was it in good sooth. In a twinkling, she lugged from the fire a huge iron pot, that might have rivalled one of the famous flesh-pots of Egypt, or the witches' caldron in Macbeth. Placing a brown earthen dish on the floor, she inclined the corpulent caldron on one side, and out leaped sundry great morsels of beef, with a regiment of turnips tumbling after them, and a rich cascade of broth overflowing the whole. This she handed me with an ivory smile that extended from ear to ear; apologizing for our humble fare, and the humble style in which it was served up Humble fare! humble style! Boiled beef and turnips, and an earthen dish to eat them from! To think of apologizing for such a treat to a half-starved man from the prairies; and then such magnificent slices of bread and butter! Head of Apicius, what a banquet!

"The rage of hunger" being appeased, I began to think of my horse. He, however, like an old campaigner, had taken good care of himself. I found him paying assiduous attention to the crib of Indian corn, and dexterously drawing forth and munching the ears that protruded between the bars. It was with great regret that I interrupted his repast, which he abandoned with a heavy sigh, or rather a rumbling groan. I was anxious, however to rejoin my travelling companions, who had passed by the farmhouse without stopping, and proceeded to the banks of the Arkansas; being in hopes of arriving before night at the Osage Agency. Leaving the Captain and his troop, therefore, amidst the abundance of the farm, where they had determined to quarter themselves for the night, I bade adieu to our sable hostess, and again pushed forward.

A ride of about a mile brought me to where my comrades were waiting on the banks of the Arkansas, which here poured along between beautiful forests. A number of Creek Indians, in their brightly colored dresses, looking like so many gay tropical birds, were busy aiding our men to transport the baggage across the river in a canoe. While this was doing, our horses had another regale from two great cribs heaped up with ears of Indian corn, which stood near the edge of the river. We had to keep a check upon the poor half famished animals, lest they should injure themselves by their voracity.

The baggage being all carried to the opposite bank, we embarked in the canoe, and swam our horses across the river. I was fearful, lest in their enfeebled state, they should not be able to stem the current; but their banquet of Indian corn had already infused fresh life and spirit into them, and it would appear as if they were cheered by the instinctive consciousness of their approach to home, where they would soon be at rest, and in plentiful quarters; for no sooner had we landed and resumed our route, than they set off on a hand-gallop, and continued so for a great part of seven miles, that we had to ride through the woods.

It was an early hour in the evening when we arrived at the Agency, on the banks of the Verdigris River, whence we had set off about a month before. Here we passed the night comfortably quartered; yet, after having been accustomed to sleep in the open air, the confinement of a chamber was, in some respects, irksome. The atmosphere seemed close, and destitute of freshness; and when I woke in the night and gazed about me upon complete darkness, I missed the glorious companionship of the stars.

The next morning after breakfast, I again set forward in company with the worthy Commissioner, for Fort Gibson, where we arrived much tattered, travel-stained and weather-beaten, but in high health and spirits;—and thus ended my foray into the Pawnee Hunting Grounds.

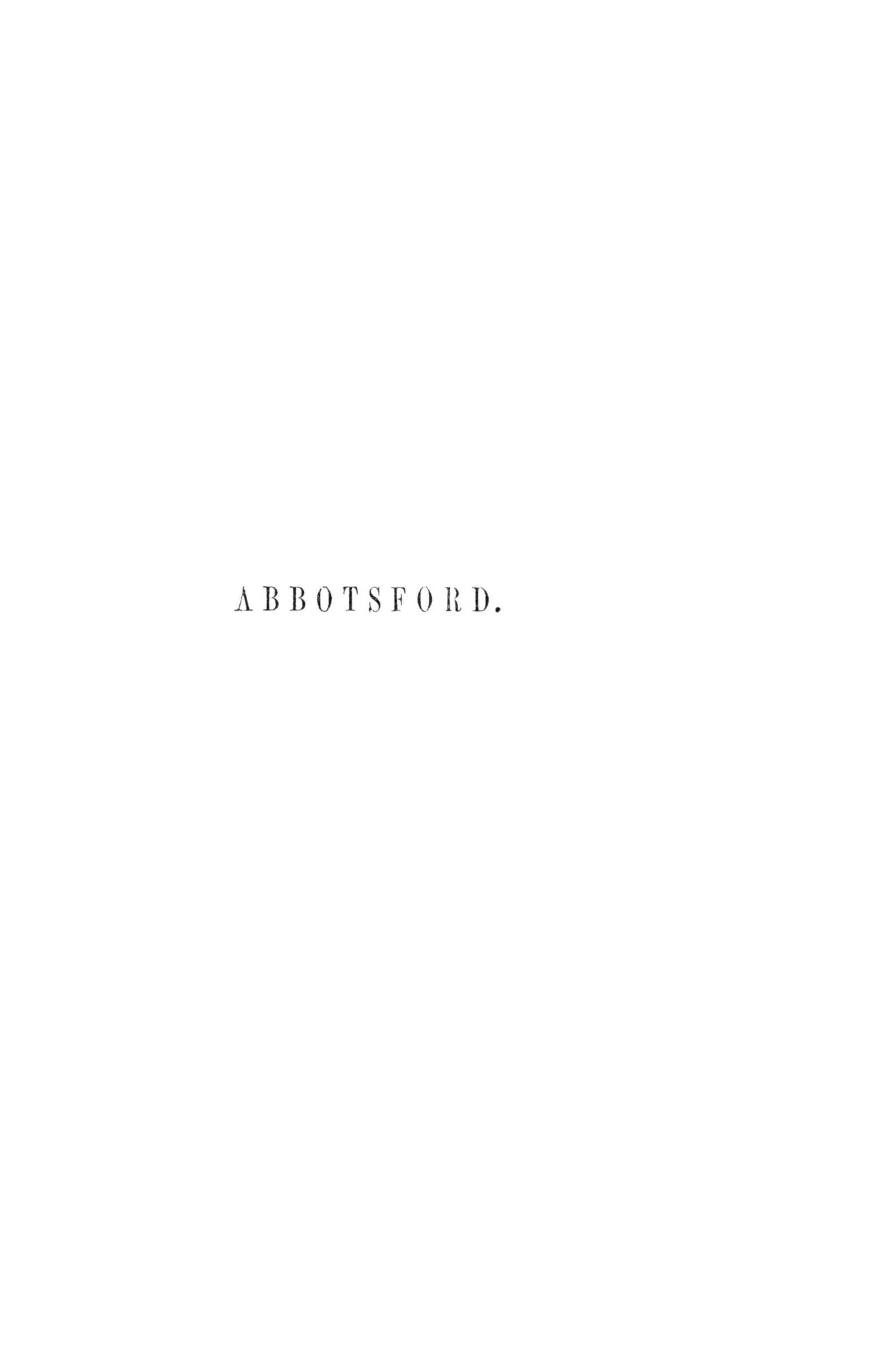

ABBOTSFORD.

ABBOTSFORD.

I SIT down to perform my promise of giving you an account of a visit made many years since to Abbotsford. I hope, however, that you do not expect much from me, for the travelling notes taken at the time are so scanty and vague, and my memory so extremely fallacious, that I fear I shall disappoint you with the meagreness and crudeness of my details.

Late in the evening of the 29th of August, 1817, I arrived at the ancient little border town of Selkirk, where I put up for the night. I had come down from Edinburgh, partly to visit Melrose Abbey and its vicinity, but chiefly to get a sight of the "mighty minstrel of the north." I had a letter of introduction to him from Thomas Campbell the poet, and had reason to think, from the interest he had taken in some of my earlier scribblings, that a visit from me would not be deemed an intrusion.

On the following morning, after an early breakfast, I set off in a postchaise for the Abbey. On the way thither I stopped at the gate of Abbotsford, and sent the postillion to the house with the letter of introduction and my card, on which I had written that I was on my way to the ruins of Melrose Abbey, and wished to know whether it would be agreeable to Mr Scott (he had not yet been made a Baronet) to receive a visit from me in the course of the morning.

While the postillion was on his errand, I had time to survey the mansion. It stood some short distance below the road, on the side of a hill sweeping down to the Tweed; and was as yet but a snug gentleman's cottage, with something rural and picturesque in its appearance. The whole front was overrun with evergreens, and immediately above the portal was a great pair of elk horns, branching out from beneath the foliage, and giving the cottage the look of a hunting lodge. The huge baronial pile, to which this modest mansion in a manner gave birth, was just emerging into existence: part of the walls, surrounded by scaffolding, already had risen to the height of the cottage, and the court-yard in front was encumbered by masses of hewn stone.

The noise of the chaise had disturbed the quiet of the establishment. Out sallied the warder of the castle, a black greyhound, and, leaping on one of the blocks of stone, began a furious barking. His alarum brought out the whole garrison of dogs:

> "Both mongrel, puppy, whelp, and hound,
> And curs of low degree;"

all open-mouthed and vociferous.——I should correct my quotation;—not a cur was to be seen on the premises: Scott was too true a sportsman, and had too high a veneration for pure blood, to tolerate a mongrel.

In a little while the "lord of the castle" himself made his appearance. I knew him at once by the descriptions I had read and heard, and the likenesses that had been published of him. He was tall, and of a large and powerful frame. His dress was simple, and almost rustic. An old green shooting-coat, with a dog-whistle at the button hole, brown linen pantaloons, stout shoes that tied at the ankles, and a white hat that had evidently seen service. He came limping up the gravel walk, aiding himself by a stout walking-staff, but moving rapidly and with vigor. By his side jogged along a large iron-gray stag hound of most grave demeanor, who took no part in the clamor of the canine rabble, but seemed to consider himself bound, for the dignity of the house, to give me a courteous reception.

Before Scott had reached the gate he called out in a hearty tone, welcoming me to Abbotsford, and asking news of Campbell. Arrived at the door of the chaise, he grasped me warmly by the hand: "Come, drive down, drive down to the house," said he, "ye're just in time for breakfast, and afterwards ye shall see all the wonders of the Abbey."

I would have excused myself, on the plea of having already made my breakfast. "Hout, man," cried he, "a ride in the morning in the keen air of the Scotch hills is warrant enough for a second breakfast."

I was accordingly whirled to the portal of the cottage, and in a few moments found myself seated at the breakfast table. There was no one present but the family, which consisted of Mrs. Scott, her eldest daughter Sophia, then a fine girl about seventeen, Miss Ann Scott, two or three years younger, Walter, a well-grown stripling, and Charles, a lively boy, eleven or twelve years of age. I soon felt myself quite at home, and my heart in a glow with the cordial welcome I experienced. I had thought to make a mere morning visit, but found I was not to be let off so lightly. "You must not think our neighborhood is to be read in a morning, like a newspaper," said Scott. "It takes several days of study for an observant traveller that has a relish for auld world trumpery. After breakfast you shall make your visit to Melrose Abbey; I shall not be able to accompany you, as I have some household affairs to attend to, but I will put you in charge of my son Charles, who is very learned in all things touching the old ruin and the neighborhood it stands in, and he and my friend Johnny Bower will tell you the whole truth about it, with a good deal more that you are not called upon to believe—unless you be a true and nothing-doubting antiquary. When you come back, I'll take you out on a ramble about the neighborhood. To-morrow we will take a look at the Yarrow, and the next day we will drive over to Dryburgh Abbey, which is a fine old ruin well worth your seeing"—in a word, before Scott had got through with his plan, I found myself committed for a visit of several days, and it seemed as if a little realm of romance was suddenly opened before me.

After breakfast I accordingly set off for the Abbey with my little friend Charles, whom I found a most sprightly and entertaining companion. He had an ample stock of anecdote about the neighborhood, which he had learned from his father, and many quaint remarks and sly jokes, evidently derived from the same source, all which were uttered with a Scottish accent and a mixture of Scottish phraseology, that gave them additional favor.

On our way to the Abbey he gave me some anecdotes of Johnny Bower to whom his father had alluded; he was sexton of the parish and custodian of the ruin, employed to keep it in order and show it to strangers;—a worthy little man, not without ambition in his humble sphere. The death of his predecessor had been mentioned in the newspapers, so that his name had appeared in print throughout the land. When Johnny succeeded to the guardianship of the ruin, he stipulated that, on his death, his name should receive like honorable blazon; with this addition, that it should be from the pen of Scott. The latter gravely pledged himself to pay this tribute to his memory, and Johnny now lived in the proud anticipation of a poetic immortality.

I found Johnny Bower a decent looking little old man, in blue coat and red waistcoat. He received us with much greeting, and seemed delighted to see my young companion, who was full of merriment and waggery, drawing out his peculiarities for my amusement. The old man was one of the most authentic and particular of cicerones; he pointed out every thing in the Abbey that had been described by Scott in his Lay of the Last Minstrel: and would repeat, with broad Scottish accent, the passage which celebrated it.

Thus, in passing through the cloisters, he made me remark the beautiful carvings of leaves and flowers wrought in stone with the most exquisite delicacy, and, notwithstanding the lapse of centuries, retaining their sharpness as if fresh from the chisel; rivalling, as Scott has said, the real objects of which they were imitations:

> " Nor herb nor flowret glistened there
> But was carved in the cloister arches as fair."

He pointed out also among the carved work a nun's head of much beauty, which he said Scott always stopped to admire— "for the shirra had a wonderful eye for all sic matters."

I would observe, that Scott seemed to derive more consequence in the neighborhood from being sheriff of the county, than from being poet.

In the interior of the Abbey, Johnny Bower conducted me to the identical stone on which Stout William of Deloraine and the Monk took their seat on that memorable night when the wizard's book was to be rescued from the grave. Nay, Johnny had even gone beyond Scott in the minuteness of his antiquarian research, for he had discovered the very tomb of the wizard, the position of which had been left in doubt by the poet. This he boasted to have ascertained by the position of the Oriel window, and the direction in which the moonbeams fell at night, through the stained glass, casting the shadow to the red cross on the spot; as had all been specified in the poem. "I pointed out the whole to the shirra," said he, "and he could na' gainsay but it was varra clear." I found afterwards, that Scott used to amuse himself with the simplicity of the old man, and his zeal in verifying every passage of the poem, as though it had been authentic history, and that he always acquiesced in his deductions. I subjoin the description of the wizard's grave, which called forth the antiquarian research of Johnny Bower.

"Lo warrior! now the cross of red,
Points to the grave of the mighty dead;
Slow moved the monk to the broad flag-stone,
Which the bloody cross was traced upon:
He pointed to a sacred nook:
An iron bar the warrior took;
And the monk made a sign with his withered hand,
The grave's huge portal to expand.

It was by dint of passing strength,
That he moved the massy stone at length.

I would you had been there, to see
How the light broke forth so gloriously,
Streamed upward to the chancel roof,
And through the galleries far aloof!
  And, issuing from the tomb,
Showed the monk's cowl and visage pale,
Danced on the dark brown warrior's mail,
  And kissed his waving plume.

Before their eyes the wizard lay,
As if he had not been dead a day.
His hoary beard in silver rolled,
He seemed some seventy winters old;
A palmer's amice wrapped him round;
With a wrought Spanish baldric bound,
  Like a pilgrim from beyond the sea;
His left hand held his book of might;
A silver cross was in his right:
  The lamp was placed beside his knee."

The fictions of Scott had become facts with honest Johnny Bower. From constantly living among the ruins of Melrose Abbey, and pointing out the scenes of the poem, the Lay of the Last Minstrel had, in a manner, become interwoven with his whole existence, and I doubt whether he did not now and then mix up his own identity with the personages of some of its cantos.

He could not bear that any other production of the poet should be preferred to the Lay of the Last Minstrel. "Faith," said he to me, "it's just e'en as gude a thing as Mr. Scott has written—an if he were stannin there I'd tell him so—an' then he'd lauff."

He was loud in his praises of the affability of Scott. "He'll come here sometimes," said he, "with great folks in his company, an the first I know of it is his voice, calling out Johnny!—Johnny Bower!—and when I go out, I am sure to be greeted with a joke or a pleasant word. He'll stand and crack and lauff wi' me, just like an auld wife—and to think that of a man that has such an awfu' knowledge o' history!"

One of the ingenious devices on which the worthy little man prided himself, was to place a visitor opposite to the Abbey, with his back to it, and bid him bend down and look at it between his legs. This, he said, gave an entire different aspect to the ruin. Folks admired the plan amazingly, but as to the "leddies," they were dainty on the matter, and contented themselves with looking from under their arms.

As Johnny Bower piqued himself upon showing every thing laid down in the poem, there was one passage that perplexed him sadly. It was the opening of one of the cantos:

"If thou would'st view fair Melrose aright,
Go visit it by the pale moonlight;
For the gay beams of lightsome day,
Gild but to flout the ruins gray," &c.

In consequence of this admonition, many of the most devout pilgrims to the ruin could not be contented with a daylight inspection, and insisted it could be nothing, unless seen by the light of the moon. Now, unfortunately, the moon shines but for a part of the month; and what is still more unfortunate, is very apt in Scotland to be obscured by clouds and mists. Johnny was sorely puzzled, therefore, how to accommodate his poetry-struck visitors with this indispensable moonshine. At length, in a lucky moment, he devised a substitute. This was a great double tallow candle stuck upon the end of a pole, with which he could conduct his visitors about the ruins on dark nights, so much to their satisfaction that, at length, he began to think it even preferable to the moon itself. "It does na light up a' the Abbey at aince, to be sure," he would say, "but then you can shift it about and show the auld ruin bit by bit, whiles the moon only shines on one side."

Honest Johnny Bower! so many years have elapsed since the time I treat of, that it is more than probable his simple head lies beneath the walls of his favorite Abbey. It is to be hoped his humble ambition has been gratified, and his name recorded by the pen of the man he so loved and honored.

After my return from Melrose Abbey, Scott proposed a ramble to show me something of the surrounding country. As we sallied forth, every dog in the establishment turned out to attend us. There was the old stag-hound Maida, that I have already mentioned, a noble animal, and a great favorite of Scott's, and Hamlet, the black greyhound, a wild thoughtless youngster, not yet arrived to the years of discretion; and Finette, a beautiful setter, with soft silken hair, long pendent ears, and a mild eye, the parlor favorite. When in front of the house, we were joined by a superannuated greyhound, who came from the kitchen wagging his tail, and was cheered by Scott as an old friend and comrade.

In our walks, Scott would frequently pause in conversation to notice his dogs and speak to them, as if rational companions;

and indeed there appears to be a vast deal of rationality in these faithful attendants on man, derived from their close intimacy with him. Maida deported himself with a gravity becoming his age and size, and seemed to consider himself called upon to preserve a great degree of dignity and decorum in our society. As he jogged along a little distance ahead of us, the young dogs would gambol about him, leap on his neck, worry at his ears, and endeavor to tease him into a frolic. The old dog would keep on for a long time with imperturbable solemnity, now and then seeming to rebuke the wantonness of his young companions. At length he would make a sudden turn, seize one of them, and tumble him in the dust; then giving a glance at us, as much as to say, "You see, gentlemen, I can't help giving way to this nonsense," would resume his gravity and jog on as before.

Scott amused himself with these peculiarities. "I make no doubt," said he, "when Maida is alone with these young dogs, he throws gravity aside, and plays the boy as much as any of them; but he is ashamed to do so in our company, and seems to say, 'Ha' done with your nonsense, youngsters; what will the laird and that other gentleman think of me if I give way to such foolery?'"

Maida reminded him, he said, of a scene on board an armed yacht in which he made an excursion with his friend Adam Ferguson. They had taken much notice of the boatswain, who was a fine sturdy seaman, and evidently felt flattered by their attention. On one occasion the crew were "piped to fun," and the sailors were dancing and cutting all kinds of capers to the music of the ship's band. The boatswain looked on with a wistful eye, as if he would like to join in; but a glance at Scott and Ferguson showed that there was a struggle with his dignity, fearing to lessen himself in their eyes. At length one of his messmates came up, and seizing him by the arm, challenged him to a jig. The boatswin, continued Scott, after a little hesitation complied, made an awkward gambol or two, like our friend Maida, but soon gave it up. "It's of no use," said he, jerking up his waistband and giving a side glance at us, "one can't dance always nouther."

Scott amused himself with the peculiarities of another of his dogs, a little shamefaced terrier, with large glassy eyes, one of the most sensitive little bodies to insult and indignity in the world. If ever he whipped him, he said, the little fellow would sneak off and hide himself from the light of day, in a lumber garret, whence there was no drawing him forth but by the sound of the chopping-knife, as if chopping up his victuals, when he would steal forth with humbled and downcast look, but would skulk away again if any one regarded him.

While we were discussing the humors and peculiarities of our canine companions, some object provoked their spleen, and produced a sharp and petulant barking from the smaller fry, but it was some time before Maida was sufficiently aroused to ramp forward two or three bounds and join in the chorus, with a deep-mouthed bow-wow!

It was but a transient outbreak, and he returned instantly, wagging his tail, and looking up dubiously in his master's face; uncertain whether he would censure or applaud.

"Aye, aye, old boy!" cried Scott, "you have done wonders. You have shaken the Eildon hills with your roaring; you may now lay by your artillery for the rest of the day. Maida is like the great gun at Constantinople," continued he; "it takes so long to get it ready, that the small guns can fire off a dozen times first, but when it does go off it plays the very d—l."

These simple anecdotes may serve to show the delightful play of Scott's humors and feelings in private life. His domestic animals were his friends; every thing about him seemed to rejoice in the light of his countenance: the face of the humblest dependent brightened at his approach, as if he anticipated a cordial and cheering word. I had occasion to observe this particularly in a visit which we paid to a quarry, whence several men were cutting stone for the new edifice; who all paused from their labor to have a pleasant "crack wi' the laird." One of them was a burgess of Selkirk, with whom Scott had some joke about the old song:

> "Up with the Souters o' Selkirk,
> And down with the Earl of Home."

Another was precentor at the Kirk, and, beside leading the psalmody on Sunday, taught the lads and lasses of the neighborhood dancing on week days, in the winter time, when out-of-door labor was scarce.

Among the rest was a tall, straight old fellow, with a healthful complexion and silver hair, and a small round-crowned white hat. He had been about to shoulder a hod, but paused, and stood looking at Scott, with a slight sparkling of his blue eye, as if waiting his turn; for the old fellow knew himself to be a favorite.

Scott accosted him in an affable tone, and asked for a pinch of snuff. The old man drew forth a horn snuff-box. "Hoot, man," said Scott, "not that old mull: where's the bonnie French one that I brought you from Paris?" "Troth, your honor," replied the old fellow, "sic a mull as that is nae for week days."

On leaving the quarry, Scott informed me that when absent

at Paris, he had purchased several trifling articles as presents for his dependents, and among others the gay snuff-box in question, which was so carefully reserved for Sundays, by the veteran. "It was not so much the value of the gifts," said he, "that pleased them, as the idea that the laird should think of them when so far away."

The old man in question, I found, was a great favorite with Scott. If I recollect right, he had been a soldier in early life, and his straight, erect person, his ruddy yet rugged countenance, his gray hair, and an arch gleam in his blue eye, reminded me of the description of Edie Ochiltree. I find that the old fellow has since been introduced by Wilkie, in his picture of the Scott family.

We rambled on among scenes which had been familiar in Scottish song, and rendered classic by the pastoral muse, long before Scott had thrown the rich mantle of his poetry over them. What a thrill of pleasure did I feel when first I saw the broom-covered tops of the Cowden Knowes, peeping above the gray hills of the Tweed: and what touching associations were called up by the sight of Ettrick Vale, Galla Water, and the Braes of Yarrow! Every turn brought to mind some household air—some almost forgotten song of the nursery, by which I had been lulled to sleep in my childhood; and with them the looks and voices of those who had sung them, and who were now no more. It is these melodies, chanted in our ears in the days of infancy, and connected with the memory of those we have loved, and who have passed away, that clothe Scottish landscape with such tender associations. The Scottish songs, in general, have something intrinsically melancholy in them; owing, in all probability, to the pastoral and lonely life of those who composed them; who were often mere shepherds, tending their flocks in the solitary glens, or folding them among the naked hills. Many of these rustic bards have passed away, without leaving a name behind them; nothing remains of them but their sweet and touching songs, which live, like echoes, about the places they once inhabited. Most of these simple effusions of pastoral poets are linked with some favorite haunt of the poet; and in this way, not a mountain or valley, a town or tower, green shaw or running stream, in Scotland, but has some popular air connected with it, that makes its very name a key note to a whole train of delicious fancies and feelings.

Let me step forward in time, and mention how sensible I was to the power of these simple airs, in a visit which I made to Ayr, the birthplace of Robert Burns. I passed a whole morning about "the banks and braes of bonnie Doon," with his tender little love verses running in my head. I found a poor Scotch carpenter at work among the ruins of Kirk Alloway, which was to be converted into a school-house. Finding the purpose of my visit, he left his work, sat down with me on a grassy grave, close by where Burns' father was buried, and talked of the poet, whom he had known personally. He said his songs were familiar to the poorest and most illiterate of the country folk, "*and it seemed to him as if the country had grown more beautiful, since Burns had written his bonnie little songs about it.*"

I found Scott was quite an enthusiast on the subject of the popular songs of his country, and he seemed gratified to find me so alive to them. Their effect in calling up in my mind the recollections of early times and scenes in which I had first heard them, reminded him, he said, of the lines of his poor friend, Leyden, to the Scottish muse:

"In youth's first morn, alert and gay,
Ere rolling years had passed away,
  Remembered like a morning dream,
I heard the dulcet measures float,
In many a liquid winding note,
  Along the bank of Teviot's stream.

Sweet sounds! that oft have soothed to rest
The sorrows of my guileless breast,
  And charmed away mine infant tears;
Fond memory shall your strains repeat,
Like distant echoes, doubly sweet,
  That on the wild the traveller hears."

Scott went on to expatiate on the popular songs of Scotland. "They are a part of our national inheritance," said he, "and something that we may truly call our own. They have no foreign taint; they have the pure breath of the heather and the mountain breeze. All the genuine legitimate races that have descended from the ancient Britons; such as the Scotch, the Welsh, and the Irish, have national airs. The English have none, because they are not natives of the soil, or, at least, are mongrels. Their music is all made up of foreign scraps, like a harlequin jacket, or a piece of mosaic. Even in Scotland, we have comparatively few national songs in the eastern part, where we have had most influx of strangers. A real old Scottish song is a cairn gorm—a gem of our own mountains: or rather, it is a precious relic of old times, that bears the national character stamped upon it;—like a cameo, that shows what the national visage was in former days, before the breed was crossed."

While Scott was thus discoursing, we were passing up a narrow glen, with the dogs beating about, to right and left, when suddenly a black cock burst upon the wing.

"Aha!" cried Scott, "there will be a good shot for master Walter; we must send him this way with his gun, when we go home. Walter's the family sportsman now, and keeps us in game. I have pretty nigh resigned my gun to him; for I find I cannot trudge about as briskly as formerly."

Our ramble took us on the hills commanding an extensive prospect. "Now," said Scott, "I have brought you, like the pilgrim in the Pilgrim's Progress, to the top of the Delectable Mountains, that I may show you all the goodly regions hereabouts. Yonder is Lammermuir, and Smalholme; and there you have Gallashiels, and Torwoodlie, and Gallawater; and in that direction you see Teviotdale, and the Braes of Yarrow; and Ettrick stream, winding along, like a silver thread, to throw itself into the Tweed."

He went on thus to call over names celebrated in Scottish song, and most of which had recently received a romantic interest from his own pen. In fact, I saw a great part of the border country spread out before me, and could trace the scenes of those poems and romances which had, in a manner, bewitched the world. I gazed about me for a time with mute surprise, I may almost say with disappointment. I beheld a mere succession of gray waving hills, line beyond line, as far as my eye could reach; monotonous in their aspect, and so destitute of trees, that one could almost see a stout fly walking along their profile; and the far-famed Tweed appeared a naked stream, flowing between bare hills, without a tree or thicket on its banks; and yet, such had been the magic web of poetry and romance thrown over the whole, that it had a greater charm for me than the richest scenery I beheld in England.

I could not help giving utterance to my thoughts. Scott hummed for a moment to himself, and looked grave; he had no idea of having his muse complimented at the expense of his native hills. "It may be partiality," said he, at length; "but to my eye, these gray hills and all this wild border country have beauties peculiar to themselves. I like the very nakedness of the land; it has something bold, and stern, and solitary about it. When I have been for some time in the rich scenery about Edinburgh, which is like ornamented garden land, I begin to wish myself back again among my own honest gray hills; and if I did not see the heather at least once a year, *I think I should die!*"

The last words were said with an honest warmth, accompanied with a thump on the ground with his staff, by way of emphasis, that showed his heart was in his speech. He vindicated the Tweed, too, as a beautiful stream in itself, and observed that he did not dislike it for being bare of trees, probably from having been much of an angler in his time, and an angler does not like to have a stream overhung by trees, which embarrass him in the exercise of his rod and line.

I took occasion to plead, in like manner, the associations of early life, for my disappointment, in respect to the surrounding scenery. I had been so accustomed to hills crowned with forests, and streams breaking their way through a wilderness of trees, that all my ideas of romantic landscape were apt to be well wooded.

"Aye, and that's the great charm of your country," cried Scott. "You love the forest as I do the heather—but I would not have you think I do not feel the glory of a great woodland prospect. There is nothing I should like more than to be in the midst of one of your grand, wild, original forests; with the idea of hundreds of miles of untrodden forest around me. I once saw, at Leith, an immense stick of timber, just landed from America. It must have been an enormous tree when it stood on its native soil, at its full height, and with all its branches. I gazed at it with admiration; it seemed like one of the gigantic obelisks which are now and then brought from Egypt, to shame the pigmy monuments of Europe; and, in fact, these vast aboriginal trees, that have sheltered the Indians before the intrusion of the white men, are the monuments and antiquities of your country."

The conversation here turned upon Campbell's poem of Gertrude of Wyoming, as illustrative of the poetic materials furnished by American scenery. Scott spoke of it in that liberal style in which I always found him to speak of the writings of his contemporaries. He cited several passages of it with great delight. "What a pity it is," said he, "that Campbell does not write more and oftener, and give full sweep to his genius. He has wings that would bear him to the skies; and he does now and then spread them grandly, but folds them up again and resumes his perch, as if he was afraid to launch away. He don't know or won't trust his own strength. Even when he has done a thing well, he has often misgivings about it. He left out several fine passages of his Lochiel, but I got him to restore some of them." Here Scott repeated several passages in a magnificent style. "What a grand idea is that," said he, "about prophetic boding, or, in common parlance, second sight—

'Coming events cast their shadows before.'

It is a noble thought, and nobly expressed. And there's that glorious little poem, too, of Hohenlinden; after he had written it, he did not seem to think much of it, but considered some of it 'd—d drum and trumpet lines.' I got him to recite it to me, and I believe that the delight I felt and expressed had an effect in inducing him to print it. The fact is," added he, "Campbell is, in a manner, a bugbear to himself. The brightness of his early success is a detriment to all his further efforts. *He is afraid of the shadow that his own fame casts before him.*"

While we were thus chatting, we heard the report of a gun among the hills. "That's Walter, I think," said Scott, "he has finished his morning's studies, and is out with his gun. I should not be surprised if he had met with the black cock; if so, we shall have an addition to our larder, for Walter is a pretty sure shot."

I inquired into the nature of Walter's studies. "Faith," said Scott, "I can't say much on that head. I am not over bent upon making prodigies of any of my children. As to Walter, I taught him, while a boy, to ride, and shoot, and speak the truth; as to the other parts of his education, I leave them to a very worthy young man, the son of one of our clergymen, who instructs all my children."

I afterwards became acquainted with the young man in question, George Thomson, son of the minister of Melrose, and found him possessed of much learning, intelligence, and modest worth He used to come every day from his father's residence at Melrose to superintend the studies of the young folks, and occasionally took his meals at Abbotsford, where he was highly esteemed Nature had cut him out, Scott used to say, for a stalwart soldier for he was tall, vigorous, active, and fond of athletic exercises, but accident had marred her work, the loss of a limb in boyhood having reduced him to a wooden leg. He was brought up, there fore, for the church, whence he was occasionally called the Dominie, and is supposed, by his mixture of learning, simplicity, and amiable eccentricity, to have furnished many traits for the character of Dominie Sampson. I believe he often acted as Scott's amanuensis, when composing his novels. With him the young people were occupied, in general, during the early part of the day, after which they took all kinds of healthful recreations in the open air; for Scott was as solicitous to strengthen their bodies as their minds.

We had not walked much further before we saw the two Miss Scotts advancing along the hill side to meet us. The morning's studies being over, they had set off to take a ramble on the hills, and gather heather blossoms with which to decorate their hair for dinner. As they came bounding lightly like young fawns, and their dresses fluttering in the pure summer breeze, I was reminded of Scott's own description of his children in his introduction to one of the cantos of Marmion—

"My imps, though hardy, bold, and wild,
As best befits the mountain child,
Their summer gambols tell and mourn,
And anxious ask will spring return,
And birds and lambs again be gay,
And blossoms clothe the hawthorn spray?

Yes, prattlers, yes, the daisy's flower
Again shall paint your summer bower;
Again the hawthorn shall supply
The garlands you delight to tie;

The lambs upon the lea shall bound,
The wild birds carol to the round,
And while you frolic light as they,
Too short shall seem the summer day."

As they approached, the dogs all sprang forward and gambolled around them. They played with them, for a time, and then joined us with countenances full of health and glee. Sophia, the eldest, was the most lively and joyous, having much of her father's varied spirit in conversation, and seeming to catch excitement from his words and looks. Ann was of quieter mood, rather silent, owing, in some measure, no doubt, to her being some years younger.

At dinner Scott had laid by his half rustic dress, and appeared clad in black. The girls, too, in completing their toilet, had twisted in their hair the sprigs of purple heather which they had gathered on the hill side, and looked all fresh and blooming from their breezy walk.

There was no guest at dinner but myself. Around the table were two or three dogs in attendance. Maida, the old stag hound, took his seat at Scott's elbow, looking up wistfully in his master's eye, while Finette, the pet spaniel, placed herself near Mrs. Scott, by whom, I soon perceived, she was completely spoiled.

The conversation happening to turn on the merits of his dogs. Scott spoke with great feeling and affection of his favorite, Camp, who is depicted by his side in the earlier engravings of him.

He talked of him as of a real friend whom he had lost, and Sophia Scott, looking up archly in his face, observed that Papa shed a few tears when poor Camp died. I may here mention another testimonial of Scott's fondness for his dogs, and his humorous mode of showing it, which I subsequently met with. Rambling with him one morning about the grounds adjacent to the house, I observed a small antique monument, on which was inscribed, in Gothic characters—

"Cy git le preux Percy."
(Here lies the brave Percy.)

I paused, supposing it to be the tomb of some stark warrior of the olden time, but Scott drew me on, "Pooh!" cried he, "it's nothing but one of the monuments of my nonsense, of which you'll find enough hereabouts." I learnt afterwards that it was the grave of a favorite greyhound.

Among the other important and privileged members of the household who figured in attendance at the dinner, was a large gray cat, who, I observed, was regaled from time to time with tit bits from the table. This sage grimalkin was a favorite of both master and mistress, and slept at night in their room; and Scott laughingly observed, that one of the least wise parts of their establishment was, that the window was left open at night for puss to go in and out The cat assumed a kind of ascendency among the quadrupeds—sitting in state in Scott's arm-chair, and occasionally stationing himself on a chair beside the door, as if to review his subjects as they passed, giving each dog a cuff beside the ears as he went by. This clapper-clawing was always taken in good part; it appeared to be, in fact, a mere act of sovereignty on the part of grimalkin, to remind the others of their vassalage; which they acknowledged by the most perfect acquiescence. A general harmony prevailed between sovereign and subjects, and they would all sleep together in the sunshine.

Scott was full of anecdote and conversation during dinner. He made some admirable remarks upon the Scottish character, and spoke strongly in praise of the quiet, orderly, honest conduct of his neighbors, which one would hardly expect, said he, from the descendants of moss troopers, and borderers, in a neighborhood famed in old times for brawl and feud, and violence of all kinds. He said he had, in his official capacity of sheriff, administered the laws for a number of years, during which there had been very few trials. The old feuds and local interests, and rivalries, and animosities of the Scotch, however, still slept, he said, in their ashes, and might easily be roused. Their hereditary feeling for names was still great. It was not always safe to have even the game of foot-ball between villages, the old clannish spirit was too apt to break out. The Scotch, he said, were more revengeful than the English; they carried their resentments longer, and would sometimes lay them by for years, but would be sure to gratify them in the end.

The ancient jealousy between the Highlanders and the Lowlanders still continued to a certain degree, the former looking upon the latter as an inferior race, less brave and hardy, but at the same time, suspecting them of a disposition to take airs upon themselves under the idea of superior refinement. This made them techy and ticklish company for a stranger on his first coming among them; ruffling up and putting themselves upon their mettle on the slightest occasion, so that he had in a manner to quarrel and fight his way into their good graces.

He instanced a case in point in a brother of Mungo Park.

who went to take up his residence in a wild neighborhood of the Highlands. He soon found himself considered as an intruder, and that there was a disposition among these cocks of the hills, to fix a quarrel on him, trusting that, being a Lowlander, he would show the white feather.

For a time he bore their flings and taunts with great coolness until one, presuming on his forbearance, drew forth a dirk, and holding it before him, asked him if he had ever seen a weapon like that in his part of the country. Park, who was a Hercules in frame, seized the dirk, and, with one blow, drove it through an oaken table :—" Yes," replied he, " and tell your friends that a man from the Lowlands drove it where the devil himself cannot draw it out again." All persons were delighted with the feat, and the words that accompanied it. They drank with Park to a better acquaintance, and were stanch friends ever afterwards.

After dinner we adjourned to the drawing-room, which served also for study and library. Against the wall on one side was a long writing-table, with drawers ; surmounted by a small cabinet of polished wood, with folding doors richly studded with brass ornaments, within which Scott kept his most valuable papers. Above the cabinet, in a kind of niche, was a complete corslet of glittering steel, with a closed helmet, and flanked by gauntlets and battle-axes. Around were hung trophies and relics of various kinds : a cimeter of Tippoo Saib ; a Highland broadsword from Floddenfield ; a pair of Rippon spurs from Bannockburn ; and above all, a gun which had belonged to Rob Roy, and bore his initials, R. M. G , an object of peculiar interest to me at the time, as it was understood Scott was actually engaged in printing a novel founded on the story of that famous outlaw.

On each side of the cabinet were book-cases, well stored with works of romantic fiction in various languages, many of them rare and antiquated. This, however, was merely his cottage library, the principal part of his books being at Edinburgh.

From this little cabinet of curiosities Scott drew forth a manuscript picked up on the field of Waterloo, containing copies of several songs popular at the time in France. The paper was dabbled with blood—"the very life-blood, very possibly," said Scott, "of some gay young officer, who had cherished these songs as a keepsake from some lady love in Paris."

He adverted in a mellow and delightful manner to the little half gay, half melancholy campaigning song, said to have been composed by General Wolfe, and sung by him at the mess table, on the eve of the storming of Quebec, in which he fell so gloriously.

"Why, soldiers, why,
Should we be melancholy, boys?
Why, soldiers, why,
Whose business 'tis to die!
For should next campaign
Send us to him who made us, boys,
We're free from pain:
But should we remain,
A bottle and kind landlady
Makes all well again."

"So, added he, "the poor lad who fell at Waterloo, in all probability, had been singing these songs in his tent the night before the battle, and thinking of the fair dame who had taught him them, and promising himself, should he outlive the campaign, to return to her all glorious from the wars."

I find since that Scott published translations of these songs among some of his smaller poems.

The evening passed away delightfully in this quaint-looking apartment, half study, half drawing-room. Scott read several passages from the old romance of Arthur, with a fine deep sonorous voice, and a gravity of tone that seemed to suit the antiquated, black-letter volume. It was a rich treat to hear such a work, read by such a person, and in such a place; and his appearance as he sat reading, in a large armed chair, with his favorite hound Maida at his feet, and surrounded by books and relics, and border trophies, would have formed an admirable and most characteristic picture.

While Scott was reading, the sage grimalkin already mentioned had taken his seat in a chair beside the fire, and remained with fixed eye and grave demeanor, as if listening to the reader. I observed to Scott that his cat seemed to have a black-letter taste in literature.

"Ah," said he, "these cats are a very mysterious kind of folk. There is always more passing in their minds than we are aware of. It comes no doubt from their being so familiar with witches and warlocks." He went on to tell a little story about a gude man who was returning to his cottage one night, when, in a lonely out of the way place, he met with a funeral procession of cats all in mourning, bearing one of their race to the grave in a coffin covered with a black velvet pall. The worthy man, astonished and half frightened at so strange a pageant, hastened home and told what he had seen to his wife and children. Scarce had he finished, when a great black cat that sat beside the fire raised himself up, exclaimed "Then I am king of the cats!" and vanished up the chimney. The funeral seen by the gude man, was one of the cat dynasty.

"Our grimalkin here," added Scott, "sometimes reminds me of the story, by the airs of sovereignty which he assumes; and I am apt to treat him with respect from the idea that he may be a great prince incog., and may some time or other come to the throne."

In this way Scott would make the habits and peculiarities of even the dumb animals about him, subjects for humorous remark or whimsical story.

Our evening was enlivened also by an occasional song from Sophia Scott, at the request of her father. She never wanted to be asked twice, but complied frankly and cheerfully. Her songs were all Scotch, sung without any accompaniment, in a simple manner, but with great spirit and expression, and in their native dialects, which gave them an additional charm. It was delightful to hear her carol off in sprightly style, and with an animated air, some of those generous-spirited old Jacobite songs, once current among the adherents of the Pretender in Scotland, in which he is designated by the appellation of "The Young Chevalier."

These songs were much relished by Scott, notwithstanding his loyalty; for the unfortunate "Chevalier" has always been a hero of romance with him, as he has with many other stanch adherents to the House of Hanover, now that the Stuart line has lost all its terrors. In speaking on the subject, Scott mentioned as a curious fact, that, among the papers of the "Chevalier," which had been submitted by government to his inspection, he had found a memorial to Charles from some adherents in America, dated 1778, proposing to set up his standard in the back settlements. I regret that, at the time, I did not make more particular inquiries of Scott on the subject; the document in question, however, in all probability, still exists among the Pretender's papers, which are in the possession of the British Government.

In the course of the evening, Scott related the story of a whimsical picture hanging in the room, which had been drawn for him by a lady of his acquaintance. It represented the doleful perplexity of a wealthy and handsome young English knight of the olden time, who, in the course of a border foray, had been captured and carried off to the castle of a hard-headed and high-handed old baron. The unfortunate youth was thrown into a dungeon, and a tall gallows erected before the castle gate for his execution. When all was ready, he was brought into the castle hall where the grim baron was seated in state, with his warriors armed to the teeth around him, and was given his choice, either to swing on the gibbet or to marry the baron's daughter. The last may be thought an easy alternative, but unfortunately, the baron's young lady was hideously ugly, with a mouth from ear to ear, so that not a suitor was to be had for her, either for love or money, ana she was known throughout the border country by the name of Muckle-mouthed Mag!

The picture in question represented the unhappy dilemma of the handsome youth. Before him sat the grim baron, with a face worthy of the father of such a daughter, and looking daggers and rat's-bane. On one side of him was Muckle-mouthed Mag, with an amorous smile across the whole breadth of her countenance, and a leer enough to turn a man to stone; on the other side was the father confessor, a sleek friar, jogging the youth's elbow, and pointing to the gallows, seen in perspective through the open portal.

The story goes, that after long laboring in mind, between the altar and the halter, the love of life prevailed, and the youth resigned himself to the charms of Muckle-mouthed Mag. Contrary to all the probabilities of romance, the match proved a happy one. The baron's daughter, if not beautiful, was a most exemplary wife; her husband was never troubled with any of those doubts and jealousies which sometimes mar the happiness of connubial life, and was made the father of a fair and undoubtedly legitimate line, which still flourishes on the border.

I give but a faint outline of the story from vague recollection; it may, perchance, be more richly related elsewhere, by some one who may retain something of the delightful humor with which Scott recounted it.

When I retired for the night, I found it almost impossible to sleep; the idea of being under the roof of Scott; of being on the borders of the Tweed, in the very centre of that region which had for some time past been the favorite scene of romantic fiction; and above all, the recollections of the ramble I had taken, the company in which I had taken it, and the conversation which had passed, all fermented in my mind, and nearly drove sleep from my pillow.

On the following morning, the sun darted his beams from over the hills through the low lattice window. I rose at an early hour, and looked out between the branches of eglantine which overhung the casement. To my surprise Scott was already up and forth, seated on a fragment of stone, and chatting with the workmen employed on the new building. I had supposed, after the time he had wasted upon me yesterday, he would be closely occupied this morning: but he appeared like a man of leisure, who had nothing to do but bask in the sunshine and amuse himself.

I soon dressed myself and joined him. He talked about his proposed plans of Abbotsford: happy would it have been for him could he have contented himself with his delightful little vine-covered cottage, and the simple, yet hearty and hospitable style, in which he lived at the time of my visit. The great pile of Abbotsford, with the huge expense it entailed upon him, of servants, retainers, guests, and baronial style, was a drain upon his purse, a tax upon his exertions, and a weight upon his mind, that finally crushed him.

As yet, however, all was in embryo and perspective, and Scott pleased himself with picturing out his future residence, as he would one of the fanciful creations of his own romances. "It was one of his air castles," he said, "which he was reducing to solid stone and mortar." About the place were strewed various morsels from the ruins of Melrose Abbey, which were to be incorporated in his mansion. He had already constructed out of similar materials a kind of Gothic shrine over a spring, and had surmounted it by a small stone cross.

Among the relics from the Abbey which lay scattered before us, was a most quaint and antique little lion, either of red stone, or painted red, which hit my fancy. I forget whose cognizance it was; but I shall never forget the delightful observations concerning old Melrose to which it accidentally gave rise.

The Abbey was evidently a pile that called up all Scott's poetic and romantic feelings; and one to which he was enthusiastically attached by the most fanciful and delightful of his early associations. He spoke of it, I may say, with affection. "There is no telling," said he, "what treasures are hid in that glorious old pile. It is a famous place for antiquarian plunder; there are such rich bits of old time sculpture for the architect, and old time story for the poet. There is as rare picking in it as in a Stilton cheese, and in the same taste—the mouldier the better."

He went on to mention circumstances of "mighty import" connected with the Abbey, which had never been touched, and which had even escaped the researches of Johnny Bower. The heart of Robert Bruce, the hero of Scotland, had been buried in it. He dwelt on the beautiful story of Bruce's pious and chivalrous request in his dying hour, that his heart might be carried to the Holy Land and placed in the Holy Sepulchre, in fulfilment of a vow of pilgrimage; and of the loyal expedition of Sir James Douglas to convey the glorious relic. Much might be made, he said, out of the adventures of Sir James in that adventurous age; of his fortunes in Spain, and his death in a crusade against the Moors; with the subsequent fortunes of the heart of Robert Bruce, until it was brought back to its native land, and inshrined within the holy walls of old Melrose.

As Scott sat on a stone talking in this way, and knocking with his staff against the little red lion which lay prostrate before him, his gray eyes twinkled beneath his shagged eyebrows; scenes. images, incidents, kept breaking upon his mind as he proceeded, mingled with touches of the mysterious and supernatural as connected with the heart of Bruce. It seemed as if a poem or romance were breaking vaguely on his imagination. That he subsequently contemplated something of the kind, as connected with this subject, and with his favorite ruin of Melrose, is evident from his introduction to 'The Monastery;' and it is a pity that he never succeeded in following out these shadowy but enthusiastic conceptions.

A summons to breakfast broke off our conversation, when I begged to recommend to Scott's attention my friend the little red lion, who had led to such an interesting topic, and hoped he might receive some niche or station in the future castle, worthy of his evident antiquity and apparent dignity. Scott assured me, with comic gravity, that the valiant little lion should be most honorably entertained; I hope, therefore, that he still flourishes at Abbotsford.

Before dismissing the theme of the relics from the Abbey, I will mention another, illustrative of Scott's varied humors. This was a human skull, which had probably belonged of yore to one of those jovial friars, so honorably mentioned in the old border ballad:

> "O the monks of Melrose made gude kale
> On Fridays, when they fasted;
> They wanted neither beef nor ale,
> As long as their neighbors lasted."

This skull Scott had caused to be cleaned and varnished, and placed it on a chest of drawers in his chamber, immediately opposite his bed; where I have seen it, grinning most dismally. It was an object of great awe and horror to the superstitious housemaids; and Scott used to amuse himself with their apprehensions. Sometimes, in changing his dress, he would leave his neckcloth coiled round it like a turban, and none of the "lasses" dared to remove it. It was a matter of great wonder and speculation among them that the laird should have such an "awsome fancy for an auld girning skull."

At breakfast that morning, Scott gave an amusing account of a little Highlander called Campbell of the North, who had a lawsuit of many years' standing with a nobleman in his neighborhood about the boundaries of their estates. It was the leading object of the little man's life; the running theme of all his conversations; he used to detail all the circumstances at full length to every body he met, and, to aid him in his description of the premises, and make his story "mair preceese," he had a great map made of his estate, a huge roll several feet long, which he used to carry about on his shoulder. Campbell was a long-bodied, but short and bandy-legged little man, always clad in the Highland garb; and as he went about with this great roll on his shoulder, and his little legs curving like a pair of parentheses below his kilt, he was an odd figure to behold. He was like little David shouldering the spear of Goliath, which was "like unto a weaver's beam."

Whenever sheep-shearing was over, Campbell used to set out for Edinburgh to attend to his lawsuit. At the inns he paid double for all his meals and his nights' lodgings; telling the landlords to keep it in mind until his return, so that he might come back that way at free cost; for he knew, he said, that he would spend all his money among the lawyers at Edinburgh, so he thought it best to secure a retreat home again.

On one of his visits he called upon his lawyer, but was told he was not at home, but his lady was. "It is just the same thing," said little Campbell. On being shown into the parlor, he unrolled his map, stated his case at full length, and, having gone through with his story, gave her the customary fee. She would have declined it, but he insisted on her taking it. "I ha' had just as much pleasure," said he, "in telling the whole tale to you, as I should have had in telling it to your husband, and I believe full as much profit."

The last time he saw Scott, he told him he believed he and the laird were near a settlement, as they agreed to within a few miles of the boundary. If I recollect right, Scott added that he advised the little man to consign his cause and his map to the care of "Slow Willie Mowbray," of tedious memory; an Edinburgh worthy, much employed by the country people, for he tired out every body in office by repeated visits and drawling, endless prolixity, and gained every suit by dint of boring.

These little stories and anecdotes, which abounded in Scott's conversation, rose naturally out of the subject, and were perfectly unforced; though in thus relating them in a detached way, without the observations or circumstances which led to them, and which have passed from my recollection, they want their setting to give them proper relief. They will serve, however, to show the natural play of his mind, in its familiar moods, and its fecundity in graphic and characteristic detail.

His daughter Sophia and his son Charles were those of his family who seemed most to feel and understand his humors, and to take delight in his conversation. Mrs. Scott did not always pay the same attention, and would now and then make a casual remark which would operate a little like a damper. Thus, one morning at breakfast, when Dominie Thompson the tutor was present, Scott was going on with great glee to relate an anecdote of the laird of Macnab, "who, poor fellow!" premised he, "is dead and gone—" "Why," Mr. Scott," exclaimed the good lady, "Macnab's not dead, is he?" "Faith, my dear," replied Scott, with humorous gravity, "if he's not dead they've done him great injustice,—for they've buried him."

The joke passed harmless and unnoticed by Mrs. Scott, but hit the poor Dominie just as he had raised a cup of tea to his lips, causing a burst of laughter which sent half of the contents about the table.

After breakfast, Scott was occupied for some time correcting proof sheets, which he had received by the mail. The novel of Rob Roy, as I have already observed, was at that time in the press, and I supposed them to be the proof sheets of that work. The authorship of the Waverly novels was still a matter of conjecture and uncertainty; though few doubted their being principally written by Scott. One proof to me of his being the author, was that he never adverted to them. A man so fond of any thing Scottish, and any thing relating to national history or local legend, could not have been mute respecting such productions, had they been written by another. He was fond of quoting the works of his contemporaries; he was continually reciting scraps of border songs, or relating anecdotes of border story. With respect to his own poems, and their merits, however, he was mute, and while with him I observed a scrupulous silence on the subject.

I may here mention a singular fact, of which I was not aware at the time, that Scott was very reserved with his children respecting his own writings, and was even disinclined to their reading his romantic poems. I learnt this, some time after, from a passage in one of his letters to me, adverting to a set of the American miniature edition of his poems, which, on my return to England, I forwarded to one of the young ladies. "In my hurry," writes he, "I have not thanked you, in Sophia's name, for the kind attention which furnished her with the American volumes. I am not quite sure I can add my own, since you have made her acquainted with much more of papa's folly, than she would otherwise have learned; for I have taken special care they should never see any of these things during their earlier years."

To return to the thread of my narrative. When Scott had got through his brief literary occupation, we set out on a ramble. The young ladies started to accompany us, but had not gone far, when they met a poor old laborer and his distressed family, and turned back to take them to the house, and relieve them.

On passing the bounds of Abbotsford, we came upon a bleak-looking farm, with a forlorn crazy old manse, or farmhouse, standing in naked desolation. This, however, Scott told me was an ancient hereditary property called Lauckend, about as valuable as the patrimonial estate of Don Quixote, and which, in like manner, conferred an hereditary dignity upon its proprietor, who was a laird, and, though poor as a rat, prided himself upon his ancient blood, and the standing of his house. He was accordingly called Lauckend, according to the Scottish custom of naming a man after his family estate, but he was more generally known through the country round by the name of Lauckie Long Legs, from the length of his limbs. While Scott was giving this account of him, we saw him at a distance striding along one of his fields, with his plaid fluttering about him, and he seemed well to deserve his appellation, for he looked all legs and tartan.

Lauckie knew nothing of the world beyond his neighborhood. Scott told me that on returning to Abbotsford from his visit to France, immediately after the war, he was called on by his neighbors generally, to inquire after foreign parts. Among the number, came Lauckie Long Legs and an old brother as ignorant as himself. They had many inquiries to make about the French, whom they seemed to consider some remote and semi-barbarous horde—"And what like are thae barbarians in their own country?" said Lauckie, "can they write?—can they cipher?" He was quite astonished to learn that they were nearly as much advanced in civilization as the gude folks of Abbotsford.

After living for a long time in single blessedness, Lauckie all at once, and not long before my visit to the neighborhood, took it into his head to get married. The neighbors were all surprised; but the family connection, who were as proud as they were poor, were grievously scandalized, for they thought the young woman on whom he had set his mind quite beneath him. It was in vain, however, that they remonstrated on the misalliance he was about to make: he was not to be swayed from his determination. Arraying himself in his best, and saddling a gaunt steed that might have rivalled Rosinante, and placing a pillion behind his saddle, he departed to wed and bring home the humble lassie who was to be made mistress of the venerable hovel of Lauckend, and who lived in a village on the opposite side of the Tweed.

A small event of the kind makes a great stir in a little quiet country neighborhood. The word soon circulated through the village of Melrose, and the cottages in its vicinity, that Lauckie Long Legs had gone over the Tweed to fetch home his bride. All the good folks assembled at the bridge to await his return. Lauckie, however, disappointed them; for he crossed the river at a distant ford, and conveyed his bride safe to his mansion, without being perceived.

Let me step forward in the course of events and relate the

fate of poor Lauckie, as it was communicated to me a year or two afterwards in letter by Scott. From the time of his marriage he had no longer any peace, owing to the constant intermeddlings of his relations, who would not permit him to be happy in his own way, but endeavored to set him at variance with his wife. Lauckie refused to credit any of their stories to her disadvantage; but the incessant warfare he had to wage, in defence of her good name, wore out both flesh and spirit. His last conflict was with his own brothers, in front of his paternal mansion. A furious scolding match took place between them; Lauckie made a vehement profession of faith in favor of her immaculate honesty, and then fell dead at the threshold of his own door. His person, his character, his name, his story, and his fate, entitled him to be immortalized in one of Scott's novels, and I looked to recognize him in some of the succeeding works from his pen; but I looked in vain.

After passing by the domains of honest Lauckie, Scott pointed out, at a distance, the Eildon stone. There in ancient days stood the Eildon tree, beneath which Thomas the Rhymer, according to popular tradition, dealt forth his prophecies, some of which still exist in antiquated ballads.

Here we turned up a little glen with a small burn or brook whimpering and dashing along it, making an occasional waterfall, and overhung in some places with mountain ash and weeping birch. We are now, said Scott, treading classic, or rather fairy ground. This is the haunted glen of Thomas the Rhymer, where he met with the queen of fairy land, and this the bogle burn, or goblin brook, along which she rode on her dapple-gray palfrey, with silver bells ringing at the bridle.

"Here," said he, pausing, "is Huntley Bank, on which Thomas the Rhymer lay musing and sleeping when he saw, or dreamt he saw, the queen of Elfland:

"True Thomas lay on Huntlie bank;
A ferlie he spied wi' his e'e;
And there he saw a ladye bright,
Come riding down by the Eildon tree.

Her skirt was o' the grass green silk,
Her mantle o' the velvet fyne;
At ilka tett of her horse's mane
Hung fifty siller bells and nine."

Here Scott repeated several of the stanzas and recounted the circumstance of Thomas the Rhymer's interview with the fairy, and his being transported by her to fairy land—

"And til seven years were gone and past,
True Thomas on earth was never seen."

It is a fine old story, said he, and might be wrought up into a capital tale.

Scott continued on, leading the way as usual, and limping up the wizard glen, talking as he went, but as his back was toward me, I could only hear the deep growling tones of his voice, like the low breathing of an organ, without distinguishing the words, until pausing, and turning his face towards me, I found he was reciting some scrap of border minstrelsy about Thomas the Rhymer. This was continually the case in my ramblings with him about this storied neighborhood. His mind was fraught with the traditionary fictions connected with every object around him, and he would breathe it forth as he went, apparently as much for his own gratification as for that of his companion.

> " Nor hill, nor brook, we paced along,
> But had its legend or its song."

His voice was deep and sonorous, he spoke with a Scottish accent, and with somewhat of the Northumbrian " burr," which, to my mind, gave a doric strength and simplicity to his elocution. His recitation of poetry was, at times, magnificent.

I think it was in the course of this ramble that my friend Hamlet, the black greyhound, got into a sad scrape. The dogs were beating about the glens and fields as usual, and had been for some time out of sight, when we heard a barking at some distance to the left. Shortly after we saw some sheep scampering on the hills, with the dogs after them. Scott applied to his lips the ivory whistle, always hanging at his button-hole, and soon called in the culprits, excepting Hamlet. Hastening up a bank which commanded a view along a fold or hollow of the hills, we beheld the sable prince of Denmark standing by the bleeding body of a sheep. The carcass was still warm, the throat bore marks of the fatal grip, and Hamlet's muzzle was stained with blood. Never was culprit more completely caught in *flagrante delictu.* I supposed the doom of poor Hamlet to be sealed; for no higher offence can be committed by a dog in a country abounding with sheep walks. Scott, however, had a greater value for his dogs than for his sheep. They were his companions and friends Hamlet, too, though an irregular, impertinent kind of youngster, was evidently a favorite. He would not for some time believe it could be he who had killed the sheep. It must have been some cur of the neighborhood, that had made off on our approach, and left poor Hamlet in the lurch. Proofs, however, were too strong, and Hamlet was generally condemned. "Well, well," said Scott, "it's partly my own fault. I have given up coursing for some time past, and the poor dog has had no chance after game to take the fire edge off of him. If he was put after a hare occasionally he never would meddle with sheep."

I understood, afterwards, that Scott actually got a pony, and went out now and then coursing with Hamlet, who, in consequence, showed no further inclination for mutton.

A further stroll among the hills brought us to what Scott pronounced the remains of a Roman camp, and as we sat upon a hillock which had once formed a part of the ramparts, he pointed out the traces of the lines and bulwarks, and the prætorium, and showed a knowledge of castramatation that would not have disgraced the antiquarian Oldbuck himself. Indeed, various circumstances that I observed about Scott during my visit, concurred to persuade me that many of the antiquarian humors of Monkbarns were taken from his own richly compounded character, and that some of the scenes and personages of that admirable novel were furnished by his immediate neighborhood.

He gave me several anecdotes of a noted pauper named Andrew Gemmells, or Gammel, as it was pronounced, who had once flourished on the banks of Galla Water, immediately opposite Abbotsford, and whom he had seen and talked and joked with when a boy; and I instantly recognized the likeness of that mirror of philosophic vagabonds and Nestor of beggars, Edie Ochiltree. I was on the point of pronouncing the name and recognizing the portrait, when I recollected the incognito observed by Scott with respect to novels, and checked myself; but it was one among many things that tended to convince me of his authorship.

His picture of Andrew Gemmells exactly accorded with that of Edie as to his height, carriage, and soldier-like air, as well as his arch and sarcastic humor. His home, if home he had, was at Gallashiels; but he went "daundering" about the country, along the green shaws and beside the burns, and was a kind of walking chronicle throughout the valleys of the Tweed, the Ettrick, and the Yarrow; carrying the gossip from house to house, commenting on the inhabitants and their concerns, and never hesitating to give them a dry rub as to any of their faults or follies.

A shrewd beggar like Andrew Gemmells, Scott added, who could sing the old Scotch airs, tell stories and traditions, and gossip away the long winter evenings, was by no means an unwelcome visitor at a lonely manse or cottage. The children would run to welcome him, and place his stool in a warm corner of the ingle nook, and the old folks would receive him as a privileged guest.

As to Andrew, he looked upon them all as a parson does upon his parishioners, and considered the alms he received as much his due as the other does his tithes. I rather think, added Scott, Andrew considered himself more of a gentleman than those who toiled for a living, and that he secretly looked down upon the painstaking peasants that fed and sheltered him.

He had derived his aristocratical notions in some degree from being admitted occasionally to a precarious sociability with some of the small country gentry, who were sometimes in want of company to help while away the time. With these Andrew would now and then play at cards and dice, and he never lacked "siller in pouch" to stake on a game, which he did with a perfect air of a man to whom money was a matter of little moment, and no one could lose his money with more gentlemanlike coolness.

Among those who occasionally admitted him to this familiarity, was old John Scott of Galla, a man of family, who inhabited his paternal mansion of Torwoodlee. Some distinction of rank, however, was still kept up. The laird sat on the inside of the window and the beggar on the outside, and they played cards on the sill.

Andrew now and then told the laird a piece of his mind very freely; especially on one occasion, when he had sold some of his paternal lands to build himself a larger house with the proceeds. The speech of honest Andrew smacks of the shrewdness of Edie Ochiltree.

"It's a' varra weel—it's a' varra weel, Torwoodlee," said he; "but who would ha' thought that your father's son would ha' sold two gude estates to build a shaw's (cuckoo's) nest on the side of a hill?"

That day there was an arrival at Abbotsford of two English tourists; one a gentleman of fortune and landed estate, the other a young clergyman whom he appeared to have under his patronage, and to have brought with him as a travelling companion.

The patron was one of those well-bred, commonplace gentlemen with which England is overrun. He had great deference for Scott, and endeavored to acquit himself learnedly in his company, aiming continually at abstract disquisitions, for which Scott had little relish. The conversation of the latter, as usual, was studded with anecdotes and stories, some of them of great pith and humor: the well-bred gentleman was either too dull to feel their point, or too decorous to indulge in hearty merriment; the honest parson, on the contrary, who was not too refined to be happy, laughed loud and long at every joke, and enjoyed them with the zest of a man who has more merriment in his heart than coin in his pocket.

After they were gone, some comments were made upon their different deportments. Scott spoke very respectfully of the good breeding and measured manners of the man of wealth, but with a kindlier feeling of the honest parson, and the homely but hearty enjoyment with which he relished every pleasantry. "I doubt," said he, "whether the parson's lot in life is not the best; if he cannot command as many of the good things of this world by his own purse as his patron can, he beats him all hollow in his enjoyment of them when set before him by others. Upon the whole," added he, "I rather think I prefer the honest parson's good humor to his patron's good breeding; I have a great regard for a hearty laugher."

He went on to speak of the great influx of English travellers, which of late years had inundated Scotland; and doubted whether they had not injured the old-fashioned Scottish character. "Formerly, they came here occasionally as sportsmen," said he, "to shoot moor game, without any idea of looking at scenery; and they moved about the country in hardy simple style, coping with the country people in their own way; but now they come rolling about in their equipages, to see ruins, and spend money, and their lavish extravagance has played the vengeance with the common people. It has made them rapacious in their dealings with strangers, greedy after money, and extortionate in their demands for the most trivial services. Formerly," continued he, "the poorer classes of our people were, comparatively, disinterested; they offered their services gratuitously, in promoting the amusement, or aiding the curiosity of strangers, and were gratified by the smallest compensation; but now they make a trade of showing rocks and ruins, and are as greedy as Italian cicerones. They look upon the English as so many walking money-bags; the more they are shaken and poked, the more they will leave behind them."

I told him that he had a great deal to answer for on that head, since it was the romantic associations he had thrown by his writings over so many out of the way places in Scotland, that had brought in the influx of curious travellers.

Scott laughed, and said he believed I might be in some measure in the right, as he recollected a circumstance in point. Being one time at Glenross, an old woman who kept a small inn, which had but little custom, was uncommonly officious in her attendance upon him, and absolutely incommoded him with her civilities. The secret at length came out. As he was about to depart, she addressed him with many curtsies, and said she understood he was the gentleman that had written a bonnie book about Loch Katrine. She begged him to write a little about their lake also, for she understood his book had done the inn at Loch Katrine a muckle deal of good.

On the following day, I made an excursion with Scott and the young ladies, to Dryburgh Abbey. We went in an open carriage, drawn by two sleek old black horses, for which Scott seemed to have an affection, as he had for every dumb animal that belonged to him. Our road lay through a variety of scenes, rich in poetical and historical associations, about most of which Scott had something to relate. In one part of the drive, he pointed to an old border keep, or fortress, on the summit of a naked hill, several miles off, which he called Smallholm Tower, and a rocky knoll on which it stood, the "Sandy Knowe crags." It was a place, he said, peculiarly dear to him, from the recollections of childhood. His grandfather had lived there in the old Smallholm Grange, or farmhouse: and he had been sent there, when but two years old, on account of his lameness, that he might have the benefit of the pure air of the hills, and be under the care of his grandmother and aunts.

In the introduction of one of the cantos of Marmion, he has depicted his grandfather, and the fireside of the farm-house; and has given an amusing picture of himself in his boyish years.

"Still with vain fondness could I trace
Anew each kind familiar face,
That brightened at our evening fire;
From the thatched mansion's gray-haired sire
Wise without learning, plain and good,
And sprung of Scotland's gentler blood;
Whose eye in age, quick, clear and keen,
Showed what in youth its glance had been;
Whose doom discording neighbors sought,
Content with equity unbought;

To him the venerable priest,
Our frequent and familiar guest,
Whose life and manners well could paint
Alike the student and the saint;
Alas! whose speech too oft I broke
With gambol rude and timeless joke;
For I was wayward, bold, and wild,
A self-willed imp, a grandame s child;
But half a plague, and half a jest,
Was still endured, beloved, carest."

It was, he said, during his residence at Smallholm crags, that he first imbibed his passion for legendary tales, border traditions, and old national songs and ballads. His grandmother and aunts were well versed in that kind of lore, so current in Scottish country life. They used to recount them in long, gloomy, winter days, and about the ingle nook at night, in conclave with their gossip visitors; and little Walter would sit and listen with greedy ear; thus taking into his infant mind the seeds of many a splendid fiction.

There was an old shepherd, he said, in the service of the family, who used to sit under the sunny wall, and tell marvellous stories, and recite old time ballads, as he knitted stockings. Scott used to be wheeled out in his chair, in fine weather, and would sit beside the old man, and listen to him for hours.

The situation of Sandy Knowe was favorable both for story-teller and listener. It commanded a wide view over all the border country, with its feudal towers, its haunted glens, and wizard streams. As the old shepherd told his tales, he could point out the very scene of action. Thus, before Scott could walk, he was made familiar with the scenes of his future stories; they were all seen as through a magic medium, and took that tinge of romance, which they ever after retained in his imagination. From the height of Sandy Knowe, he may be said to have had the first look-out upon the promised land of his future glory.

On referring to Scott's works, I find many of the circumstances related in this conversation, about the old tower, and the boyish scenes connected with it, recorded in the introduction to Marmion, already cited. This was frequently the case with Scott; incidents and feelings that had appeared in his writings, were apt to be mingled up in his conversation, for they had been taken from what he had witnessed and felt in real life, and were connected with those scenes among which he lived, and moved, and had his being. I make no scruple at quoting the passage relative to the tower, though it repeats much of the foregone imagery, and with vastly superior effect.

"Thus, while I ape the measure wild
Of tales that charmed me yet a child,
Rude though they be, still with the chime
Return the thoughts of early time;
And feelings roused in life's first day,
Glow in the line, and prompt the lay.
Then rise those crags, that mountain tower,
Which charmed my fancy's wakening hour,
Though no broad river swept along
To claim perchance heroic song;
Though sighed no groves in summer gale
To prompt of love a softer tale;
Though scarce a puny streamlet's speed
Claimed homage from a shepherd's reed;
Yet was poetic impulse given,
By the green hill and clear blue heaven.

It was a barren scene, and wild,
Where naked cliffs were rudely piled;
But ever and anon between
Lay velvet tufts of loveliest green;
And well the lonely infant knew
Recesses where the wall-flower grew,
And honey-suckle loved to crawl
Up the low crag and ruined wall.
I deemed such nooks the sweetest shade
The sun in all his round surveyed;
And still I thought that shattered tower
The mightiest work of human power;
And marvelled as the aged hind
With some strange tale bewitched my mind
Of forayers, who, with headlong force,
Down from that strength had spurred their horse,
Their southern rapine to renew,
Far in the distant Cheviot's blue,
And, nome returning, filled the hall
With revel, wassail-rout, and brawl—
Methought that still with tramp and clang
The gate-way's broken arches rang;
Methought grim features, seamed with scars.
Glared through the window's rusty bars.
And ever by the winter hearth,
Old tales I heard of woe or mirth,
Of lovers' slights, of ladies' charms,
Of witches' spells, of warriors' arms;
Of patriot battles, won of old,
By Wallace wight and Bruce the bold;
Of later fields of feud and fight,
When pouring from the Highland height,
The Scottish clans, in headlong sway,
Had swept the scarlet ranks away.

While stretched at length upon the floor,
Again I fought each combat o'er,
Pebbles and shells, in order laid,
The mimic ranks of war displayed ;
And onward still the Scottish Lion bore,
And still the scattered Southron fled before."

Scott eyed the distant height of Sandy Knowe with an earnest gaze as we rode along, and said he had often thought of buying the place, repairing the old tower, and making it his residence. He has in some measure, however, paid off his early debt of gratitude, in clothing it with poetic and romantic associations, by his tale of "The Eve of St. John." It is to be hoped that those who actually possess so interesting a monument of Scott's early days, will preserve it from further dilapidation.

Not far from Sandy Knowe, Scott pointed out another old border hold, standing on the summit of a hill, which had been a kind of enchanted castle to him in his boyhood. It was the tower of Bemerside, the baronial residence of the Haigs, or De Hagas, one of the oldest families of the border. "There had seemed to him," he said, "almost a wizard spell hanging over it, in consequence of a prophecy of Thomas the Rhymer, in which, in his young days, he most potently believed :"

"Betide, betide, whate'er betide,
Haig shall be Haig of Bemerside."

Scott added some particulars which showed that, in the present instance, the venerable Thomas had not proved a false prophet, for it was a noted fact, that, amid all the changes and chances of the border; through all the feuds, and forays, and sackings, and burnings, which had reduced most of the castles to ruins, and the proud families that once possessed them to poverty, the tower of Bemerside still remained unscathed, and was still the strong-hold of the ancient family of Haig.

Prophecies, however, often insure their own fulfilment. It is very probable that the prediction of Thomas the Rhymer has linked the Haigs to their tower, as their rock of safety, and has induced them to cling to it, almost superstitiously, through hardships and inconveniences that would, otherwise, have caused its abandonment.

I afterwards saw, at Dryburgh Abbey, the burying place of this predestinated and tenacious family, the inscription of which showed the value they set upon their antiquity :—

"Locus Sepulturæ,
Antiquessimæ Familiæ
De Haga
De Bemerside.

In reverting to the days of his childhood, Scott observed that the lameness which had disabled him in infancy gradually decreased; he soon acquired strength in his limbs, and though he always limped, he became, even in boyhood, a great walker. He used frequently to stroll from home and wander about the country for days together, picking up all kinds of local gossip, and observing popular scenes and characters. His father used to be vexed with him for this wandering propensity, and, shaking his head, would say he fancied the boy would make nothing but a pedler. As he grew older, he became a keen sportsman, and passed much of his time hunting and shooting. His field sports led him into the most wild and unfrequented parts of the country, and in this way he picked up much of that local knowledge which he has since evinced in his writings.

His first visit to Loch Katrine, he said, was in his boyish days, on a shooting excursion. The island, which he has made the romantic residence of the Lady of the Lake, was then garrisoned by an old man and his wife. Their house was vacant: they had put the key under the door, and were absent fishing It was at that time a peaceful residence, but became afterwards a resort of smugglers, until they were ferreted out.

In after years, when Scott began to turn this local knowledge to literary account, he revisited many of those scenes of his early ramblings, and endeavored to secure the fugitive remains of the traditions and songs that had charmed his boyhood. When collecting materials for his Border Minstrelsy, he used, he said, to go from cottage to cottage and make the old wives repeat all they knew, if but two lines; and by putting these scraps together, he retrieved many a fine characteristic old ballad or tradition from oblivion.

I regret to say that I can recollect scarce any thing of our visit to Dryburgh Abbey. It is on the estate of the Earl of Buchan. The religious edifice is a mere ruin, rich in Gothic antiquities, but especially interesting to Scott, from containing the family vault, and the tombs and monuments of his ancestors. He appeared to feel much chagrin at their being in the possession, and subject to the intermeddlings of the Earl, who was represented as a nobleman of an eccentric character. The latter, however, set great value on these sepulchral relics, and had expressed a lively anticipation of one day or other having the honor of burying Scott, and adding his monument to the collection, which he intended should be worthy of the "mighty minstrel of the north,"—a prospective compliment which was by no means relished by the object of it.

One of my pleasant rambles with Scott, about the neighborhood of Abbotsford, was taken in company with Mr. William Laidlaw, the steward of his estate. This was a gentleman for whom Scott entertained a particular value. He had been born to a competency, had been well educated, his mind was richly stored with varied information, and he was a man of sterling moral worth. Having been reduced by misfortune, Scott had got him to take charge of his estate. He lived at a small farm on the hill-side above Abbotsford, and was treated by Scott as a cherished and confidential friend, rather than a dependent.

As the day was showery, Scott was attended by one of his retainers, named Tommie Purdie, who carried his plaid, and who deserves especial mention. Sophia Scott used to call him her father's grand vizier, and she gave a playful account one evening, as she was hanging on her father's arm, of the consultations which he and Tommie used to have about matters relative to farming. Purdie was tenacious of his opinions, and he and Scott would have long disputes in front of the house, as to something that was to be done on the estate, until the latter, fairly tired out, would abandon the ground and the argument, exclaiming, "Well, well, Tom, have it your own way."

After a time, however, Purdie would present himself at the door of the parlor, and observe, "I ha' been thinking over the matter, and upon the whole, I think I'll take your honor's advice."

Scott laughed heartily when this anecdote was told of him. "It was with him and Tom," he said, "as it was with an old laird and a pet servant, whom he had indulged until he was positive beyond all endurance. 'This won't do!' cried the old laird, in a passion, 'we can't live together any longer—we must part.' 'An' where the deil does your honor mean to go?' replied the other."

I would, moreover, observe of Tom Purdie, that he was a firm believer in ghosts, and warlocks, and all kinds of old wives' fable. He was a religious man, too, mingling a little degree of Scottish pride in his devotion; for though his salary was but twenty pounds a year, he had managed to afford seven pounds for a family Bible. It is true, he had one hundred pounds clear of the world, and was looked up to by his comrades as a man of property.

In the course of our morning's walk, we stopped at a small house belonging to one of the laborers on the estate. The object of Scott's visit was to inspect a relic which had been digged up in the Roman camp, and which, if I recollect right, he pronounced to have been a tongs. It was produced by the cottager's wife, a ruddy, healthy-looking dame, whom Scott addressed by the name of Ailie. As he stood regarding the relic, turning it round and round, and making comments upon it, half grave, half comic, with the cottage group around him, all joining occasionally in the colloquy, the inimitable character of Monkbarns was again brought to mind, and I seemed to see before me that prince of antiquarians and humorists holding forth to his unlearned and unbelieving neighbors.

Whenever Scott touched, in this way, upon local antiquities, and in all his familiar conversations about local traditions and superstitions, there was always a sly and quiet humor running at the bottom of his discourse, and playing about his countenance, as if he sported with the subject. It seemed to me as if he distrusted his own enthusiasm, and was disposed to droll upon his own humors and peculiarities, yet, at the same time, a poetic gleam in his eye would show that he really took a strong relish and interest in them. "It was a pity," he said, "that antiquarians were generally so dry, for the subjects they handled were rich in historical and poetic recollections, in picturesque details, in quaint and heroic characteristics, and in all kinds of curious and obsolete ceremonials. They are always groping among the rarest materials for poetry, but they have no idea of turning them to poetic use. Now every fragment from old times has, in some degree, its story with it, or gives an inkling of something characteristic of the circumstances and manners of its day, and so sets the imagination at work."

For my own part I never met with antiquarian so delightful, either in his writings or his conversation; and the quiet subacid humor that was prone to mingle in his disquisitions, gave them, to me, a peculiar and an exquisite flavor. But he seemed, in fact, to undervalue every thing that concerned himself. The play of his genius was so easy that he was unconscious of its mighty power, and made light of those sports of intellect that shamed the efforts and labors of other minds.

Our ramble this morning took us again up the Rhymer's Glen, and by Huntley Bank, and Huntley Wood, and the silver waterfall overhung with weeping birches and mountain ashes, those delicate and beautiful trees which grace the green shaws and burnsides of Scotland. The heather, too, that closely woven robe of Scottish landscape which covers the nakedness of its hills and mountains, tinted the neighborhood with soft and rich colors. As we ascended the glen, the prospects opened upon us; Melrose, with its towers and pinnacles, lay below; beyond was the Eildon hills, the Cowden Knowes, the Tweed, the Galla Water, and all the storied vicinity; the whole landscape varied by gleams of sunshine and driving showers.

Scott, as usual, took the lead, limping along with great activity, and in joyous mood, giving scraps of border rhymes and border stories; two or three times in the course of our walk there were drizzling showers, which I supposed would put an end to our ramble, but my companions trudged on as unconcernedly as if it had been fine weather.

At length, I asked whether we had not better seek some shelter. "True," said Scott, "I did not recollect that you were not accustomed to our Scottish mists. This is a lachrymose climate, evermore showering. We, however, are children of the mist, and must not mind a little whimpering of the clouds any more than a man must mind the weeping of an hysterical wife. As you are not accustomed to be wet through, as a matter of course, in a morning's walk, we will bide a bit under the lee of this bank until the shower is over." Taking his seat under shelter of a thicket, he called to his man George for his tartan, then turning to me, "come," said he, "come under my plaidy, as the old song goes;" so, making me nestle down beside him, he wrapped a part of the plaid round me, and took me, as he said, under his wing.

While we were thus nestled together, he pointed to a hole in the opposite bank of the glen. That, he said, was the hole of an old gray badger, who was, doubtless, snugly housed in this bad weather. Sometimes he saw him at the entrance of his hole, like a hermit at the door of his cell, telling his beads, or reading a homily. He had a great respect for the venerable anchorite, and would not suffer him to be disturbed. He was a kind of successor to Thomas the Rhymer, and perhaps might be Thomas himself returned from fairy land, but still under fairy spell.

Some accident turned the conversation upon Hogg, the poet, in which Laidlaw, who was seated beside us, took a part. Hogg had once been a shepherd in the service of his father, and Laidlaw gave many interesting anecdotes of him, of which I now retain no recollection. They used to tend the sheep together when Laidlaw was a boy, and Hogg would recite the first struggling conceptions of his muse. At night when Laidlaw was quartered comfortably in bed, in the farmhouse, poor Hogg would take to the shepherd's hut, in the field on the hillside, and there lie awake for hours together, and look at the stars and make poetry, which he would repeat the next day to his companion.

Scott spoke in warm terms of Hogg, and repeated passages from his beautiful poem of Kelmeny, to which he gave great and well-merited praise. He gave, also, some amusing anecdotes of Hogg and his publisher, Blackwood, who was at that time just rising into the bibliographical importance which he has since enjoyed.

Hogg in one of his poems, I believe the Pilgrims of the Sun, had dabbled a little in metaphysics, and like his heroes, had got into the clouds. Blackwood, who began to affect criticism, argued stoutly with him as to the necessity of omitting or elucidating some obscure passage. Hogg was immovable.

"But, man," said Blackwood, "I dinna ken what ye mean in this passage." "Hout tout, man," replied Hogg, impatiently,

"I dinna ken always what I mean mysel." There is many a metaphysical poet in the same predicament with honest Hogg.

Scott promised to invite the Shepherd to Abbotsford during my visit, and I anticipated much gratification in meeting with him, from the account I had received of his character and manners, and the great pleasure I had derived from his works. Circumstances, however, prevented Scott from performing his promise; and to my great regret I left Scotland without seeing one of its most original and national characters.

When the weather held up, we continued our walk until we came to a beautiful sheet of water, in the bosom of the mountain, called, if I recollect right, the lake of Cauldshiel. Scott prided himself much upon this little Mediterranean sea in his dominions, and hoped I was not too much spoiled by our great lakes in America to relish it. He proposed to take me out to the centre of it, to a fine point of view: for which purpose we embarked in a small boat, which had been put on the lake by his neighbor, Lord Somerville. As I was about to step on board, I observed in large letters on one of the benches, "Search No. 2." I paused for a moment and repeated the inscription aloud, trying to recollect something I had heard or read to which it alluded. "Pshaw," cried Scott, "it is only some of Lord Somerville's nonsense—get in!" In an instant scenes in the Antiquary connected with "Search No. 1," flashed upon my mind. "Ah! I remember now," said I, and with a laugh took my seat, but adverted no more to the circumstance.

We had a pleasant row about the lake, which commanded some pretty scenery. The most interesting circumstance connected with it, however, according to Scott, was, that it was haunted by a bogle in the shape of a water bull, which lived in the deep parts, and now and then came forth upon dry land and made a tremendous roaring, that shook the very hills. This story had been current in the vicinity from time immemorial;—there was a man living who declared he had seen the bull,—and he was believed by many of his simple neighbors. "I don't choose to contradict the tale," said Scott, "for I am willing to have my lake stocked with any fish, flesh, or fowl that my neighbors think proper to put into it; and these old wives' fables are a kind of property in Scotland that belong to the estates and go with the soil. Our streams and lochs are like the rivers and pools in Germany, that have all their Wasser Nixe, or water witches, and I have a fancy for these kind of amphibious bogles and hobgoblins."

Scott went on after we had landed to make many remarks, mingled with picturesque anecdotes, concerning the fabulous beings with which the Scotch were apt to people the wild streams and lochs that occur in the solemn and lonely scenes of their mountains; and to compare them with similar superstitions among the northern nations of Europe; but Scotland, he said, was above all other countries for this wild and vivid progeny of the fancy, from the nature of the scenery, the misty magnificence and vagueness of the climate, the wild and gloomy events of its history; the clannish divisions of its people; their local feelings, notions, and prejudices; the individuality of their dialect, in which all kinds of odd and peculiar notions were incorporated; by the secluded life of their mountaineers; the lonely habits of their pastoral people, much of whose time was passed on the solitary hillsides; their traditional songs, which clothed every rock and stream with old world stories, handed down from age to age, and generation to generation. The Scottish mind, he said, was made up of poetry and strong common sense; and the very strength of the latter gave perpetuity and luxuriance to the former. It was a strong tenacious soil, into which, when once a seed of poetry fell, it struck deep root and brought forth abundantly. "You will never weed these popular stories and songs and superstitions out of Scotland," said he. "It is not so much that the people believe in them, as that they delight in them. They belong to the native hills and streams of which they are fond, and to the history of their forefathers, of which they are proud."

"It would do your heart good," continued he, "to see a number of our poor country people seated round the ingle nook, which is generally capacious enough, and passing the long dark dreary winter nights listening to some old wife, or strolling gaberlunzie, dealing out auld world stories about bogles and warlocks, or about raids and forays, and border skirmishes; or reciting some ballad stuck full of those fighting names that stir up a true Scotchman's blood like the sound of a trumpet. These traditional tales and ballads have lived for ages in mere oral circulation, being passed from father to son, or rather from grandam to grandchild, and are a kind of hereditary property of the poor peasantry, of which it would be hard to deprive them, as they have not circulating libraries to supply them with works of fiction in their place."

I do not pretend to give the precise words, but, as nearly as I can from scanty memorandums and vague recollections, the leading ideas of Scott. I am constantly sensible, however, how far I fall short of his copiousness and richness.

He went on to speak of the elves and sprites, so frequent in Scottish legend. "Our fairies, however," said he, "though they dress in green, and gambol by moonlight about the banks, and shaws, and burnsides, are not such pleasant little folks as the English fairies, but are apt to bear more of the warlock in their natures, and to play spiteful tricks. When I was a boy, I used to look wistfully at the green hillocks that were said to be haunted by fairies, and felt sometimes as if I should like to lie down by them and sleep, and be carried off to Fairy Land, only that I did not like some of the cantrips which used now and then to be played off upon visitors."

Here Scott recounted, in graphic style, and with much humor, a little story which used to be current in the neighborhood, of an honest burgess of Selkirk, who, being at work upon the hill of Peatlaw, fell asleep upon one of these 'fairy knowes,' or hillocks. When he awoke, he rubbed his eyes and gazed about him with astonishment, for he was in the market-place of a great city, with a crowd of people bustling about him, not one of whom he knew. At length he accosted a bystander, and asked him the name of the place. "Hout man," replied the other, "are ye in the heart o' Glasgow, and speer the name of it?" The poor man was astonished, and would not believe either ears or eyes; he insisted that he had laid down to sleep but half an hour before on the Peatlaw, near Selkirk. He came well nigh being taken up for a madman, when, fortunately, a Selkirk man came by, who knew him, and took charge of him, and conducted him back to his native place. Here, however, he was likely to fare no better, when he spoke of having been whisked in his sleep from the Peatlaw to Glasgow. The truth of the matter at length came out; his coat, which he had taken off when at work on the Peatlaw, was found lying near a "fairy knowe," and his bonnet, which was missing, was discovered on the weathercock of Lanark steeple. So it was as clear as day that he had been carried through the air by the fairies while he was sleeping, and his bonnet had been blown off by the way.

I give this little story but meagerly from a scanty memorandum; Scott has related it in somewhat different style in a note to one of his poems; but in narration these anecdotes derived their chief zest, from the quiet but delightful humor, the bonhommie with which he seasoned them, and the sly glance of the eye from under his bushy eyebrows, with which they were accompanied.

That day at dinner, we had Mr. Laidlaw and his wife, and a female friend who accompanied them. The latter was a very intelligent, respectable person, about the middle age, and was treated with particular attention and courtesy by Scott. Our dinner was a most agreeable one; for the guests were evidently cherished visitors to the house, and felt that they were appreciated.

When they were gone, Scott spoke of them in the most cordial manner. "I wished to show you," said he, "some of our really excellent, plain Scotch people; not fine gentlemen and ladies, for such you can meet every where, and they are every where the same. The character of a nation is not to be learnt from its fine folks."

He then went on with a particular eulogium on the lady who had accompanied the Laidlaws. She was the daughter, he said.

of a poor country clergyman, who had died in debt, and left her an orphan and destitute. Having had a good plain education, she immediately set up a child's school, and had soon a numerous flock under her care, by which she earned a decent maintenance. That, however, was not her main object. Her first care was to pay off her father's debts, that no ill word or ill will might rest upon his memory. This, by dint of Scottish economy, backed by filial reverence and pride, she accomplished, though in the effort, she subjected herself to every privation. Not content with this, she in certain instances refused to take pay for the tuition of the children of some of her neighbors, who had befriended her father in his need, and had since fallen into poverty. "In a word," added Scott, "she is a fine old Scotch girl; and I delight in her, more than in many a fine lady I have known, and I have known many of the finest."

It is time, however, to draw this rambling narrative to a close. Several days were passed by me, in the way I have attempted to describe, in almost constant, familiar, and joyous conversation with Scott; it was, as if I were admitted to a social communion with Shakspeare, for it was with one of a kindred, if not equal genius. Every night I retired with my mind filled with delightful recollections of the day, and every morning I rose with the certainty of new enjoyment. The days thus spent, I shall ever took back to, as among the very happiest of my life; for I was conscious at the time of being happy.

The only sad moment that I experienced at Abbotsford, was that of my departure; but it was cheered with the prospect of soon returning; for I had promised, after making a tour in the

Highlands, to come and pass a few more days on the banks of the Tweed, when Scott intended to invite Hogg the poet to meet me. I took a kind farewell of the family, with each of whom I had been highly pleased; if I have refrained from dwelling particularly on their several characters, and giving anecdotes of them individually, it is because I consider them shielded by the sanctity of domestic life: Scott, on the contrary, belongs to history. As he accompanied me on foot, however, to a small gate on the confines of his premises, I could not refrain from expressing the enjoyment I had experienced in his domestic circle, and passing some warm eulogiums on the young folks from whom I had just parted. I shall never forget his reply. "They have kind hearts," said he, "and that is the main point as to human happiness. They love one another, poor things, which is every thing in domestic life. The best wish I can make you, my friend," added he, laying his hand upon my shoulder, "is, that when you return to your own country, you may get married, and have a family of young bairns about you. If you are happy, there they are to share your happiness—and if you are otherwise—there they are to comfort you."

By this time we had reached the gate, when he halted, and took my hand. "I will not say farewell," said he, "for it is always a painful word, but I will say, come again. When you have made your tour to the Highlands, come here and give me a few more days—but come when you please, you will always find Abbotsford open to you, and a hearty welcome."

I have thus given, in a rude style, my main recollections of what occurred during my sojourn at Abbotsford, and I feel mortified that I can give but such meager, scattered, and colorless details of what was so copious, rich, and varied. During several days that I passed there Scott was in admirable vein. From early morn until dinner time he was rambling about, showing me the neighborhood, and during dinner, and until late at night, engaged in social conversation. No time was reserved for himself; he seemed as if his only occupation was to entertain me; and yet I was almost an entire stranger to him, one of whom he knew nothing, but an idle book I had written, and which, some years before, had amused him. But such was Scott—he appeared to have nothing to do but lavish his time, attention, and conversation on those around. It was difficult to imagine what time he found to write those volumes that were incessantly issuing from the press; all of which, too, were of a nature to require reading and research. I could not find that his life was ever otherwise than a life of leisure and hap-hazard recreation, such as it was during my visit. He scarce ever balked a party of pleasure, or a sporting excursion, and rarely pleaded his own concerns as an excuse for rejecting those of others. During my visit I heard of other visitors who had preceded me, and who must have kept him occupied for many days, and I have had an opportunity of knowing the course of his daily life for some time subsequently. Not long after my departure from Abbotsford, my friend Wilkie arrived there, to paint a picture of the Scott family. He found the house full of guests. Scott's whole time was taken up in riding and driving about the country, or in social conversation at home. "All this time," said Wilkie to me, "I did not presume to ask Mr. Scott to sit for his portrait, for I saw he had not a moment to spare; I waited for the guests to go away, but as fast as one went another arrived, and so it continued for several days, and with each set he was completely occupied. At length all went off, and we were quiet. I thought, however, Mr. Scott will now shut himself up among his books and papers, for he has to make up for lost time; it won't do for me to ask him now to sit for his picture. Laidlaw, who managed his estate, came in, and Scott turned to him, as I supposed, to consult about business. 'Laidlaw,' said he, 'to-morrow morning we'll go across the water and take the dogs with us—there's a place where I think we shall be able to find a hare.'

"In short," added Wilkie, "I found that instead of business, he was thinking only of amusement, as if he had nothing in the world to occupy him; so I no longer feared to intrude upon him."

The conversation of Scott was frank, hearty, picturesque, and dramatic. During the time of my visit he inclined to the comic rather than the grave, in his anecdotes and stories, and such, I was told, was his general inclination. He relished a joke, or a trait of humor in social intercourse, and laughed with right good will. He talked not for effect, nor display, but from the flow of his spirits, the stores of his memory, and the vigor of his imagination. He had a natural turn for narration, and his narratives and descriptions were without effort, yet wonderfully graphic. He placed the scene before you like a picture; he gave the dialogue with the appropriate dialect or peculiarities, and described the appearance and characters of his personages with that spirit and felicity evinced in his writings. Indeed, his conversation reminded me continually of his novels; and it seemed to me, that during the whole time I was with him, he talked enough to fill volumes, and that they could not have been filled more delightfully.

He was as good a listener as talker, appreciating every thing that others said, however humble might be their rank or pretensions, and was quick to testify his perception of any point in their discourse. He arrogated nothing to himself, but was perfectly unassuming and unpretending, entering with heart and soul into the business, or pleasure, or, I had almost said, folly, of the hour and the company. No one's concerns, no one's thoughts, no one's opinions, no one's tastes and pleasures seemed beneath him. He made himself so thoroughly the companion of those with whom he happened to be, that they forgot for a time his vast superiority, and only recollected and wondered, when all was over, that it was Scott with whom they had been on such familiar terms, and in whose society they had felt so perfectly at their ease.

It was delightful to observe the generous spirit in which he spoke of all his literary contemporaries, quoting the beauties of their works, and this, too, with respect to persons with whom he might have been supposed to be at variance in literature or politics. Jeffrey, it was thought, had ruffled his plumes in one of his reviews, yet Scott spoke of him in terms of high and warm eulogy, both as an author and as a man.

His humor in conversation, as in his works, was genial and free from all causticity. He had a quick perception of faults and foibles, but he looked upon poor human nature with an indulgent eye, relishing what was good and pleasant, tolerating what was frail, and pitying what was evil. It is this beneficent spirit which gives such an air of bonhommie to Scott's humor throughout all his works. He played with the foibles and errors of his fellow beings, and presented them in a thousand whimsical and characteristic lights, but the kindness and generosity of his nature would not allow him to be a satirist. I do not recollect a sneer throughout his conversation any more than there is throughout his works.

Such is a rough sketch of Scott, as I saw him in private life, not merely at the time of the visit here narrated, but in the casual intercourse of subsequent years. Of his public character and merits, all the world can judge. His works have incorporated themselves with the thoughts and concerns of the whole civilized world, for a quarter of a century, and have had a controlling influence over the age in which he lived. But when did a human being ever exercise an influence more salutary and benignant? Who is there that, on looking back over a great portion of his life, does not find the genius of Scott administering to his pleasures, beguiling his cares, and soothing his lonely sorrows? Who does not still regard his works as a treasury of pure enjoyment, an armory to which to resort in time of need, to find weapons with which to fight off the evils and the griefs of life? For my own part, in periods of dejection, I have hailed the announcement of a new work from his pen as an earnest of certain pleasure in store for me, and have looked forward to it as a traveller in a waste looks to a green spot at a distance, where he feels assured of solace and refreshment. When I consider how much he has thus contributed to the better hours of my past existence, and how independent his works still make me, at times, of all the world for my enjoyment, I bless my stars that cast my lot in his days, to be thus cheered and gladdened by the outpourings of his genius. I consider it one of the greatest advantages that I have derived from my literary career, that it has elevated me into genial communion with such a spirit; and as a tribute of gratitude for his friendship, and veneration for his memory, I cast this humble stone upon his cairn, which will soon, I trust, be piled aloft with the contributions of abler hands.

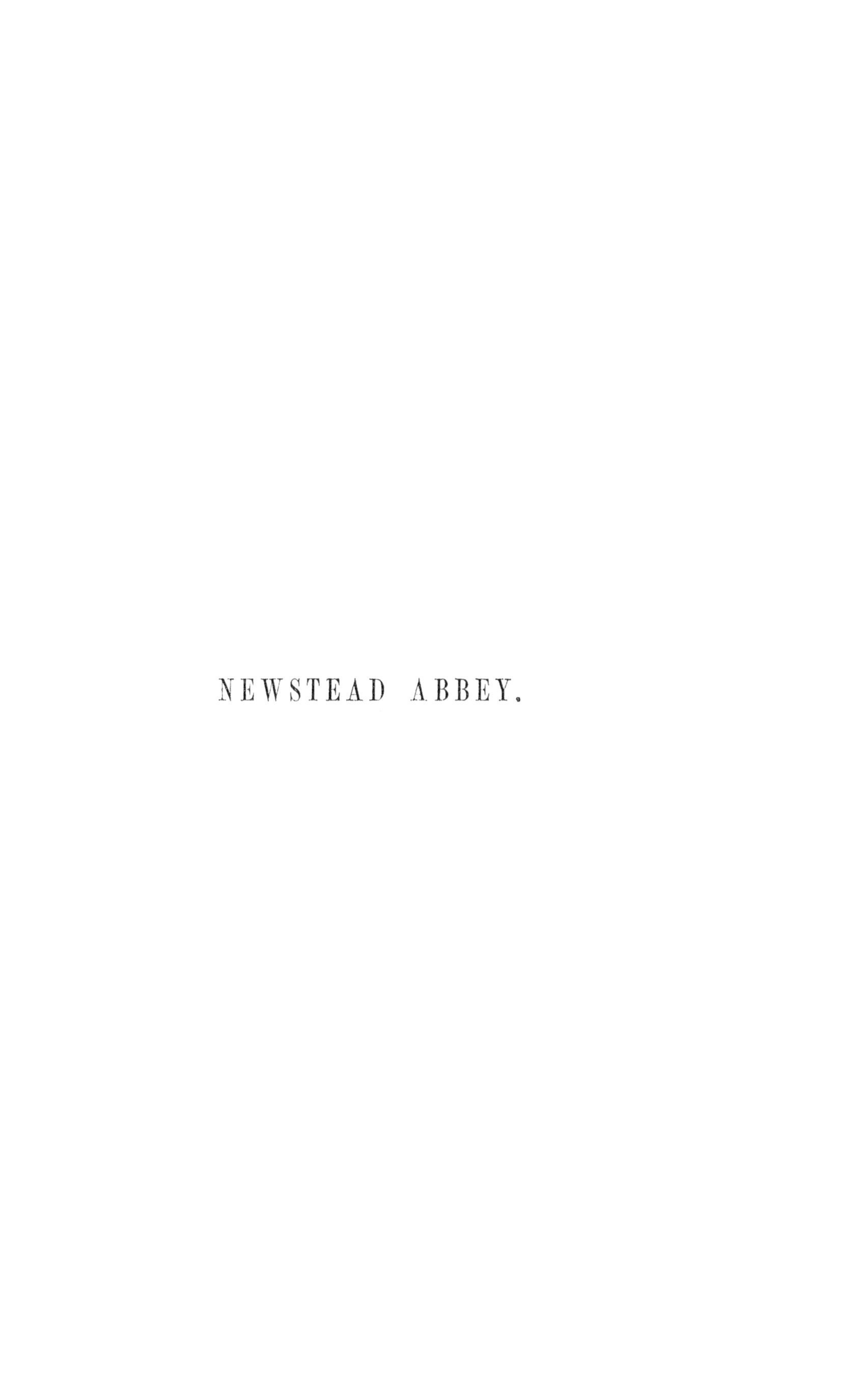

NEWSTEAD ABBEY.

NEWSTEAD ABBEY.

HISTORICAL NOTICE.

Being about to give a few sketches taken during a three weeks' sojourn in the ancestral mansion of the late Lord Byron, I think it proper to premise some brief particulars concerning its history.

Newstead Abbey is one of the finest specimens in existence of those quaint and romantic piles, half castle, half convent, which remain as monuments of the olden times of England. It stands, too, in the midst of a legendary neighborhood; being in the heart of Sherwood Forest, and surrounded by the haunts of Robin Hood and his band of outlaws, so famous in ancient ballad and nursery tale. It is true, the forest scarcely exists but in name, and the tract of country over which it once extended its broad solitudes and shades, is now an open and smiling region, cultivated with parks and farms, and enlivened with villages.

Newstead, which probably once exerted a monastic sway over this region, and controlled the consciences of the rude foresters, was originally a priory, founded in the latter part of the twelfth century, by Henry II, at the time when he sought, by building of shrines and convents, and by other acts of external piety, to expiate the murder of Thomas a Becket. The priory was dedicated to God and the Virgin, and was inhabited by a fraternity of canons regular of St. Augustine. This order was originally simple and abstemious in its mode of living, and exemplary in its conduct; but it would seem that it gradually lapsed into those abuses which disgraced too many of the wealthy monastic establishments; for there are documents among its archives which intimate the prevalence of gross misrule and dissolute sensuality among its members.

At the time of the dissolution of the convents during the reign of Henry VIII, Newstead underwent a sudden reverse, being given, with the neighboring manor and rectory of Papelwick, to Sir John Byron, Steward of Manchester and Rochdale, and Lieutenant of Sherwood Forest. This ancient family worthy figures in the traditions of the Abbey, and in the ghost stories with which it abounds, under the quaint and graphic appellation of "Sir John Byron the Little, with the great Beard." He converted the saintly edifice into a castellated dwelling, making it his favorite residence and the seat of his forest jurisdiction.

The Byron family being subsequently ennobled by a baronial title, and enriched by various possessions, maintained great style and retinue at Newstead. The proud edifice partook, however, of the vicissitudes of the times, and Lord Byron, in one of his poems, represents it as alternately the scene of lordly wassailing and of civil war:

"Hark, how the hall resounding to the strain,
Shakes with the martial music's novel din!
The heralds of a warrior's haughty reign,
High crested banners wave thy walls within.

Of changing sentinels the distant hum,
  The mirth of feasts, the clang of burnish'd arms,
The braying trumpet, and the hoarser drum,
  Unite in concert with increased alarms."

About the middle of the last century, the Abbey came into the possession of another noted character, who makes no less figure in its shadowy traditions than Sir John the Little with the great Beard. This was the grand-uncle of the poet, familiarly known among the gossiping chroniclers of the Abbey as "the Wicked Lord Byron." He is represented as a man of irritable passions and vindictive temper, in the indulgence of which an incident occurred which gave a turn to his whole character and life, and in some measure affected the fortunes of the Abbey. In his neighborhood lived his kinsman and friend, Mr. Chaworth, proprietor of Annesley Hall. Being together in London in 1765, in a chamber of the Star and Garter tavern in Pall Mall, a quarrel rose between them. Byron insisted upon settling it upon the spot by single combat. They fought without seconds, by the dim light of a candle, and Mr. Chaworth, although the most expert swordsman, received a mortal wound. With his dying breath he related such particulars of the contest as induced the coroner's jury to return a verdict of wilful murder. Lord Byron was sent to the tower, and subsequently tried before the House of Peers, where an ultimate verdict was given of manslaughter.

He retired after this to the Abbey, where he shut himself up to brood over his disgraces; grew gloomy, morose, and fantastical, and indulged in fits of passion and caprice, that made him the theme of rural wonder and scandal. No tale was too wild or too monstrous for vulgar belief. Like his successor the poet, he was accused of all kinds of vagaries and wickedness. It was said that he always went armed, as if prepared to commit murder on the least provocation. At one time, when a gentleman of his neighborhood was to dine *tete a tete* with him, it is said a brace of pistols were gravely laid with the knives and forks upon the table, as part of the regular table furniture, and implements that might be needed in the course of the repast. Another rumor states that being exasperated at his coachman for disobedience to orders, he shot him on the spot, threw his body into the coach where Lady Byron was seated, and, mounting the box, officiated in his stead. At another time, according to the same vulgar rumors, he threw her ladyship into the lake in front of the Abbey, where she would have been drowned, but for the timely aid of the gardener. These stories are doubtless exaggerations of trivial incidents which may have occurred; but it is certain that the wayward passions of this unhappy man caused a separation from his wife, and finally spread a solitude around him. Being displeased at the marriage of his son, and heir, he displayed an inveterate malignity towards him. Not being able to cut off his succession to the Abbey estate, which descended to him by entail, he endeavored to injure it as much as possible, so that it might come a mere wreck into his hands. For this purpose he suffered the Abbey to fall out of repair, and every thing to go to waste about it, and cut down all the timber on the estate, laying low many a tract of old Sherwood Forest, so that the Abbey lands lay stripped and bare of all their ancient honors. He was baffled in his unnatural revenge by the premature death of his son, and passed the remainder of his days in his deserted and dilapidated halls, a gloomy misanthrope, brooding amidst the scenes he had laid desolate.

His wayward humors drove from him all neighborly society,

and for a part of the time he was almost without domestics. In his misanthropic mood, when at variance with all human kind, he took to feeding crickets, so that in process of time the Abbey was overrun with them, and its lonely halls made more lonely at night by their monotonous music. Tradition adds that, at his death, the crickets seemed aware that they had lost their patron and protector, for they one and all packed up bag and baggage, and left the Abbey, trooping across its courts and corridors in all directions.

The death of the "Old Lord," or "The Wicked Lord Byron," for he is known by both appellations, occurred in 1798; and the Abbey then passed into the possession of the poet. The latter was but eleven years of age, and living in humble style with his mother in Scotland. They came soon after to England, to take possession. Moore gives a simple but striking anecdote of the first arrival of the poet at the domains of his ancestors.

They had arrived at the Newstead toll-bar, and saw the woods of the Abbey stretching out to receive them, when Mrs. Byron, affecting to be ignorant of the place, asked the woman of the toll-house to whom that seat belonged? She was told that the owner of it, Lord Byron, had been some months dead. "And who is the next heir?" asked the proud and happy mother. "They say," answered the old woman, "it is a little boy who lives at Aberdeen." "And this is he, bless him!" exclaimed the nurse, no longer able to contain herself, and turning to kiss with delight the young lord who was seated on her lap.*

During Lord Byron's minority, the Abbey was let to Lord Grey de Ruthen, but the poet visited it occasionally during the Harrow vacations, when he resided with his mother at lodgings

* Moore's Life of Lord Byron.

in Nottingham. It was treated little better by its present tenant than by the old lord who preceded him; so that when, in the autumn of 1808, Lord Byron took up his abode there, it was in a ruinous condition. The following lines from his own pen, may give some idea of its condition:

"Through thy battlements, Newstead, the hollow winds whistle,
Thou, the hall of my fathers, art gone to decay;
In thy once smiling garden, the hemlock and thistle
Have choked up the rose which once bloomed in the way.

Of the mail-covered barons who, proudly, to battle
Led thy vassals from Europe to Palestine's plain,
The escutcheon and shield, which with every wind rattle,
Are the only sad vestiges now that remain."*

In another poem he expresses the melancholy feeling with which he took possession of his ancestral mansion:

"Newstead! That saddening scene of change is thine,
Thy yawning arch betokens sure decay:
The last and youngest of a noble line,
Now holds thy mouldering turrets in his sway.

Deserted now, he scans thy gray-worn towers,
Thy vaults, where dead of feudal ages sleep,
Thy cloisters, pervious to the wintry showers,
These—these he views, and views them but to weep.

Yet he prefers thee to the gilded domes,
Or gewgaw grottoes of the vainly great;
Yet lingers mid thy damp and mossy tombs,
Nor breathes a murmur 'gainst the will of fate."†

* Lines on leaving Newstead Abbey. † Elegy on Newstead Abbey.

Lord Byron had not fortune sufficient to put the pile in extensive repair, nor to maintain any thing like the state of his ancestors. He restored some of the apartments, so as to furnish his mother with a comfortable habitation, and fitted up a quaint study for himself, in which, among books and busts, and other library furniture, were two skulls of the ancient friars, grinning on each side of an antique cross. One of his gay companions gives a picture of Newstead when thus repaired, and the picture is sufficiently desolate.

"There are two tiers of cloisters, with a variety of cells and rooms about them, which, though not inhabited, nor in an inhabitable state, might easily be made so; and many of the original rooms, among which is a fine stone hall, are still in use. Of the Abbey church, one end only remains; and the old kitchen, with a long range of apartments, is reduced to a heap of rubbish. Leading from the Abbey to the modern part of the habitation is a noble room, seventy feet in length, and twenty-three in breadth; but every part of the house displays neglect and decay, save those which the present lord has lately fitted up."*

Even the repairs thus made were but of transient benefit, for the roof being left in its dilapidated state, the rain soon penetrated into the apartments which Lord Byron had restored and decorated, and in a few years rendered them almost as desolate as the rest of the Abbey.

Still he felt a pride in the ruinous old edifice; its very dreary and dismantled state, addressed itself to his poetical imagination, and to that love of the melancholy and the grand which is evinced in all his writings. "Come what may," said he in one

* Letter of the late Charles Skinner Mathews, Esq.

of his letters, "Newstead and I stand or fall together. I have now lived on the spot. I have fixed my heart upon it, and no pressure, present or future, shall induce me to barter the last vestige of our inheritance. I have that pride within me which will enable me to support difficulties: could I obtain in exchange for Newstead Abbey, the first fortune in the country, I would reject the proposition."

His residence at the Abbey, however, was fitful and uncertain. He passed occasional portions of time there, sometimes studiously and alone, oftener idly and recklessly, and occasionally with young and gay companions, in riot and revelry, and the indulgence of all kinds of mad caprice. The Abbey was by no means benefited by these roystering inmates, who sometimes played off monkish mummeries about the cloisters, at other times turned the state chambers into schools for boxing and single-stick, and shot pistols in the great hall. The country people of the neighborhood were as much puzzled by these madcap vagaries of the new incumbent, as by the gloomier habits of the "old lord," and began to think that madness was inherent in the Byron race, or that some wayward star ruled over the Abbey.

It is needless to enter into a detail of the circumstances which led his Lordship to sell his ancestral estate, notwithstanding the partial predilections and hereditary feeling which he had so eloquently expressed. Fortunately, it fell into the hands of a man who possessed something of a poetical temperament, and who cherished an enthusiastic admiration for Lord Byron. Colonel (at that time Major) Wildman had been a schoolmate of the poet, and sat with him on the same form at Harrow. He had subsequently distinguished himself in the war of the Peninsula, and at the battle of Waterloo, and it was a great consolation to

Lord Byron, in parting with his family estate, to know that it would be held by one capable of restoring its faded glories, and who would respect and preserve all the monuments and memorials of his line.*

The confidence of Lord Byron in the good feeling and good taste of Colonel Wildman has been justified by the event. Under his judicious eye and munificent hand the venerable and romantic pile has risen from its ruins in all its old monastic and baronial splendor, and additions have been made to it in perfect conformity of style. The groves and forests have been replanted; the lakes and fish-ponds cleaned out, and the gardens rescued from the "hemlock and thistle," and restored to their pristine and dignified formality.

* The following letter, written in the course of the transfer of the estate, has never been published:—

Venice, Nov. 18, 1818.

My Dear Wildman,

Mr. Hanson is on the eve of his return, so that I have only time to return a few inadequate thanks for your very kind letter. I should regret to trouble you with any requests of mine, in regard to the preservation of any signs of my family, which may still exist at Newstead, and leave every thing of that kind to your own feelings, present or future, upon the subject. The portrait which you flatter me by desiring, would not be worth to you your trouble and expense of such an expedition, but you may rely upon having the very first that may be painted, and which may seem worth your acceptance.

I trust that Newstead will, being yours, remain so, and that it may see you as happy, as I am very sure that you will make your dependents. With regard to myself, you may be sure that whether in the fourth, or fifth, or sixth form at Harrow, or in the fluctuations of after life, I shall always remember with regard my old schoolfellow—fellow monitor, and friend, and recognize with respect the gallant soldier, who, with all the advantages of fortune and allurements of youth to a life of pleasure, devoted himself to duties of a nobler order, and will receive his reward in the esteem and admiration of his country.

Ever yours most truly and affectionately,

BYRON.

The farms on the estate have been put in complete order, new farmhouses built of stone, in the picturesque and comfortable style of the old English granges; the hereditary tenants secured in their paternal homes, and treated with the most considerate indulgence; every thing, in a word, gives happy indications of a liberal and beneficent landlord.

What most, however, will interest the visitors to the Abbey in favor of its present occupant, is the reverential care with which he has preserved and renovated every monument and relic of the Byron family, and every object in any wise connected with the memory of the poet. Eighty thousand pounds have already been expended upon the venerable pile, yet the work is still going on, and Newstead promises to realize the hope faintly breathed by the poet when bidding it a melancholy farewell--

> "Haply thy sun emerging, yet may shine,
> Thee to irradiate with meridian ray;
> Hours splendid as the past may still be thine,
> And bless thy future, as thy former day."

ARRIVAL AT THE ABBEY.

I HAD been passing a merry Christmas in the good old style at Barlboro' Hall, a venerable family mansion in Derbyshire, and set off to finish the holidays with the hospitable proprietor of Newstead Abbey. A drive of seventeen miles through a pleasant country, part of it the storied region of Sherwood Forest, brought me to the gate of Newstead Park. The aspect of the park was by no means imposing, the fine old trees that once adorned it having been laid low by Lord Byron's wayward predecessor.

Entering the gate, the postchaise rolled heavily along a sandy road, between naked declivities, gradually descending into one of those gentle and sheltered valleys, in which the sleek monks of old loved to nestle themselves. Here a sweep of the road round an angle of a garden wall brought us full in front of the venerable edifice, embosomed in the valley, with a beautiful sheet of water spreading out before it.

The irregular gray pile, of motley architecture, answered to the description given by Lord Byron :

> "An old, old monastery once, and now
> Still older mansion, of a rich and rare
> Mixed Gothic———"

One end was fortified by a castellated tower, bespeaking the baronial and warlike days of the edifice; the other end maintained its primitive monastic character. A ruined chapel, flanked by a solemn grove, still reared its front entire. It is true, the threshold of the once frequented portal was grass-grown, and the great lancet window, once glorious with painted glass, was now entwined and overhung with ivy; but the old convent cross still braved both time and tempest on the pinnacle of the chapel, and below, the blessed effigies of the Virgin and child, sculptured in gray stone, remained uninjured in their niche, giving a sanctified aspect to the pile.*

A flight of rooks, tenants of the adjacent grove, were hovering about the ruin, and balancing themselves upon every airy projection, and looked down with curious eye and cawed as the postchaise rattled along below.

The chamberlain of the Abbey, a most decorous personage, dressed in black, received us at the portal. Here, too, we encountered a memento of Lord Byron, a great black and white Newfoundland dog, that had accompanied his remains from Greece. He was descended from the famous Boatswain, and inherited his generous qualities. He was a cherished inmate of the Abbey, and honored and caressed by every visitor. Conducted by the chamberlain, and followed by the dog, who assisted in doing the honors of the house, we passed through a long low

* "—— in a higher niche, alone, but crown'd,
The Virgin Mother of the God-born child
With her son in her blessed arms, looked round,
Spared by some chance, when all beside was spoil'd:
She made the earth below seem holy ground."

DON JUAN, Canto III.

vaulted hall, supported by massive Gothic arches, and not a little resembling the crypt of a cathedral, being the basement story of the Abbey.

From this we ascended a stone staircase, at the head of which a pair of folding doors admitted us into a broad corridor that ran round the interior of the Abbey. The windows of the corridor looked into a quadrangular grass-grown court, forming the hollow centre of the pile. In the midst of it rose a lofty and fantastic fountain, wrought of the same gray stone as the main edifice, and which has been well described by Lord Byron.

> " Amidst the court a Gothic fountain play'd,
>   Symmetrical, but deck'd with carvings quaint,
> Strange faces, like to men in masquerade,
>   And here perhaps a monster, there a saint:
> The spring rush'd through grim mouths of granite made,
>   And sparkled into basins, where it spent
> Its little torrent in a thousand bubbles,
> Like man's vain glory, and his vainer troubles." *

Around this quadrangle were low vaulted cloisters, with Gothic arches, once the secluded walks of the monks: the corridor along which we were passing was built above these cloisters, and their hollow arches seemed to reverberate every footfall. Every thing thus far had a solemn monastic air; but, on arriving at an angle of the corridor, the eye, glancing along a shadowy gallery, caught a sight of two dark figures in plate armor, with closed visors, bucklers braced, and swords drawn, standing motionless against the wall. They seemed two phantoms of the chivalrous era of the Abbey.

* Don Juan, Canto III.

Here the chamberlain, throwing open a folding door, ushered us at once into a spacious and lofty saloon, which offered a brilliant contrast to the quaint and sombre apartments we had traversed. It was elegantly furnished, and the walls hung with paintings, yet something of its original architecture had been preserved and blended with modern embellishments. There were the stone-shafted casements and the deep bow-window of former times. The carved and panelled wood work of the lofty ceiling had likewise been carefully restored, and its Gothic and grotesque devices painted and gilded in their ancient style.

Here, too, were emblems of the former and latter days of the Abbey, in the effigies of the first and last of the Byron line that held sway over its destinies. At the upper end of the saloon, above the door, the dark Gothic portrait of "Sir John Byron the Little with the great Beard," looked grimly down from his canvas, while, at the opposite end, a white marble bust of the *genius loci*, the noble poet, shone conspicuously from its pedestal.

The whole air and style of the apartment partook more of the palace than the monastery, and its windows looked forth on a suitable prospect, composed of beautiful groves, smooth verdant lawns, and silver sheets of water. Below the windows was a small flower-garden, inclosed by stone balustrades, on which were stately peacocks, sunning themselves and displaying their plumage. About the grass-plots in front, were gay cock pheasants, and plump partridges, and nimble-footed water hens, feeding almost in perfect security.

Such was the medley of objects presented to the eye on first visiting the Abbey, and I found the interior fully to answer the pescription of the poet—

"The mansion's self was vast and venerable,
With more of the monastic than has been
Elsewhere preserved; the cloisters still were stable,
The cells, too, and refectory, I ween;
An exquisite small chapel had been able,
Still unimpair'd, to decorate the scene;
The rest had been reformed, replaced, or sunk,
And spoke more of the friar than the monk.

Huge halls, long galleries, spacious chambers, joined
By no quite lawful marriage of the arts,
Might shock a connoisseur; but when combined
Formed a whole, which, irregular in parts,
Yet left a grand impression on the mind,
At least of those whose eyes were in their hearts."

It is not my intention to lay open the scenes of domestic life at the Abbey, nor to describe the festivities of which I was a partaker during my sojourn within its hospitable walls. I wish merely to present a picture of the edifice itself, and of those personages and circumstances about it, connected with the memory of Byron.

I forbear, therefore, to dwell on my reception by my excellent and amiable host and hostess, or to make my reader acquainted with the elegant inmates of the mansion that I met in the saloon; and I shall pass on at once with him to the chamber allotted me, and to which I was most respectfully conducted by the chamberlain.

It was one of a magnificent suite of rooms, extending between the court of the cloisters and the Abbey garden, the windows looking into the latter. The whole suite formed the ancient state apartment, and had fallen into decay during the neglected days of the Abbey, so as to be in a ruinous condition in the time of Lord Byron. It had since been restored to its ancient splendor, of which my chamber may be cited as a specimen. It was lofty and well proportioned; the lower part of the walls was panelled with ancient oak, the upper part hung with goblin tapestry, representing oriental hunting scenes, wherein the figures were of the size of life, and of great vivacity of attitude and color.

The furniture was antique, dignified, and cumbrous. High-backed chairs curiously carved, and wrought in needlework; a massive clothes-press of dark oak, well polished, and inlaid with landscapes of various tinted woods; a bed of state, ample and lofty, so as only to be ascended by a movable flight of steps, the huge posts supporting a high tester with a tuft of crimson plumes at each corner, and rich curtains of crimson damask hanging in broad and heavy folds.

A venerable mirror of plate glass stood on the toilet, in which belles of former centuries may have contemplated and decorated their charms. The floor of the chamber was of tesselated oak, shining with wax, and partly covered by a Turkey carpet. In the centre stood a massy oaken table, waxed and polished as smooth as glass, and furnished with a writing desk of perfumed rosewood.

A sober light was admitted into the room through Gothic stone-shafted casements, partly shaded by crimson curtains, and partly overshadowed by the trees of the garden. This solemnly tempered light added to the effect of the stately and antiquated interior.

Two portraits, suspended over the doors, were in keeping with the scene. They were in ancient Vandyke dresses; one was a cavalier, who may have occupied this apartment in days of yore, the other was a lady with a black velvet mask in her hand, who may once have arrayed herself for conquest at the very mirror I have described.

The most curious relic of old times, however, in this quaint but richly dight apartment, was a great chimney-piece of panel-work, carved in high relief, with niches or compartments, each containing a human bust, that protruded almost entirely from the wall. Some of the figures were in ancient Gothic garb; the most striking among them was a female, who was earnestly regarded by a fierce Saracen from an adjoining niche.

This panel-work is among the mysteries of the Abbey, and causes as much wide speculation as the Egyptian hieroglyphics. Some suppose it to illustrate an adventure in the Holy Land, and that the lady in effigy had been rescued by some crusader of the family from the turbaned Turk who watches her so earnestly. What tends to give weight to these suppositions is, that similar pieces of panel-work exist in other parts of the Abbey, in all of which are to be seen the Christian lady and her Saracen guardian or lover. At the bottom of these sculptures are emblazoned the armorial bearings of the Byrons.

I shall not detain the reader, however, with any further description of my apartment, or of the mysteries connected with it. As he is to pass some days with me at the Abbey, we shall have time to examine the old edifice at our leisure, and to make ourselves acquainted, not merely with its interior, but likewise with its environs.

THE ABBEY GARDEN.

The morning after my arrival, I rose at an early hour. The daylight was peering brightly between the window curtains, and drawing them apart, I gazed through the Gothic casement upon a scene that accorded in character with the interior of the ancient mansion. It was the old Abbey garden, but altered to suit the tastes of different times and occupants. In one direction were shady walks and alleys, broad terraces and lofty groves; in another, beneath a gray monastic-looking angle of the edifice, overrun with ivy and surmounted by a cross, lay a small French garden, with formal flower-pots, gravelled walks, and stately stone balustrades.

The beauty of the morning, and the quiet of the hour, tempted me to an early stroll; for it is pleasant to enjoy such old-time places alone, when one may indulge poetical reveries, and spin cobweb fancies, without interruption. Dressing myself, therefore, with all speed, I descended a small flight of steps from the state apartment into the long corridor over the cloisters, along which I passed to a door at the farther end. Here I emerged into the open air, and, descending another flight of stone steps, found myself in the centre of what had once been the Abbey chapel.

Nothing of the sacred edifice remained, however, but the Gothic front, with its deep portal and grand lancet window, already described. The nave, the side walls, the choir, the sacristy, all had disappeared. The open sky was over my head, a smooth shaven grass-plot beneath my feet. Gravel walks and shrubberies had succeeded to the shadowy aisles, and stately trees to the clustering columns.

> "Where now the grass exhales a murky dew,
>   The humid pall of life extinguished clay,
> In sainted fame the sacred fathers grew,
>   Nor raised their pious voices but to pray.
> Where now the bats their wavering wings extend,
>   Soon as the gloaming spreads her warning shade,
> The choir did oft their mingling vespers blend,
>   Or matin orisons to Mary paid."

Instead of the matin orisons of the monks, however, the ruined walls of the chapel now resounded to the cawing of innumerable rooks that were fluttering and hovering about the dark grove which they inhabited, and preparing for their morning flight.

My ramble led me along quiet alleys, bordered by shrubbery, where the solitary water-hen would now and then scud across my path, and take refuge among the bushes. From hence I entered upon a broad terraced walk, once a favorite resort of the friars, which extended the whole length of the old Abbey garden, passing along the ancient stone wall which bounded it. In the centre of the garden lay one of the monkish fish-pools, an oblong sheet of water, deep set like a mirror, in green sloping banks of turf. In its glassy bosom was reflected the dark mass of a neighboring grove, one of the most important features of the garden.

This grove goes by the sinister name of "the Devil's Wood,"

and enjoys but an equivocal character in the neighborhood. It was planted by "The Wicked Lord Byron," during the early part of his residence at the Abbey, before his fatal duel with Mr. Chaworth. Having something of a foreign and classical taste, he set up leaden statues of satyrs or fawns at each end of the grove. The statues, like every thing else about the old Lord, fell under the suspicion and obloquy that overshadowed him in the latter part of his life. The country people, who knew nothing of heathen mythology and its sylvan deities, looked with horror at idols invested with the diabolical attributes of horns and cloven feet. They probably supposed them some object of secret worship of the gloomy and secluded misanthrope and reputed murderer, and gave them the name of "The old Lord's Devils."

I penetrated the recesses of the mystic grove. There stood the ancient and much slandered statues, overshadowed by tall larches, and stained by dank green mould. It is not a matter of surprise that strange figures, thus behoofed and behorned, and set up in a gloomy grove, should perplex the minds of the simple and superstitious yeomanry. There are many of the tastes and caprices of the rich, that in the eyes of the uneducated must savor of insanity.

I was attracted to this grove, however, by memorials of a more touching character. It had been one of the favorite haunts of the late Lord Byron. In his farewell visit to the Abbey, after he had parted with the possession of it, he passed some time in this grove, in company with his sister; and as a last memento, engraved their names on the bark of a tree.

The feelings that agitated his bosom during this farewell visit, when he beheld round him objects dear to his pride, and dear to his juvenile recollections, but of which the narrowness of his for tune would not permit him to retain possession, may be gathered from a passage in a poetical epistle, written to his sister in after years:

> "I did remind you of our own dear lake
> By the old hall, *which may be mine no more;*
> Leman's is fair; but think not I forsake
> The sweet remembrance of a dearer shore:
> Sad havoc Time must with my memory make
> Ere *that* or *thou* can fade these eyes before;
> Though, like all things which I have loved, they are
> Resign'd for ever, or divided far.
>
> I feel almost at times as I have felt
> In happy childhood; trees, and flowers, and brooks,
> Which do remember me of where I dwelt
> Ere my young mind was sacrificed to books,
> Come as of yore upon me, and can melt
> My heart with recognition of their looks;
> And even at moments I would think I see
> Some living things I love—but none like thee."

I searched the grove for some time, before I found the tree on which Lord Byron had left his frail memorial. It was an elm of peculiar form, having two trunks, which sprang from the same root, and, after growing side by side, mingled their branches together. He had selected it, doubtless, as emblematical of his sister and himself. The names of BYRON and AUGUSTA were still visible. They had been deeply cut in the bark, but the natural growth of the tree was gradually rendering them illegible, and a few years hence, strangers will seek in vain for this record of fraternal affection.

Leaving the grove, I continued my ramble along a spacious terrace, overlooking what had once been the kitchen garden of the Abbey. Below me lay the monks' stew, or fish pond, a dark pool, overhung by gloomy cypresses, with a solitary water-hen swimming about in it.

A little further on, and the terrace looked down upon the stately scene on the south side of the Abbey; the flower garden, with its stone balustrades and stately peacocks, the lawn, with its pheasants and partridges, and the soft valley of Newstead beyond.

At a distance, on the border of the lawn, stood another memento of Lord Byron; an oak planted by him in his boyhood, on his first visit to the Abbey. With a superstitious feeling inherent in him, he linked his own destiny with that of the tree. "As it fares," said he, "so will fare my fortunes." Several years elapsed, many of them passed in idleness and dissipation. He returned to the Abbey a youth scarce grown to manhood, but, as he thought, with vices and follies beyond his years. He found his emblem oak almost choked by weeds and brambles, and took the lesson to himself.

"Young oak, when I planted thee deep in the ground,
I hoped that thy days would be longer than mine,
That thy dark waving branches would flourish around,
And ivy thy trunk with its mantle entwine.

Such, such was my hope—when in infancy's years
On the land of my fathers I reared thee with pride;
They are past, and I water thy stem with my tears—
Thy decay not the weeds that surround thee can hide."

I leaned over the stone balustrade of the terrace, and gazed upon the valley of Newstead, with its silver sheets of water gleaming in the morning sun. It was a Sabbath morning, which always seems to have a hallowed influence over the landscape, probably from the quiet of the day, and the cessation of all kinds of week-day labor. As I mused upon the mild and beautiful scene, and the wayward destinies of the man, whose stormy temperament forced him from this tranquil paradise to battle with the passions and perils of the world, the sweet chime of bells from a village a few miles distant came stealing up the valley. Every sight and sound this morning seemed calculated to summon up touching recollections of poor Byron. The chime was from the village spire of Hucknall Torkard, beneath which his remains lie buried !

——— I have since visited his tomb. It is in an old gray country church, venerable with the lapse of centuries. He lies buried beneath the pavement, at one end of the principal aisle. A light falls on the spot through the stained glass of a Gothic window, and a tablet on the adjacent wall announces the family vault of the Byrons. It had been the wayward intention of the poet to be entombed, with his faithful dog, in the monument erected by him in the garden of Newstead Abbey. His executors showed better judgment and feeling, in consigning his ashes to the family sepulchre, to mingle with those of his mother and his kindred. Here,

> "After life's fitful fever, he sleeps well.
> Malice domestic, foreign levy, nothing
> Can touch him further !"

How nearly did his dying hour realize the wish made by him, but a few years previously, in one of his fitful moods of melancholy and misanthropy :

"When time, or soon or late, shall bring
The dreamless sleep that lulls the dead,
Oblivion! may thy languid wing
Wave gently o'er my dying bed!

No band of friends or heirs be there,
To weep or wish the coming blow:
No maiden with dishevelled hair,
To feel, or feign decorous woe.

But silent let me sink to earth,
With no officious mourners near:
I woul not mar one hour of mirth,
Nor startle friendship with a tear."

He died among strangers, in a foreign land, without a kindred hand to close his eyes; yet he did not die unwept. With all his faults and errors, and passions and caprices, he had the gift of attaching his humble dependents warmly to him. One of them, a poor Greek, accompanied his remains to England, and followed them to the grave. I am told that, during the ceremony, he stood holding on by a pew in an agony of grief, and when all was over, seemed as if he would have gone down into the tomb with the body of his master.—A nature that could inspire such attachments, must have been generous and beneficent.

PLOUGH MONDAY.

SHERWOOD Forest is a region that still retains much of the quaint customs and holiday games of the olden time. A day or two after my arrival at the Abbey, as I was walking in the cloisters, I heard the sound of rustic music, and now and then a burst of merriment, proceeding from the interior of the mansion. Presently the chamberlain came and informed me that a party of country lads were in the servants' hall, performing Plough Monday antics, and invited me to witness their mummery. I gladly assented, for I am somewhat curious about these relics of popular usages. The servants' hall was a fit place for the exhibition of an old Gothic game. It was a chamber of great extent, which, in monkish times had been the refectory of the Abbey. A row of massive columns extended lengthwise through the centre, whence sprung Gothic arches, supporting the low vaulted ceiling. Here was a set of rustics dressed up in something of the style represented in the books concerning popular antiquities. One was in a rough garb of frieze, with his head muffled in bear-skin, and a bell dangling behind him, that jingled at every movement. He was the clown, or fool of the party, probably a tradi tional representative of the ancient satyr. The rest were decorated with ribands and armed with wooden swords. The leader of the troop recited the old ballad of St. George and the Dragon, which had been current among the country people for ages; his companions accompanied the recitation with some rude attempt at acting, while the clown cut all kinds of antics.

To these succeeded a set of morris-dancers, gayly dressed up with ribands and hawks'-bells. In this troop we had Robin Hood and Maid Marian, the latter represented by a smooth-faced boy: also, Beelzebub, equipped with a broom, and accompanied by his wife Bessy, a termagant old beldame. These rude pageants are the lingering remains of the old customs of Plough Monday, when bands of rustics, fantastically dressed, and furnished with pipe and tabor, dragged what was called the "fool plough" from house to house, singing ballads and performing antics, for which they were rewarded with money and good cheer.

But it is not in "merry Sherwood Forest" alone that these remnants of old times prevail. They are to be met with in most of the counties north of the Trent, which classic stream seems to be the boundary line of primitive customs. During my recent Christmas sojourn at Barlboro' Hall, on the skirts of Derbyshire and Yorkshire, I had witnessed many of the rustic festivities peculiar to that joyous season, which have rashly been pronounced obsolete, by those who draw their experience merely from city life. I had seen the great Yule clog put on the fire on Christmas Eve, and the wassail bowl sent round, brimming with its spicy beverage. I had heard carols beneath my window by the choristers of the neighboring village, who went their rounds about the ancient Hall at midnight, according to immemorial custom. We had mummers and mimers too, with the story of St. George and the Dragon, and other ballads and traditional dialogues, together with the famous old interlude of the Hobby Horse, all represented in the antechamber and servants' hall by rustics, who inherited the custom and the poetry from preceding generations.

The boar's head, crowned with rosemary, had taken its honored station among the Christmas cheer; the festal board had been attended by glee singers and minstrels from the village to entertain the company with hereditary songs and catches during their repast; and the old Pyrrhic game of the sword dance, handed down since the time of the Romans, was admirably performed in the court-yard of the mansion by a band of young men, lithe and supple in their forms and graceful in their movements, who, I was told, went the rounds of the villages and country seats during the Christmas holidays.

I specify these rural pageants and ceremonials, which I saw during my sojourn in this neighborhood, because it has been deemed that some of the anecdotes of holiday customs given in my preceding writings, related to usages which have entirely passed away. Critics who reside in cities have little idea of the primitive manners and observances, which still prevail in remote and rural neighborhoods.

In fact, in crossing the Trent one seems to step back into old times; and in the villages of Sherwood Forest we are in a black-letter region. The moss-green cottages, the lowly mansions of gray stone, the Gothic crosses at each end of the villages, and the tall May pole in the centre, transport us in imagination to foregone centuries; every thing has a quaint and antiquated air.

The tenantry on the Abbey estate partake of this primitive character. Some of the families have rented farms there for nearly three hundred years; and, notwithstanding that their mansions fell to decay, and every thing about them partook of the general waste and misrule of the Byron dynasty, yet nothing could uproot them from their native soil. I am happy to say, that Colonel Wildman has taken these stanch loyal families under his peculiar care. He has favored them in their rents, repaired, or rather rebuilt their farmhouses, and has enabled families that had almost sunk into the class of mere rustic laborers, once more to hold up their heads among the yeomanry of the land.

I visited one of these renovated establishments that had but lately been a mere ruin, and now was a substantial grange. It was inhabited by a young couple. The good woman showed every part of the establishment with decent pride, exulting in its comfort and respectability. Her husband, I understood, had risen in consequence with the improvement of his mansion, and now began to be known among his rustic neighbors by the appellation of "the young Squire."

OLD SERVANTS.

In an old, time-worn, and mysterious looking mansion like Newstead Abbey, and one so haunted by monkish, and feudal, and poetical associations, it is a prize to meet with some ancient crone, who has passed a long life about the place, so as to have become a living chronicle of its fortunes and vicissitudes. Such a one is Nanny Smith, a worthy dame, near seventy years of age, who for a long time served as housekeeper to the Byrons. The Abbey and its domains comprise her world, beyond which she knows nothing, but within which she has ever conducted herself with native shrewdness and old-fashioned honesty. When Lord Byron sold the Abbey her vocation was at end, still she lingered about the place, having for it the local attachment of a cat. Abandoning her comfortable housekeeper's apartment, she took shelter in one of the "rock houses," which are nothing more than a little neighborhood of cabins, excavated in the perpendicular walls of a stone quarry, at no great distance from the Abbey. Three cells cut in the living rock, formed her dwelling; these she fitted up humbly but comfortably; her son William labored in the neighborhood, and aided to support her, and Nanny Smith maintained a cheerful aspect and an independent spirit. One of her gossips suggested to her that William should marry, and bring home a young wife to help her and take care of her

"Nay, nay," replied Nanny, tartly, "I want no young mistress in *my house.*" So much for the love of rule—poor Nanny's house was a hole in a rock!

Colonel Wildman, on taking possession of the Abbey, found Nanny Smith thus humbly nestled. With that active benevolence which characterizes him, he immediately set William up in a small farm on the estate, where Nanny Smith has a comfortable mansion in her old days. Her pride is roused by her son's advancement. She remarks with exultation that people treat William with much more respect now that he is a farmer, than they did when he was a laborer. A farmer of the neighborhood has even endeavored to make a match between him and his sister, but Nanny Smith has grown fastidious, and interfered. The girl, she said, was too old for her son, besides, she did not see that he was in any need of a wife.

"No," said William, "I ha' no great mind to marry the wench: but if the Colonel and his lady wish it, I am willing. They have been so kind to me that I should think it my duty to please them." The Colonel and his lady, however, have not thought proper to put honest William's gratitude to so severe a test.

Another worthy whom Colonel Wildman found vegetating upon the place, and who had lived there for at least sixty years, was old Joe Murray. He had come there when a mere boy in the train of the "old lord," about the middle of the last century, and had continued with him until his death. Having been a cabin boy when very young, Joe always fancied himself a bit of a sailor, and had charge of all the pleasure-boats on the lake, though he afterwards rose to the dignity of butler. In the latter days of the old Lord Byron, when he shut himself up from all the world, Joe Murray was the only servant retained by him, excepting his housekeeper, Betty Hardstaff, who was reputed to have an undue sway over him, and was derisively called Lady Betty among the country folk.

When the Abbey came into the possession of the late Lord Byron, Joe Murray accompanied it as a fixture. He was reinstated as butler in the Abbey, and high admiral on the lake, and his sturdy honest mastiff qualities won so upon Lord Byron as even to rival his Newfoundland dog in his affections. Often when dining, he would pour out a bumper of choice Madeira, and hand it to Joe as he stood behind his chair. In fact, when he built the monumental tomb which stands in the Abbey garden, he intended it for himself, Joe Murray, and the dog. The two latter were to lie on each side of him. Boatswain died not long afterwards, and was regularly interred, and the well-known epitaph inscribed on one side of the monument. Lord Byron departed for Greece; during his absence, a gentleman to whom Joe Murray was showing the tomb, observed, "Well, old boy, you will take your place here some twenty years hence."

"I don't know that, sir," growled Joe, in reply, "if I was sure his Lordship would come here, I should like it well enough, but I should not like to lie alone with the dog."

Joe Murray was always extremely neat in his dress, and attentive to his person, and made a most respectable appearance. A portrait of him still hangs in the Abbey, representing him a hale fresh looking fellow, in a flaxen wig, a blue coat and buff waistcoat, with a pipe in his hand. He discharged all the duties of his station with great fidelity, unquestionable honesty, and much outward decorum, but, if we may believe his contemporary, Nanny Smith, who, as housekeeper, shared the sway of the household with him, he was very lax in his minor morals, and used to sing loose and profane songs as he presided at the table in the servants' hall, or sat taking his ale and smoking his pipe by the evening fire. Joe had evidently derived his convivial notions from the race of English country squires who flourished in the days of his juvenility. Nanny Smith was scandalized at his ribald songs, but being above harm herself, endured them in silence. At length, on his singing them before a young girl of sixteen, she could contain herself no longer, but read him a lecture that made his ears ring, and then flounced off to bed. The lecture seems, by her account, to have staggered Joe, for he told her the next morning that he had had a terrible dream in the night. An Evangelist stood at the foot of his bed with a great Dutch Bible, which he held with the printed part towards him, and after a while pushed it in his face. Nanny Smith undertook to interpret the vision, and read from it such a homily, and deduced such awful warnings, that Joe became quite serious, left off singing, and took to reading good books for a month; but after that, continued Nanny, he relapsed and became as bad as ever, and continued to sing loose and profane songs to his dying day.

When Colonel Wildman became proprietor of the Abbey he found Joe Murray flourishing in a green old age, though upwards of fourscore, and continued him in his station as butler. The old man was rejoiced at the extensive repairs that were immediately commenced, and anticipated with pride the day when the Abbey should rise out of its ruins with renovated splendor, its gates be thronged with trains and equipages, and its halls once more echo to the sound of joyous hospitality.

What chiefly, however, concerned Joe's pride and ambition,

was a plan of the Colonel's to have the ancient refectory of the convent, a great vaulted room, supported by Gothic columns, converted into a servants' hall. Here Joe looked forward to rule the roast at the head of the servants' table, and to make the Gothic arches ring with those hunting and hard-drinking ditties which were the horror of the discreet Nanny Smith. Time, however, was fast wearing away with him, and his great fear was that the hall would not be completed in his day. In his eagerness to hasten the repairs, he used to get up early in the morning, and ring up the workmen. Notwithstanding his great age, also, he would turn out half-dressed in cold weather to cut sticks for the fire. Colonel Wildman kindly remonstrated with him for thus risking his health, as others would do the work for him.

"Lord, sir," exclaimed the hale old fellow, "it's my air bath, I'm all the better for it."

Unluckily, as he was thus employed one morning a splinter flew up and wounded one of his eyes. An inflammation took place; he lost the sight of that eye, and subsequently of the other. Poor Joe gradually pined away, and grew melancholy. Colonel Wildman kindly tried to cheer him up—"Come, come, old boy," cried he, "be of good heart, you will yet take your place in the servants' hall."

"Nay, nay, sir," replied he, "I did hope once that I should live to see it—I looked forward to it with pride, I confess, but it is all over with me now—I shall soon go home!"

He died shortly afterwards, at the advanced age of eighty-six, seventy of which had been passed as an honest and faithful servant at the Abbey. Colonel Wildman had him decently interred in the church of Hucknall Torkard, near the vault of Lord Byron.

SUPERSTITIONS OF THE ABBEY.

THE anecdotes I had heard of the quondam housekeeper of Lord Byron, rendered me desirous of paying her a visit. I rode in company with Colonel Wildman, therefore, to the cottage of her son William, where she resides, and found her seated by her fire-side, with a favorite cat perched upon her shoulder and purring in her ear. Nanny Smith is a large, good-looking woman, a specimen of the old-fashioned country housewife, combining antiquated notions and prejudices, and very limited information, with natural good sense. She loves to gossip about the Abbey and Lord Byron, and was soon drawn into a course of anecdotes, though mostly of an humble kind, such as suited the meridian of the housekeeper's room and servants' hall. She seemed to entertain a kind recollection of Lord Byron, though she had evidently been much perplexed by some of his vagaries; and especially by the means he adopted to counteract his tendency to corpulency. He used various modes to sweat himself down; sometimes he would lie for a long time in a warm bath, sometimes he would walk up the hills in the park, wrapped up and loaded with great coats; "a sad toil for the poor youth," added Nanny, "he being so lame."

His meals were scanty and irregular, consisting of dishes which Nanny seemed to hold in great contempt, such as pilaw, maccaroni, and light puddings.

She contradicted the report of the licentious life which he was reported to lead at the Abbey, and of the paramours said to have been brought with him from London. "A great part of his time used to be passed lying on a sofa reading. Sometimes he had young gentlemen of his acquaintance with him, and they played some mad pranks; but nothing but what young gentlemen may do, and no harm done."

"Once, it is true," she added, "he had with him a beautiful boy as a page, which the housemaids said was a girl. For my part, I know nothing about it. Poor soul, he was so lame he could not go out much with the men; all the comfort he had was to be a little with the lasses. The housemaids, however, were very jealous; one of them, in particular, took the matter in great dudgeon. Her name was Lucy; she was a great favorite with Lord Byron, and had been much noticed by him, and began to have high notions. She had her fortune told by a man who squinted, to whom she gave two-and-sixpence. He told her to hold up her head and look high, for she would come to great things. Upon this," added Nanny, "the poor thing dreamt of nothing less than becoming a lady, and mistress of the Abbey; and promised me, if such luck should happen to her, she would be a good friend to me. Ah well-a-day! Lucy never had the fine fortune she dreamt of; but she had better than I thought for; she is now married, and keeps a public house at Warwick."

Finding that we listened to her with great attention, Nanny Smith went on with her gossiping. "One time," said she, "Lord Byron took a notion that there was a deal of money buried about the Abbey by the monks in old times, and nothing would serve him but he must have the flagging taken up in the cloisters; and they digged and digged, but found nothing but stone coffins full of bones. Then he must needs have one of the coffins put in one end of the great hall, so that the servants were afraid to go there of nights. Several of the skulls were cleaned and put in frames in his room. I used to have to go into the room at night to shut the windows, and if I glanced an eye at them, they all seemed to grin; which I believe skulls always do. I can't say but I was glad to get out of the room.

"There was at one time (and for that matter there is still) a good deal said about ghosts haunting about the Abbey. The keeper's wife said she saw two standing in a dark part of the cloisters just opposite the chapel, and one in the garden by the lord's well. Then there was a young lady, a cousin of Lord Byron, who was staying in the Abbey and slept in the room next the clock; and she told me that one night when she was lying in bed, she saw a lady in white come out of the wall on one side of the room, and go into the wall on the opposite side.

"Lord Byron one day said to me, 'Nanny, what nonsense they tell about ghosts, as if there ever were any such things. I have never seen any thing of the kind about the Abbey, and I warrant you have not.' This was all done, do you see, to draw me out; but I said nothing, but shook my head. However, they say his lordship did once see something. It was in the great hall—something all black and hairy: he said it was the devil.

"For my part," continued Nanny Smith, "I never saw any thing of the kind—but I heard something once. I was one evening scrubbing the floor of the little dining-room at the end of the long gallery; it was after dark; I expected every moment to be called to tea, but wished to finish what I was about. All at once I heard heavy footsteps in the great hall. They sounded like the tramp of a horse. I took the light and went to see what it was. I heard the steps come from the lower end of the hall to the fireplace in the centre, where they stopped; but I could see nothing. I returned to my work, and in a little time heard the same noise again. I went again with the light; the footsteps stopped by the fireplace as before; still I could see nothing. I returned to my work, when I heard the steps for a third time. I then went into the hall without a light, but they stopped just the same, by the fireplace half way up the hall. I thought this rather odd, but returned to my work. When it was finished, I took the light and went through the hall, as that was my way to the kitchen. I heard no more footsteps, and thought no more of the matter, when, on coming to the lower end of the hall, I found the door locked, and then, on one side of the door, I saw the stone coffin with the skull and bones that had been digged up in the cloisters."

Here Nanny paused: I asked her if she believed that the mysterious footsteps had any connection with the skeleton in the coffin; but she shook her head, and would not commit herself. We took our leave of the good old dame shortly after, and the story she had related gave subject for conversation on our ride homeward. It was evident she had spoken the truth as to what she had heard, but had been deceived by some peculiar effect of sound. Noises are propagated about a huge irregular edifice of the kind in a very deceptive manner; footsteps are prolonged and reverberated by the vaulted cloisters and echoing halls; the creaking and slamming of distant gates, the rushing of the blast through the groves and among the ruined arches of the chapel, have all a strangely delusive effect at night.

Colonel Wildman gave an instance of the kind from his own experience. Not long after he had taken up his residence at the

Abbey, he heard one moonlight night a noise as if a carriage was passing at a distance. He opened the window and leaned out. It then seemed as if the great iron roller was dragged along the gravel walks and terrace, but there was nothing to be seen. When he saw the gardener on the following morning, he questioned him about working so late at night. The gardener declared that no one had been at work, and the roller was chained up. He was sent to examine it, and came back with a countenance full of surprise. The roller had been moved in the night, but he declared no mortal hand could have moved it. "Well," replied the Colonel, good-humoredly, "I am glad to find I have a brownie to work for me."

Lord Byron did much to foster and give currency to the superstitious tales connected with the Abbey, by believing, or pretending to believe in them. Many have supposed that his mind was really tinged with superstition, and that this innate infirmity was increased by passing much of his time in a lonely way, about the empty halls and cloisters of the Abbey, then in a ruinous melancholy state, and brooding over the skulls and effigies of its former inmates. I should rather think that he found poetical enjoyment in these supernatural themes, and that his imagination delighted to people this gloomy and romantic pile with all kinds of shadowy inhabitants. Certain it is, the aspect of the mansion under the varying influence of twilight and moonlight, and cloud and sunshine operating upon its halls, and galleries, and monkish cloisters, is enough to breed all kinds of fancies in the minds of its inmates, especially if poetically or superstitiously inclined.

I have already mentioned some of the fabled visitants of the Abbey. The goblin friar, however, is the one to whom Lord Byron has given the greatest importance. It walked the cloisters by night, and sometimes glimpses of it were seen in other parts of the Abbey. Its appearance was said to portend some impending evil to the master of the mansion. Lord Byron pretended to have seen it about a month before he contracted his ill-starred marriage with Miss Milbanke.

He has embodied this tradition in the following ballad, in which he represents the friar as one of the ancient inmates of the Abbey, maintaining by night a kind of spectral possession of it, in right of the fraternity. Other traditions, however, represent him as one of the friars doomed to wander about the place in atonement for his crimes. But to the ballad—

"Beware! beware! of the Black Friar,
  Who sitteth by Norman stone,
For he mutters his prayer in the midnight air,
  And his mass of the days that are gone.
When the Lord of the Hill, Amundeville,
  Made Norman Church his prey,
And expell'd the friars, one friar still
  Would not be driven away.

Though he came in his might, with King Henry's right,
  To turn church lands to lay,
With sword in hand, and torch to light
  Their walls, if they said nay,
A monk remain'd, unchased, unchain'd,
  And he did not seem form'd of clay,
For he's seen in the porch, and he's seen in the church,
  Though he is not seen by day.

And whether for good, or whether for ill,
  It is not mine to say;

But still to the house of Amundeville
He abideth night and day.
By the marriage bed of their lords, 'tis said,
He flits on the bridal eve;
And 'tis held as faith, to their bed of death,
He comes—but not tc grieve.

When an heir is born, he is heard to mourn,
And when aught is to befall
That ancient line, in the pale moonshine
He walks from hall to hall.
His form you may trace, but not his face,
'Tis shadow'd by his cowl;
But his eyes may be seen from the folds between,
And they seem of a parted soul.

But beware! beware of the Black Friar,
He still retains his sway,
For he is yet the church's heir,
Whoever may be the lay.
Amundeville is lord by day,
But the monk is lord by night,
Nor wine nor wassail could raise a vassal
To question that friar's right.

Say nought to him as he walks the hall,
And he'll say nought to you;
He sweeps along in his dusky pall,
As o'er the grass the dew.
Then gramercy! for the Black Friar;
Heaven sain him! fair or foul,
And whatsoe'er may be his prayer
Let ours be for his soul."

Such is the story of the goblin friar, which, partly through old tradition, and partly through the influence of Lord Byron's rhymes, has become completely established in the Abbey, and threatens to hold possession as long as the old edifice shall endure. Various visitors have either fancied, or pretended to have seen him, and a cousin of Lord Byron, Miss Sally Parkins, is even said to have made a sketch of him from memory. As to the servants at the Abbey, they have become possessed with all kinds of superstitious fancies. The long corridors and Gothic halls, with their ancient portraits and dark figures in armor, are all haunted regions to them; they even fear to sleep alone, and will scarce venture at night on any distant errand about the Abbey unless they go in couples.

Even the magnificent chamber in which I was lodged was subject to the supernatural influences which reigned over the Abbey, and was said to be haunted by "Sir John Byron the Little with the great Beard." The ancient black-looking portrait of this family worthy, which hangs over the door of the great saloon, was said to descend occasionally at midnight from the frame, and walk the rounds of the state apartments. Nay, his visitations were not confined to the night, for a young lady, on a visit to the Abbey some years since, declared that, on passing in broad day by the door of the identical chamber I have described, which stood partly open, she saw Sir John Byron the Little seated by the fireplace, reading out of a great black-letter book. From this circumstance some have been led to suppose that the story of Sir John Byron may be in some measure connected with the mysterious sculptures of the chimney-piece already mentioned; but this has no countenance from the most authentic antiquarians of the Abbey.

For my own part, the moment I learned the wonderful stories and strange suppositions connected with my apartment, it became an imaginary realm to me. As I lay in bed at night and gazed at the mysterious panel-work, where Gothic knight, and Christian dame, and Paynim lover gazed upon me in effigy, I used to weave a thousand fancies concerning them. The great figures in the tapestry, also, were almost animated by the workings of my imagination, and the Vandyke portraits of the cavalier and lady that looked down with pale aspects from the wall, had almost a spectral effect, from their immovable gaze and silent companionship—

> " For by dim lights the portraits of the dead
> Have something ghastly, desolate, and dread.
> —— Their buried looks still wave
> Along the canvas; their eyes glance like dreams
> On ours, as spars within some dusky cave,
> But death is mingled in their shadowy beams."

In this way I used to conjure up fictions of the brain, and clothe the objects around me with ideal interest and import, until, as the Abbey clock tolled midnight, I almost looked to see Sir John Byron the Little with the long Beard stalk into the room with his book under his arm, and take his seat beside the mysterious chimney-piece.

ANNESLEY HALL.

At about three miles' distance from Newstead Abbey, and contiguous to its lands, is situated Annesley Hall, the old family mansion of the Chaworths. The families, like the estates, of the Byrons and Chaworths, were connected in former times, until the fatal duel between their two representatives. The feud, however, which prevailed for a time, promised to be cancelled by the attachment of two youthful hearts. While Lord Byron was yet a boy, he beheld Mary Ann Chaworth, a beautiful girl, and the sole heiress of Annesley. With that susceptibility to female charms, which he evinced almost from childhood, he became almost immediately enamored of her. According to one of his biographers, it would appear that at first their attachment was mutual, yet clandestine. The father of Miss Chaworth was then living, and may have retained somewhat of the family hostility, for we are told that the interviews of Lord Byron and the young lady were private, at a gate which opened from her father's grounds to those of Newstead. However, they were so young at the time that these meetings could not have been regarded as of any importance: they were little more than children in years; but, as Lord Byron says of himself, his feelings were beyond his age.

The passion thus early conceived was blown into a flame,

during a six weeks' vacation which he passed with his mother at Nottingham. The father of Miss Chaworth was dead, and she resided with her mother at the old Hall of Annesley. During Byron's minority, the estate of Newstead was let to Lord Grey de Ruthen, but its youthful Lord was always a welcome guest at the Abbey. He would pass days at a time there, and make frequent visits thence to Annesley Hall. His visits were encouraged by Miss Chaworth's mother; she partook none of the family feud, and probably looked with complacency upon an attachment that might heal old differences and unite two neighboring estates.

The six weeks' vacation passed as a dream amongst the beautiful flowers of Annesley. Byron was scarce fifteen years of age, Mary Chaworth was two years older; but his heart, as I have said, was beyond his age, and his tenderness for her was deep and passionate. These early loves, like the first run of the uncrushed grape, are the sweetest and strongest gushings of the heart, and however they may be superseded by other attachments in after years, the memory will continually recur to them, and fondly dwell upon their recollections.

His love for Miss Chaworth, to use Lord Byron's own expression, was "the romance of the most romantic period of his life," and I think we can trace the effect of it throughout the whole course of his writings, coming up every now and then, like some lurking theme which runs through a complicated piece of music, and links it all in a pervading chain of melody.

How tenderly and mournfully does he recall, in after years, the feelings awakened in his youthful and inexperienced bosom by this impassioned, yet innocent attachment; feelings, he says, lost or hardened in the intercourse of life:

"The love of better things and better days;
The unbounded hope, and heavenly ignorance
Of what is called the world, and the world's ways;
The moments when we gather from a glance
More joy than from all future pride or praise,
Which kindle manhood, but can ne'er entrance
The heart in an existence of its own,
Of which another's bosom is the zone."

Whether this love was really responded to by the object, is uncertain. Byron sometimes speaks as if he had met with kindness in return, at other times he acknowledges that she never gave him reason to believe she loved him. It is probable, however, that at first she experienced some flutterings of the heart. She was of a susceptible age; had as yet formed no other attachments; her lover, though boyish in years, was a man in intellect, a poet in imagination, and had a countenance of remarkable beauty.

With the six weeks' vacation ended this brief romance. Byron returned to school deeply enamored, but if he had really made any impression on Miss Chaworth's heart, it was too slight to stand the test of absence. She was at that age when a female soon changes from the girl to the woman, and leaves her boyish lovers far behind her. While Byron was pursuing his school-boy studies, she was mingling with society, and met with a gentleman of the name of Musters, remarkable, it is said, for manly beauty. A story is told of her having first seen him from the top of Annesley Hall, as he dashed through the park, with hound and horn, taking the lead of the whole field in a fox chase, and that she was struck by the spirit of his appearance, and his admirable horsemanship. Under such favorable auspices, he wooed and won her, and when Lord Byron next met her, he learned to his dismay that she was the affianced bride of another.

With that pride of spirit which always distinguished him, he controlled his feelings and maintained a serene countenance. He even affected to speak calmly on the subject of her approaching nuptials. "The next time I see you," said he, "I suppose you will be Mrs. Chaworth," (for she was to retain her family name.) Her reply was, "I hope so."

I have given these brief details preparatory to a sketch of a visit which I made to the scene of this youthful romance. Annesley Hall I understood was shut up, neglected, and almost in a state of desolation; for Mr. Musters rarely visited it, residing with his family in the neighborhood of Nottingham. I set out for the Hall on horseback, in company with Colonel Wildman, and followed by the great Newfoundland dog Boatswain. In the course of our ride we visited a spot memorable in the love story I have cited. It was the scene of this parting interview between Byron and Miss Chaworth, prior to her marriage. A long ridge of upland advances into the valley of Newstead, like a promontory into a lake, and was formerly crowned by a beautiful grove, a landmark to the neighboring country. The grove and promontory are graphically described by Lord Byron in his "Dream," and an exquisite picture given of himself, and the lovely object of his boyish idolatry—

"I saw two beings in the hues of youth
Standing upon a hill, a gentle hill,
Green, and of mild declivity, the last
As 'twere the cape of a long ridge of such,
Save that there was no sea to lave its base,
But a most living landscape, and the wave

Of woods and corn-fields, and the abodes of men,
Scatter'd at intervals, and wreathing smoke
Arising from such rustic roofs;—the hill
Was crown'd with a peculiar diadem
Of trees, in circular array, so fixed,
Not by the sport of nature, but of man:
These two a maiden and a youth, were there
Gazing—the one on all that was beneath
Fair as herself—but the boy gazed on her;
And both were fair, and one was beautiful:
And both were young—yet not alike in youth.
As the sweet moon in the horizon's verge,
The maid was on the verge of womanhood:
The boy had fewer summers, but his heart
Had far outgrown his years, and to his eye
There was but one beloved face on earth,
And that was shining on him."

I stood upon the spot consecrated by this memorable interview. Below me extended the "living landscape," once contemplated by the loving pair; the gentle valley of Newstead, diversified by woods and corn-fields, and village spires, and gleams of water, and the distant towers and pinnacles of the venerable Abbey. The diadem of trees, however, was gone. The attention drawn to it by the poet, and the romantic manner in which he had associated it with his early passion for Mary Chaworth, had nettled the irritable feelings of her husband, who but ill brooked the poetic celebrity conferred on his wife by the enamored verses of another. The celebrated grove stood on his estate, and in a fit of spleen he ordered it to be levelled with the dust. At the time of my visit the mere roots of the trees were visible; but the hand that laid them low is execrated by every poetical pilgrim.

Descending the hill, we soon entered a part of what once was Annesley Park, and rode among time-worn and tempest-riven oaks and elms, with ivy clambering about their trunks, and rooks' nests among their branches. The park had been cut up by a post-road, crossing which, we came to the gate-house of Annesley Hall. It was an old brick building that might have served as an outpost or barbacan to the Hall during the civil wars, when every gentleman's house was liable to become a fortress. Loopholes were still visible in its walls, but the peaceful ivy had mantled the sides, overrun the roof, and almost buried the ancient clock in front, that still marked the waning hours of its decay.

An arched way led through the centre of the gate-house, secured by grated doors of open iron work, wrought into flowers and flourishes. These being thrown open, we entered a paved court-yard, decorated with shrubs and antique flower-pots, with a ruined stone fountain in the centre. The whole approach resembled that of an old French chateau.

On one side of the court-yard was a range of stables, now tenantless, but which bore traces of the fox-hunting squire; for there were stalls boxed up, into which the hunters might be turned loose when they came home from the chase.

At the lower end of the court, and immediately opposite the gate-house, extended the Hall itself; a rambling, irregular pile, patched and pieced at various times, and in various tastes, with gable ends, stone balustrades, and enormous chimneys, that strutted out like buttresses from the walls. The whole front of the edifice was overrun with evergreens.

We applied for admission at the front door, which was under a heavy porch. The portal was strongly barricadoed, and our knocking was echoed by waste and empty halls. Every thing bore an appearance of abandonment. After a time, however, our knocking summoned a solitary tenant from some remote corner of the pile. It was a decent-looking little dame, who emerged from a side door at a distance, and seemed a worthy inmate of the antiquated mansion. She had, in fact, grown old with it. Her name, she said, was Nanny Marsden; if she lived until next August, she would be seventy-one: a great part of her life had been passed in the Hall, and when the family had removed to Nottingham, she had been left in charge of it. The front of the house had been thus warily barricadoed in consequence of the late riots at Nottingham; in the course of which, the dwelling of her master had been sacked by the mob. To guard against any attempt of the kind upon the Hall, she had put it in this state of defence; though I rather think she and a superannuated gardener comprised the whole garrison. "You must be attached to the old building," said I, "after having lived so long in it." "Ah, sir!" replied she, "I am *getting in years*, and have a furnished cottage of my own in Annesley Wood, and begin to feel as if I should like to go and live in my own home."

Guided by the worthy little custodian of the fortress, we entered through the sally port by which she had issued forth, and soon found ourselves in a spacious, but somewhat gloomy hall, where the light was partially admitted through square stone-shafted windows, overhung with ivy. Every thing around us had the air of an old-fashioned country squire's establishment. In the centre of the hall was a billiard table, and about the walls were hung portraits of race-horses, hunters, and favorite dogs, mingled indiscriminately with family pictures.

Staircases led up from the hall to various apartments. In one of the rooms we were shown a couple of buff jerkins, and a pair of ancient jackboots, of the time of the cavaliers; relics which are often to be met with in the old English family mansions. These, however, had peculiar value, for the good little dame assured us they had belonged to Robin Hood. As we were in the midst of the region over which that famous outlaw once bore ruffian sway, it was not for us to gainsay his claim to any of these venerable relics, though we might have demurred that the articles of dress here shown were of a date much later than his time. Every antiquity, however, about Sherwood Forest is apt to be linked with the memory of Robin Hood and his gang.

As we were strolling about the mansion, our four-footed attendant, Boatswain, followed leisurely, as if taking a survey of the premises. I turned to rebuke him for his intrusion, but the moment the old housekeeper understood he had belonged to Lord Byron, her heart seemed to yearn towards him.

"Nay, nay," exclaimed she, "let him alone, let him go where he pleases. He's welcome. Ah, dear me! If he lived here I should take great care of him—he should want for nothing.—Well!" continued she, fondling him, "who would have thought that I should see a dog of Lord Byron in Annesley Hall!"

"I suppose, then," said I, "you recollect something of Lord Byron, when he used to visit here?" "Ah, bless him!" cried she, "that I do! He used to ride over here and stay three days at a time, and sleep in the blue room. Ah! poor fellow! He was very much taken with my young mistress; he used to walk about the garden and the terraces with her, and seemed to love the very ground she trod on. He used to call her *his bright morning star of Annesley.*"

I felt the beautiful poetic phrase thrill through me.

"You appear to like the memory of Lord Byron," said I.

"Ah, sir! why should not I! He was always main good to me when he came here. Well! well! they say it is a pity he and my young lady did not make a match. Her mother would have liked it. He was always a welcome guest, and some think it would have been well for him to have had her; but it was not to be! He went away to school, and then Mr. Musters saw her, and so things took their course."

The simple soul now showed us into the favorite sitting-room of Miss Chaworth, with a small flower-garden under the windows, in which she had delighted. In this room Byron used to sit and listen to her as she played and sang, gazing upon her with the passionate, and almost painful devotion of a love-sick stripling. He himself gives us a glowing picture of his mute idolatry:

> "He had no breath, no being, but in hers;
> She was his voice; he did not speak to her,
> But trembled on her words; she was his sight,
> For his eye followed hers, and saw with hers,
> Which colored all his objects;—he had ceased
> To live within himself; she was his life,
> The ocean to the river of his thoughts,
> Which terminated all: upon a tone,
> A touch of hers, his blood would ebb and flow,
> And his cheek change tempestuously—his heart
> Unknowing of its cause of agony."

There was a little Welsh air, called Mary Ann, which, from bearing her own name, he associated with herself, and often persuaded her to sing it over and over for him.

The chamber, like all the other parts of the house, had a look of sadness and neglect; the flower-pots beneath the window, which once bloomed beneath the hand of Mary Chaworth, were overrun with weeds; and the piano, which had once vibrated to her touch, and thrilled the heart of her stripling lover, was now unstrung and out of tune.

We continued our stroll about the waste apartments, of all shapes and sizes, and without much elegance of decoration. Some of them were hung with family portraits, among which was pointed out that of the Mr. Chaworth who was killed by the "wicked Lord Byron."

These dismal looking portraits had a powerful effect upon the imagination of the stripling poet, on his first visit to the Hall. As they gazed down from the wall, he thought they scowled upon him, as if they had taken a grudge against him on account of the duel of his ancestor. He even gave this as a reason, though probably in jest, for not sleeping at the Hall, declaring that he feared they would come down from their frames at night to haunt him.

A feeling of the kind he has embodied in one of his stanzas of Don Juan:

" The forms of the grim knights and pictured saints
  Look living in the moon; and as you turn
Backward and forward to the echoes faint
  Of your own footsteps—voices from the urn
Appear to wake, and shadows wild and quaint
  Start from the frames which fence their aspects stern,
As if to ask you how you dare to keep
A vigil there, where all but death should sleep."

Nor was the youthful poet singular in these fancies; the Hall, like most old English mansions that have ancient family portraits hanging about their dusky galleries and waste apartments, had its ghost story connected with these pale memorials of the dead. Our simple-hearted conductor stopped before the portrait of a lady, who had been a beauty in her time, and inhabited the Hall in the heyday of her charms. Something mysterious or melancholy was connected with her story; she died young, but continued for a long time to haunt the ancient mansion, to the great dismay of the servants, and the occasional disquiet of the visitors, and it was with much difficulty her troubled spirit was conjured down and put to rest.

From the rear of the Hall we walked out into the garden, about which Byron used to stroll and loiter in company with Miss Chaworth. It was laid out in the old French style. There was a long terraced walk, with heavy stone balustrades and sculptured urns, overrun with ivy and evergreens. A neglected shrubbery bordered one side of the terrace, with a lofty grove inhabited by a venerable community of rooks. Great flights of steps led down from the terrace to a flower-garden, laid out in formal plots. The rear of the Hall, which overlooked the garden, had the weather stains of centuries, and its stone-shafted casements, and an ancient sun-dial against its walls, carried back the mind to days of yore.

The retired and quiet garden, once a little sequestered world of love and romance, was now all matted and wild, yet was beautiful even in its decay. Its air of neglect and desolation was in unison with the fortune of the two beings who had once walked here in the freshness of youth, and life, and beauty. The garden, like their young hearts, had gone to waste and ruin.

Returning to the Hall we now visited a chamber built over the porch, or grand entrance; it was in a ruinous condition; the ceiling having fallen in, and the floor given away. This, however, is a chamber rendered interesting by poetical associations. It is supposed to be the oratory alluded to by Lord Byron in his Dream, wherein he pictures his departure from Annesley, after learning that Mary Chaworth was engaged to be married—

'There was an ancient mansion, and before
Its walls there was a steed caparison'd ;
Within an antique Oratory stood
The Boy of whom I spake ;—he was alone,
And pale and pacing to and fro : anon
He sate him down, and seized a pen, and traced
Words which I could not guess of ; then he lean'd
His bow'd head on his hands, and shook as 'twere
With a convulsion—then arose again,
And with his teeth and quivering hands did tear
What he had written, but he shed no tears.
And he did calm himself, and fix his brow
Into a kind of quiet ; as he paused,
The lady of his love re-entered there ;
She was serene and smiling then, and yet
She knew she was by him beloved,—she knew,
For quickly comes such knowledge, that his heart
Was darken'd with her shadow, and she saw
That he was wretched, but she saw not all.
He rose, and with a cold and gentle grasp
He took her hand ; a moment o'er his face
A tablet of unutterable thoughts
Was traced, and then it faded as it came ;
He dropp'd the hand he held, and with slow steps
Return'd, but not as bidding her adieu,
For they did part with mutual smiles :—he pass'd
From out the massy gate of that old Hall,
And mounting on his steed he went his way,
And ne'er repass'd that hoary threshold more."

In one of his journals, Lord Byron describes his feelings after thus leaving the oratory. Arriving on the summit of a hill, which commanded the last view of Annesley, he checked his horse, and gazed back with mingled pain and fondness upon the groves which embowered the Hall, and thought upon the lovely being that dwelt there, until his feelings were quite dissolved in tenderness. The conviction at length recurred that she never could be his, when, rousing himself from his reverie, he struck his spurs into his steed and dashed forward, as if by rapid motion to leave reflection behind him.

Yet, notwithstanding what he asserts in the verses last quoted, he did pass the "hoary threshold" of Annesley again. It was, however, after the lapse of several years, during which he had grown up to manhood, had passed through the ordeal of pleasures and tumultuous passions, and had felt the influence of other charms. Miss Chaworth, too, had become a wife and a mother and he dined at Annesley Hall at the invitation of her husband. He thus met the object of his early idolatry in the very scene of his tender devotions, which, as he says, her smiles had once made a heaven to him. The scene was but little changed. He was in the very chamber where he had so often listened entranced to the witchery of her voice; there were the same instruments and music; there lay her flower-garden beneath the window, and the walks through which he had wandered with her in the intoxication of youthful love. Can we wonder that amidst the tender recollections which every object around him was calculated to awaken, the fond passion of his boyhood should rush back in full current to his heart? He was himself surprised at this sudden revulsion of his feelings, but he had acquired self-possession and could command them. His firmness, however, was doomed to undergo a further trial. While seated by the object of his secret devotions, with all these recollections throbbing in his bosom, her infant daughter was brought into the room. At sight of the child he started; it dispelled the last lingerings of his dream, and he afterwards confessed, that to repress his emotion at the moment, was the severest part of his task.

The conflict of feelings that raged within his bosom throughout this fond and tender, yet painful and embarrassing visit, are touchingly depicted in lines which he wrote immediately afterwards, and which, though not addressed to her by name, are evidently intended for the eye and the heart of the fair lady of Annesley:

"Well! thou art happy, and I feel
That I should thus be happy too;
For still my heart regards thy weal
Warmly, as it was wont to do.

Thy husband's blest—and 'twill impart
Some pangs to view his happier lot:
But let them pass—Oh! how my heart
Would hate him, if he loved thee not!

When late I saw thy favorite child
I thought my jealous heart would break;
But when the unconscious infant smiled,
I kiss'd it for its mother's sake.

I kiss'd it, and repress'd my sighs
Its father in its face to see;
But then it had its mother's eyes,
And they were all to love and me.

Mary, adieu! I must away:
While thou art blest I'll not repine;
But near thee I can never stay:
My heart would soon again be thine.

I deem'd that time, I deem'd that pride
Had quench'd at length my boyish flame;
Nor knew, till seated by thy side,
My heart in all, save love, the same.

Yet I was calm: I knew the time
My breast would thrill before thy look;
But now to tremble were a crime—
We met, and not a nerve was shook.

I saw thee gaze upon my face,
Yet meet with no confusion there:
One only feeling could'st thou trace;
The sullen calmness of despair.

Away! away! my early dream
Remembrance never must awake:
Oh! where is Lethe's fabled stream?
My foolish heart, be still, or break."

The revival of this early passion, and the melancholy associations which it spread over those scenes in the neighborhood of Newstead, which would necessarily be the places of his frequent resort while in England, are alluded to by him as a principal cause of his first departure for the Continent:

"When man expell'd from Eden's bowers
A moment lingered near the gate,
Each scene recalled the vanish'd hours,
And bade him curse his future fate.

But wandering on through distant climes,
He learnt to bear his load of grief;
Just gave a sigh to other times,
And found in busier scenes relief.

Thus Mary must it be with me,
And I must view thy charms no more;
For, while I linger near to thee,
I sigh for all I knew before."

It was in the subsequent June that he set off on his pilgrimage by sea and land, which was to become the theme of his immortal poem. That the image of Mary Chaworth, as he saw and loved her in the days of his boyhood, followed him to the very shore, is shown in the glowing stanzas addressed to her on the eve of embarkation—

"'Tis done—and shivering in the gale
The bark unfurls her snowy sail;
And whistling o'er the bending mast,
Loud sings on high the fresh'ning blast;
And I must from this land be gone,
Because I cannot love but one.

And I will cross the whitening foam,
And I will seek a foreign home;
Till I forget a false fair face,
I ne'er shall find a resting place;
My own dark thoughts I cannot shun,
But ever love, and love but one.

To think of every early scene,
Of what we are, and what we've been,

Would whelm some softer hearts with woe—
But mine, alas! has stood the blow;
Yet still beats on as it begun,
And never truly loves but one.

And who that dear loved one may be
Is not for vulgar eyes to see,
And why that early love was cross'd,
Thou know'st the best, I feel the most;
But few that dwell beneath the sun
Have loved so long, and loved but one.

I've tried another's fetters too,
With charms, perchance, as fair to view;
And I would fain have loved as well,
But some unconquerable spell
Forbade my bleeding breast to own
A kindred care for aught but one.

'Twould soothe to take one lingering view,
And bless thee in my last adieu;
Yet wish I not those eyes to weep
For him who wanders o'er the deep;
His home, his hope, his youth are gone,
Yet still he loves, and loves but one."

The painful interview at Annesley Hall which revived with such intenseness his early passion, remained stamped upon his memory with singular force, and seems to have survived all his "wandering through distant climes," to which he trusted as an oblivious antidote. Upwards of two years after that event, when, having made his famous pilgrimage, he was once more an inmate of Newstead Abbey, his vicinity to Annesley Hall brought the whole scene vividly before him, and he thus recalls it in a poetic epistle to a friend—

> "I've seen my bride another's bride,—
> Have seen her seated by his side,—
> Have seen the infant which she bore,
> Wear the sweet smile the mother wore,
> When she and I in youth have smiled
> As fond and faultless as her child:—
> Have seen her eyes, in cold disdain,
> Ask if I felt no secret pain.
>
> And I have acted well my part,
> And made my cheek belie my heart,
> Return'd the freezing glance she gave,
> Yet felt the while *that* woman's slave;—
> Have kiss'd, as if without design,
> The babe which ought to have been mine,
> And show'd, alas! in each caress,
> Time had not made me love the less."

"It was about the time," says Moore in his life of Lord Byron, "when he was thus bitterly feeling and expressing the blight which his heart had suffered from a *real* object of affection, that his poems on an imaginary one, 'Thyrza,' were written." He was at the same time grieving over the loss of several of his earliest and dearest friends, the companions of his joyous school-boy hours. To recur to the beautiful language of Moore, who writes with the kindred and kindling sympathies of a true poet: 'All these recollections of the young and the dead mingled themselves in his mind with the image of her, who, though living, was, for him, as much lost as they, and diffused that general feeling of sadness and fondness through his soul, which found a vent in these poems. * * * It was the blending of the two affections in his memory and imagination, that gave birth to an ideal object combining the best features of both, and drew from him those saddest and tenderest of love poems, in which we find all the depth and intensity of real feeling, touched over with such a light as no reality ever wore."

An early, innocent, and unfortunate passion, however fruitful of pain it may be to the man, is a lasting advantage to the poet. It is a well of sweet and bitter fancies; of refined and gentle sentiments; of elevated and ennobling thoughts; shut up in the deep recesses of the heart, keeping it green amidst the withering blights of the world, and, by its casual gushings and overflowings, recalling at times all the freshness, and innocence, and enthusiasm of youthful days. Lord Byron was conscious of this effect, and purposely cherished and brooded over the remembrance of his early passion, and of all the scenes of Annesley Hall connected with it. It was this remembrance that attuned his mind to some of its most elevated and virtuous strains, and shed an inexpressible grace and pathos over his best productions.

Being thus put upon the traces of this little love-story, I cannot refrain from threading them out, as they appear from time to time in various passages of Lord Byron's works. During his subsequent rambles in the East, when time and distance had softened away his "early romance" almost into the remembrance of a pleasing and tender dream, he received accounts of the object of it, which represented her, still in her paternal Hall, among her native bowers of Annesley, surrounded by a blooming and beautiful family, yet a prey to secret and withering melancholy—

—— " In her home,
A thousand leagues from his,—her native home,
She dwelt, begirt with growing infancy,
Daughters and sons of beauty, but—behold !
Upon her face there was the tint of grief,
The settled shadow of an inward strife,
And an unquiet drooping of the eye,
As if its lids were charged with unshed tears."

For an instant the buried tenderness of early youth and the fluttering hopes which accompanied it, seemed to have revived in his bosom, and the idea to have flashed upon his mind that his image might be connected with her secret woes—but he rejected the thought almost as soon as formed.

" What could her grief be ?—she had all she loved,
And he who had so loved her was not there
To trouble with bad hopes, or evil wish,
Or ill repress'd affection, her pure thoughts.
What could her grief be ?—she had loved him not,
Nor given him cause to deem himself beloved,
Nor could he be a part of that which prey'd
Upon her mind—a spectre of the past."

The cause of her grief was a matter of rural comment in the neighborhood of Newstead and Annesley. It was disconnected from all idea of Lord Byron, but attributed to the harsh and capricious conduct of one to whose kindness and affection she had a sacred claim. The domestic sorrows which had long preyed in secret on her heart, at length affected her intellect, and the "bright morning star of Annesley" was eclipsed for ever.

> " The lady of his love,—oh! she was changed
> As by the sickness of the soul; her mind
> Had wandered from its dwelling, and her eyes,
> They had not their own lustre, but the look
> Which is not of the earth; she was become
> The queen of a fantastic realm: but her thoughts
> Were combinations of disjointed things;
> And forms impalpable and unperceived
> Of others' sight, familiar were to hers.
> And this the world calls frenzy."

Notwithstanding lapse of time, change of place, and a succession of splendid and spirit-stirring scenes in various countries, the quiet and gentle scene of his boyish love seems to have held a magic sway over the recollections of Lord Byron, and the image of Mary Chaworth to have unexpectedly obtruded itself upon his mind like some supernatural visitation. Such was the fact on the occasion of his marriage with Miss Milbanke; Annesley Hall and all its fond associations floated like a vision before his thoughts, even when at the altar, and on the point of pronouncing the nuptial vows. The circumstance is related by him with a force and feeling that persuade us of its truth.

> " A change came o'er the spirit of my dream.
> The wanderer was returned.—I saw him stand
> Before an altar—with a gentle bride;
> Her face was fair, but was not that which made
> The star-light of his boyhood;—as he stood

Even at the altar, o'er his brow there came
The self-same aspect, and the quivering shock
That in the antique oratory shook
His bosom in its solitude ; and then—
As in that hour—a moment o'er his face
The tablet of unutterable thoughts
Was traced,—and then it faded as it came,
And he stood calm and quiet, and he spoke
The fitting vows, but heard not his own words,
And all things reel'd around him : he could see
Not that which was, nor that which should have been—
But the old mansion, and the accustomed hall,
And the remember'd chambers, and the place,
The day, the hour, the sunshine, and the shade,
All things pertaining to that place and hour,
And her who was his destiny, came back,
And thrust themselves between him and the light:
What business had they there at such a time?"

The history of Lord Byron's union is too well known to need narration. The errors, and humiliations, and heart-burnings that followed upon it, gave additional effect to the remembrance of his early passion, and tormented him with the idea, that had he been successful in his suit to the lovely heiress of Annesley, they might both have shared a happier destiny. In one of his manuscripts, written long after his marriage, having accidentally mentioned Miss Chaworth as "my M. A. C." "Alas!" exclaims he, with a sudden burst of feeling, "why do I say *my?* Our union would have healed feuds in which blood had been shed by our fathers; it would have joined lands broad and rich; it would have joined at least *one* heart, and two persons not ill-matched in years—and—and—and—what has been the result?"

But enough of Annesley Hall and the poetical themes connected with it. I felt as if I could linger for hours about its ruined oratory, and silent hall, and neglected garden, and spin reveries and dream dreams, until all became an ideal world around me. The day, however, was fast declining, and the shadows of evening throwing deeper shades of melancholy about the place. Taking our leave of the worthy old housekeeper, therefore, with a small compensation and many thanks for her civilities, we mounted our horses and pursued our way back to Newstead Abbey.

THE LAKE.

"Before the mansion lay a lucid lake,
  Broad as transparent, deep, and freshly fed
By a river, which its softened way did take
  In currents through the calmer water spread
Around: the wild fowl nestled in the brake
  And sedges, brooding in their liquid bed:
The woods sloped downward to its brink, and stood
With their green faces fixed upon the flood."

Such is Lord Byron's description of one of a series of beautiful sheets of water, formed in old times by the monks by damming up the course of a small river. Here he used daily to enjoy his favorite recreations of swimming and sailing. The "wicked old Lord," in his scheme of rural devastation, had cut down all the woods that once fringed the lake; Lord Byron, on coming of age, endeavored to restore them, and a beautiful young wood, planted by him, now sweeps up from the water's edge, and clothes the hill hide opposite to the Abbey. To this woody nook Colonel Wildman has given the appropriate title of "the Poet's Corner."

The lake has inherited its share of the traditions and fables connected with every thing in and about the Abbey. It was a petty Mediterranean sea on which the "wicked old Lord" used to gratify his nautical tastes and humors. He had his mimic castles and fortresses along its shores, and his mimic fleets upon its waters, and used to get up mimic sea-fights. The remains of his petty fortifications still awaken the curious inquiries of visitors. In one of his vagaries, he caused a large vessel to be brought on wheels from the sea-coast and launched in the lake. The country people were surprised to see a ship thus sailing over dry land. They called to mind a saying of Mother Shipton, the famous prophet of the vulgar, that whenever a ship freighted with ling should cross Sherwood Forest, Newstead would pass out of the Byron family. The country people, who detested the old Lord, were anxious to verify the prophecy. Ling, in the dialect of Nottingham, is the name for heather; with this plant they heaped the fated bark as it passed, so that it arrived full freighted at Newstead.

The most important stories about the lake, however, relate to the treasures that are supposed to lie buried in its bosom. These may have taken their origin in a fact which actually occurred. There was one time fished up from the deep part of the lake a great eagle of molten brass, with expanded wings, standing on a pedestal or perch of the same metal. It had doubtless served as a stand or reading-desk, in the Abbey chapel, to hold a folio Bible or missal.

The sacred relic was sent to a braiser to be cleaned. As he was at work upon it, he discovered that the pedestal was hollow and composed of several pieces. Unscrewing these, he drew forth a number of parchment deeds and grants appertaining to the Abbey, and bearing the seals of Edward III. and Henry VIII., which had thus been concealed, and ultimately sunk in the lake by the friars, to substantiate their right and title to these domains at some future day.

One of the parchment scrolls thus discovered, throws rather an awkward light upon the kind of life led by the friars of Newstead. It is an indulgence granted to them for a certain number of months, in which plenary pardon is assured in advance for all kinds of crimes, among which, several of the most gross and sensual are specifically mentioned, and the weaknesses of the flesh to which they were prone.

After inspecting these testimonials of monkish life, in the regions of Sherwood Forest, we cease to wonder at the virtuous indignation of Robin Hood and his outlaw crew, at the sleek sensualists of the cloister:

"I never hurt the husbandman,
That use to till the ground,
Nor spill their blood that range the wood
To follow hawk and hound.

My chiefest spite to clergy is,
Who in these days bear sway;
With friars and monks with their fine spunks,
I make my chiefest prey."

OLD BALLAD OF ROBIN HOOD.

The brazen eagle has been transferred to the parochial and collegiate church of Southall, about twenty miles from Newstead, where it may still be seen in the centre of the chancel, supporting, as of yore, a ponderous Bible. As to the documents it contained, they are carefully treasured up by Colonel Wildman among his other deeds and papers, in an iron chest secured by a patent lock of nine bolts, almost equal to a magic spell.

The fishing up of this brazen relic, as I have already hinted, has given rise to the tales of treasure lying at the bottom of the lake, thrown in there by the monks when they abandoned the Abbey. The favorite story is, that there is a great iron chest there filled with gold and jewels, and chalices and crucifixes.

Nay, that it has been seen, when the water of the lake was unusually low. There were large iron rings at each end, but all attempts to move it were ineffectual; either the gold it contained was too ponderous, or what is more probable, it was secured by one of those magic spells usually laid upon hidden treasure. It remains, therefore, at the bottom of the lake to this day; and it is to be hoped, may one day or other be discovered by the present worthy proprietor.

ROBIN HOOD AND SHERWOOD FOREST.

WHILE at Newstead Abbey I took great delight in riding and rambling about the neighborhood, studying out the traces of merry Sherwood Forest, and visiting the haunts of Robin Hood. The relics of the old forest are few and scattered, but as to the bold outlaw who once held a kind of freebooting sway over it, there is scarce a hill or dale, a cliff or cavern, a well or fountain, in this part of the country, that is not connected with his memory. The very names of some of the tenants on the Newstead estate, such as Beardall and Hardstaff, sound as if they may have been borne in old times by some of the stalwart fellows of the outlaw gang.

One of the earliest books that captivated my fancy when a child, was a collection of Robin Hood ballads, "adorned with cuts," which I bought of an old Scotch pedler, at the cost of all my holiday money. How I devoured its pages, and gazed upon is uncouth wood cuts! For a time my mind was filled with picturings of "merry Sherwood," and the exploits and revelling of the bold foresters; and Robin Hood, Little John, Friar Tuck, and their doughty compeers, were my heroes of romance.

These early feelings were in some degree revived when I found myself in the very heart of the far-famed forest, and, as I said before, I took a kind of schoolboy delight in hunting up all traces of old Sherwood and its sylvan chivalry. One of the first of my antiquarian rambles was on horseback, in company with Colonel Wildman and his lady, who undertook to guide me to some of the mouldering monuments of the forest. One of these stands in front of the very gate of Newstead Park, and is known throughout the country by the name of "The Pilgrim Oak. It is a venerable tree, of great size, overshadowing a wide arena of the road. Under its shade the rustics of the neighborhood have been accustomed to assemble on certain holidays, and celebrate their rural festivals. This custom had been handed down from father to son for several generations, until the oak had acquired a kind of sacred character.

The "old Lord Byron," however, in whose eyes nothing was sacred, when he laid his desolating hand on the groves and forests of Newstead, doomed likewise this traditional tree to the axe. Fortunately the good people of Nottingham heard of the danger of their favorite oak, and hastened to ransom it from destruction. They afterwards made a present of it to the poet, when he came to the estate, and the Pilgrim Oak is likely to continue a rural gathering place for many coming generations.

From this magnificent and time-honored tree we continued on our sylvan research, in quest of another oak, of more ancient date and less flourishing condition. A ride of two or three miles, the latter part across open wastes, once clothed with forest, now bare and cheerless, brought us to the tree in question. It was the Oak of Ravenshead, one of the last survivors of old Sherwood, and which had evidently once held a high head in the forest; it was now a mere wreck, crazed by time, and blasted by lightning, and standing alone on a naked waste, like a ruined column in a desert.

"The scenes are desert now, and bare,
Where flourished once a forest fair,
When these waste glens with copse were lined,
And peopled with the hart and hind.
Yon lonely oak, would he could tell
The changes of his parent dell,
Since he, so gray and stubborn now,
Waved in each breeze a sapling bough.
Would he could tell how deep the shade
A thousand mingled branches made.
Here in my shade, methinks he'd say,
The mighty stag at noontide lay,
While doe, and roe, and red-deer good,
Have bounded by through gay green-wood."

At no great distance from Ravenshead Oak is a small cave which goes by the name of Robin Hood's stable. It is in the breast of a hill, scooped out of brown freestone, with rude attempts at columns and arches. Within are two niches, which served, it is said, as stalls for the bold outlaw's horses. To this retreat he retired when hotly pursued by the law, for the place was a secret even from his band. The cave is overshadowed by an oak and alder, and is hardly discoverable even at the present day; but when the country was overrun with forest it must have been completely concealed.

There was an agreeable wildness and loneliness in a great part of our ride. Our devious road wound down, at one time, among rocky dells, by wandering streams, and lonely pools, haunted by shy water fowl. We passed through a skirt of woodland, of more modern planting, but considered a legitimate off-spring of the ancient forest, and commonly called Jock of Sherwood In riding through these quiet, solitary scenes, the partridge and pheasant would now and then burst upon the wing, and the hare scud away before us.

Another of these rambling rides in quest of popular antiquities, was to a chain of rocky cliffs, called the Kirkby Crags, which skirt the Robin Hood hills. Here, leaving my horse at the foot of the crags, I scaled their rugged sides, and seated myself in a niche of the rocks, called Robin Hood's chair. It commands a wide prospect over the valley of Newstead, and here the bold outlaw is said to have taken his seat, and kept a look-out upon the roads below, watching for merchants, and bishops, and other wealthy travellers, upon whom to pounce down, like an eagle from his eyrie.

Descending from the cliffs and remounting my horse, a ride of a mile or two further along a narrow "robber path," as it was called, which wound up into the hills between perpendicular rocks, led to an artificial cavern cut in the face of a cliff, with a door and window wrought through the living stone. This bears the name of Friar Tuck's cell, or hermitage, where, according to tradition, that jovial anchorite used to make good cheer and boisterous revel with his freebooting comrades.

Such were some of the vestiges of old Sherwood and its renowned "yeomandrie," which I visited in the neighborhood of Newstead. The worthy clergyman who officiated as chaplain at the Abbey, seeing my zeal in the cause, informed me of a considerable tract of the ancient forest, still in existence about ten miles distant. There were many fine old oaks in it, he said, that had stood for centuries, but were now shattered and "stag-headed," that is to say, their upper branches were bare, and blasted, and straggling out like the antlers of a deer. Their trunks, too, were hollow, and full of crows and jackdaws, who

15*

made them their nestling places. He occasionally rode over to the forest in the long summer evenings, and pleased himself with loitering in the twilight about the green alleys and under the venerable trees.

The description given by the chaplain made me anxious to visit this remnant of old Sherwood, and he kindly offered to be my guide and companion. We accordingly sallied forth one morning on horseback on this sylvan expedition. Our ride took us through a part of the country where King John had once held a hunting seat; the ruins of which are still to be seen. At that time the whole neighborhood was an open royal forest, or Frank chase, as it was termed; for King John was an enemy to parks and warrens, and other inclosures, by which game was fenced in for the private benefit and recreation of the nobles and the clergy.

Here, on the brow of a gentle hill, commanding an extensive prospect of what had once been forest, stood another of those monumental trees, which, to my mind, gave a peculiar interest to this neighborhood. It was the Parliament Oak, so called in memory of an assemblage of the kind keld by King John beneath its shade. The lapse of upwards of six centuries had reduced this once mighty tree to a mere crumbling fragment, yet, like a gigantic torso in ancient statuary, the grandeur of the mutilated trunk gave evidence of what it had been in the days of its glory. In contemplating its mouldering remains, the fancy busied itself in calling up the scene that must have been presented beneath its shade, when this sunny hill swarmed with the pageantry of a warlike and hunting court. When silken pavilions and warrior tents decked its crest, and royal standards, and baronial banners, and knightly pennons rolled out to the breeze. When prelates and courtiers, and steel-clad chivalry thronged round the person of the monarch, while at a distance loitered the foresters in green, and all the rural and hunting train that waited upon his sylvan sports.

> "A thousand vassals mustered round
> With horse, and hawk, and horn, and hound;
> And through the brake the rangers stalk,
> And falc'ners hold the ready hawk;
> And foresters in green-wood trim
> Lead in the leash the greyhound grim."

Such was the phantasmagoria that presented itself for a moment to my imagination, peopling the silent place before me with empty shadows of the past. The reverie however was transient: king, courtier, and steel-clad warrior, and forester in green, with horn, and hawk, and hound, all faded again into oblivion, and I awoke to all that remained of this once stirring scene of human pomp and power—a mouldering oak, and a tradition.

> "We are such stuff as dreams are made of!"

A ride of a few miles further brought us at length among the venerable and classic shades of Sherwood. Here I was delighted to find myself in a genuine wild wood, of primitive and natural growth, so rarely to be met with in this thickly peopled and highly cultivated country. It reminded me of the aboriginal forests of my native land. I rode through natural alleys and green-wood groves, carpeted with grass and shaded by lofty and beautiful birches. What most interested me, however, was to behold around me the mighty trunks of veteran oaks, old monumental trees, the patriarchs of Sherwood Forest. They were shattered, hollow, and moss-grown, it is true, and their "leafy honors" were nearly departed; but like mouldering towers they were noble and picturesque in their decay, and gave evidence, even in their ruins, of their ancient grandeur.

As I gazed about me upon these vestiges of once "Merrie Sherwood," the picturings of my boyish fancy began to rise in my mind, and Robin Hood and his men to stand before me.

> "He clothed himself in scarlet then,
> His men were all in green;
> A finer show throughout the world
> In no place could be seen.
>
> Good lord! it was a gallant sight
> To see them all in a row;
> With every man a good broad-sword
> And eke a good yew bow."

The horn of Robin Hood again seemed to resound through the forest. I saw this sylvan chivalry, half huntsmen, half free-booters, trooping across the distant glades, or feasting and revelling beneath the trees; I was going on to embody in this way all the ballad scenes that had delighted me when a boy, when the distant sound of a wood-cutter's axe roused me from my day-dream.

The boding apprehensions which it awakened were too soon verified. I had not ridden much further, when I came to an open space where the work of destruction was going on. Around me lay the prostrate trunks of venerable oaks, once the towering and magnificent lords of the forest, and a number of wood-cutters were hacking and hewing at another gigantic tree, just tottering to its fall

Alas! for old Sherwood Forest: it had fallen into the possession of a noble agriculturist; a modern utilitarian, who had no feeling for poetry or forest scenery. In a little while and this glorious woodland will be laid low; its green glades be turned into sheep-walks; its legendary bowers supplanted by turnip-fields, and "Merrie Sherwood" will exist but in ballad and tradition.

"O for the poetical superstitions," thought I, "of the olden time! that shed a sanctity over every grove; that gave to each tree its tutelar genius or nymph, and threatened disaster to all who should molest the hamadryads in their leafy abodes. Alas! for the sordid propensities of modern days, when every thing is coined into gold, and this once holiday planet of ours is turned into a mere 'working-day world.'"

My cobweb fancies put to flight, and my feelings out of tune, I left the forest in a far different mood from that in which I had entered it, and rode silently along until, on reaching the summit of a gentle eminence, the chime of evening bells came on the breeze across the heath from a distant village.

I paused to listen.

"They are merely the evening bells of Mansfield," said my companion.

"Of Mansfield!" Here was another of the legendary names of this storied neighborhood, that called up early and pleasant associations. The famous old ballad of the King and the Miller of Mansfield came at once to mind, and the chime of the bells put me again in good humor.

A little further on, and we were again on the traces of Robin Hood. Here was Fountain Dale, where he had his encounter with that stalwart shaveling Friar Tuck, who was a kind of saint militant, alternately wearing the casque and the cowl:

"The curtal fryar kept Fountain dale
Seven long years and more,
There was neither lord, knight or earl
Could make him yield before."

The moat is still shown which is said to have surrounded the strong-hold of this jovial and fighting friar; and the place where he and Robin Hood had their sturdy trial of strength and prowess, in the memorable conflict which lasted

"From ten o'clock that very day
Until four in the afternoon,"

and ended in the treaty of fellowship. As to the hardy feats, both of sword and trencher, performed by this "curtal fryar," behold are they not recorded at length in the ancient ballads, and in the magic pages of Ivanhoe?

The evening was fast coming on, and the twilight thickening, as we rode through these haunts famous in outlaw story. A melancholy seemed to gather over the landscape as we proceeded, for our course lay by shadowy woods, and across naked heaths, and along lonely roads, marked by some of those sinister names by which the country people in England are apt to make dreary places still more dreary. The horrors of "Thieves' Wood," and the "Murderers' Stone," and "the Hag Nook," had all to be encountered in the gathering gloom of evening, and threatened to beset our path with more than mortal peril. Happily, however, we passed these ominous places unharmed, and arrived in safety at the portal of Newstead Abbey, highly satisfied with our greenwood foray.

THE ROOK CELL.

In the course of my sojourn at the Abbey, I changed my quarters from the magnificent old state apartment haunted by Sir John Byron the Little, to another in a remote corner of the ancient edifice, immediately adjoining the ruined chapel. It possessed still more interest in my eyes, from having been the sleeping apartment of Lord Byron during his residence at the Abbey. The furniture remained the same. Here was the bed in which he slept, and which he had brought with him from college; its gilded posts surmounted by coronets, giving evidence of his aristocratical feelings. Here was likewise his college sofa; and about the walls were the portraits of his favorite butler, old Joe Murray, of his fancy acquaintance, Jackson the pugilist, together with pictures of Harrow School and the College at Cambridge, at which he was educated.

The bedchamber goes by the name of the Rook Cell, from its vicinity to the Rookery which, since time immemorial, has maintained possession of a solemn grove adjacent to the chapel. This venerable community afforded me much food for speculation during my residence in this apartment. In the morning I used to hear them gradually waking and seeming to call each other up. After a time, the whole fraternity would be in a flutter; some balancing and swinging on the tree tops, others perched on the pinnacle of the Abbey church, or wheeling and hovering about in the air, and the ruined walls would reverberate with their incessant cawings. In this way they would linger about the rookery and its vicinity for the early part of the morning, when, having apparently mustered all their forces, called over the roll, and determined upon their line of march, they one and all would sail off in a long straggling flight to maraud the distant fields. They would forage the country for miles, and remain absent all day, excepting now and then a scout would come home, as if to see that all was well. Towards night the whole host might be seen, like a dark cloud in the distance, winging their way homeward. They came, as it were, with whoop and halloo, wheeling high in the air above the Abbey, making various evolutions before they alighted, and then keeping up an incessant cawing in the tree tops, until they gradually fell asleep.

It is remarked at the Abbey, that the rooks, though they sally forth on forays throughout the week, yet keep about the venerable edifice on Sundays, as if they had inherited a reverence for the day, from their ancient confreres, the monks. Indeed, a believer in the metempsychosis might easily imagine these Gothic-looking birds to be the embodied souls of the ancient friars still hovering about their sanctified abode.

I dislike to disturb any point of popular and poetic faith, and was loth, therefore, to question the authenticity of this mysterious reverence for the Sabbath, on the part of the Newstead rooks; but certainly in the course of my sojourn in the Rook Cell, I detected them in a flagrant outbreak and foray on a bright Sunday morning.

Beside the occasional clamor of the rookery, this remote apartment was often greeted with sounds of a different kind, from the neighboring ruins. The great lancet window in front of the chapel, adjoins the very wall of the chamber; and the mysterious sounds from it at night, have been well described by Lord Byron:

——— "Now loud, now frantic,
The gale sweeps through its fretwork, and oft sings
The owl his anthem, when the silent quire
Lie with their hallelujahs quenched like fire.

But on the noontide of the moon, and when
The wind is winged from one point of heaven,
There moans a strange unearthly sound, which then
Is musical—a dying accent driven
Through the huge arch, which soars and sinks again.
Some deem it but the distant echo given
Back to the night wind by the waterfall,
And harmonized by the old choral wall.

Others, that some original shape or form,
Shaped by decay perchance, hath given the power
To this gray ruin, with a voice to charm.
Sad, but serene, it sweeps o'er tree or tower;
The cause I know not, nor can solve; but such
The fact:—I've heard it,—once perhaps too much."

Never was a traveller in quest of the romantic in greater luck. I had, in sooth, got lodged in another haunted apartment of the Abbey; for in this chamber Lord Byron declared he had more than once been harassed at midnight by a mysterious visitor. A black shapeless form would sit cowering upon his bed, and after gazing at him for a time with glaring eyes, would roll off and disappear. The same uncouth apparition is said to have disturbed the slumbers of a newly married couple that once passed their honey-moon in this apartment.

I would observe, that the access to the Rook Cell is by a spiral stone staircase leading up into it, as into a turret, from the long shadowy corridor over the cloisters, one of the midnight walks of the goblin friar. Indeed, to the fancies engendered in his brain in this remote and lonely apartment, incorporated with the floating superstitions of the Abbey, we are no doubt indebted for the spectral scene in Don Juan

" Then as the night was clear, though cold, he threw
His chamber door wide open—and went forth
Into a gallery, of sombre hue,
Long furnish'd with old pictures of great worth,
Of knights and dames, heroic and chaste too
As doubtless should be people of high birth.
* * * * * *

No sound except the echo of his sigh
Or step ran sadly through that antique house,
When suddenly he heard, or thought so, nigh,
A supernatural agent—or a mouse,
Whose little nibbling rustle will embarrass
Most people, as it plays along the arras.

It was no mouse, but lo! a monk, arrayed
In cowl, and beads, and dusky garb, appeared,
Now in the moonlight, and now lapsed in shade;
With steps that trod as heavy, yet unheard;
His garments only a slight murmur made;
He moved as shadowy as the sisters weird,
But slowly; and as he passed Juan by
Glared, without pausing, on him a bright eye.

Juan was petrified; he had heard a hint
  Of such a spirit in these halls of old,
But thought, like most men, there was nothing in't
  Beyond the rumor which such spots unfold,
Coin'd from surviving superstition's mint,
  Which passes ghosts in currency like gold,
But rarely seen, like gold compared with paper.
And *did* he see this? or was it a vapor?

Once, twice, thrice pass'd, repass'd—the thing of air,
  Or earth beneath, or heaven, or t'other place;
And Juan gazed upon it with a stare,
  Yet could not speak or move; but, on its base
As stands a statue, stood: he felt his hair
  Twine like a knot of snakes around his face;
He tax'd his tongue for words, which were not granted,
To ask the reverend person what he wanted.

The third time, after a still longer pause,
  The shadow pass'd away—but where? the hall
Was long, and thus far there was no great cause
  To think his vanishing unnatural:
Doors there were many, through which, by the laws
  Of physics, bodies, whether short or tall,
Might come or go; but Juan could not state
Through which the spectre seem'd to evaporate.

He stood, how long he knew not, but it seem'd
  An age—expectant, powerless, with his eyes
Strain'd on the spot where first the figure gleam'd
  Then by degrees recall'd his energies,
And would have pass'd the whole off as a dream,
  But could not wake; he was, he did surmise,
Waking already, and return'd at length
Back to his chamber, shorn of half his strength."

As I have already observed, it is difficult to determine whether Lord Byron was really subject to the superstitious fancies which have been imputed to him, or whether he merely amused himself by giving currency to them among his domestics and dependents. He certainly never scrupled to express a belief in supernatural visitations, both verbally and in his correspondence. If such were his foible, the Rook Cell was an admirable place to engender these delusions. As I have lain awake at night, I have heard all kinds of mysterious and sighing sounds from the neighboring ruin. Distant footsteps, too, and the closing of doors in remote parts of the Abbey, would send hollow reverberations and echoes along the corridor and up the spiral staircase. Once, in fact, I was roused by a strange sound at the very door of my chamber. I threw it open, and a form "black and shapeless with glaring eyes" stood before me. It proved, however, neither ghost nor goblin, but my friend Boatswain, the great Newfoundland dog, who had conceived a companionable liking for me, and occasionally sought me in my apartment. To the hauntings of even such a visitant as honest Boatswain may we attribute some of the marvellous stories about the Goblin Friar.

THE LITTLE WHITE LADY.

In the course of a morning's ride with Colonel Wildman, about the Abbey lands, we found ourselves in one of the prettiest little wild-woods imaginable. The road to it had led us among rocky ravines overhung with thickets, and now wound through birchen dingles and among beautiful groves and clumps of elms and beeches. A limpid rill of sparkling water, winding and doubling in perplexed mazes, crossed our path repeatedly, so as to give the wood the appearance of being watered by numerous rivulets. The solitary and romantic look of this piece of woodland, and the frequent recurrence of its mazy stream, put him in mind, Colonel Wildman said, of the little German fairy tale of Undine, in which is recorded the adventures of a knight who had married a water-nymph. As he rode with his bride through her native woods, every stream claimed her as a relative; one was a brother, another an uncle, another a cousin.

We rode on amusing ourselves with applying this fanciful tale to the charming scenery around us, until we came to a lowly gray-stone farmhouse, of ancient date, situated in a solitary glen, on the margin of the brook, and overshadowed by venerable trees. It went by the name, as I was told, of the Weir Mill farmhouse. With this rustic mansion was connected a little tale of real life, some circumstances of which were related to me on the spot, and others I collected in the course of my sojourn at the Abbey.

Not long after Colonel Wildman had purchased the estate of Newstead, he made it a visit for the purpose of planning repairs and alterations. As he was rambling one evening, about dusk, in company with his architect, through this little piece of woodland, he was struck with its peculiar characteristics, and then, for the first time, compared it to the haunted wood of Undine. While he was making the remark, a small female figure, in white, flitted by without speaking a word, or indeed appearing to notice them. Her step was scarcely heard as she passed, and her form was indistinct in the twilight.

"What a figure for a fairy or sprite!" exclaimed Colonel Wildman. "How much a poet or a romance writer would make of such an apparition, at such a time and in such a place!"

He began to congratulate himself upon having some elfin inhabitant for his haunted wood, when, on proceeding a few paces, he found a white frill lying in the path, which had evidently fallen from the figure that had just passed.

"Well," said he, "after all, this is neither sprite nor fairy, but a being of flesh, and blood, and muslin."

Continuing on, he came to where the road passed by an old mill in front of the Abbey. The people of the mill were at the door. He paused and inquired whether any visitor had been at the Abbey, but was answered in the negative.

"Has nobody passed by here?"

"No one, sir."

"That's strange! Surely I met a female in white, who must have passed along this path."

"Oh, sir, you mean the Little White Lady—oh, yes, she passed by here not long since."

"The Little White Lady! And pray who is the Little White Lady?"

"Why, sir, that nobody knows; she lives in the Weir Mill farmhouse, down in the skirts of the wood. She comes to the Abbey every morning, keeps about it all day, and goes away at night. She speaks to nobody, and we are rather shy of her, for we don't know what to make of her."

Colonel Wildman now concluded that it was some artist or amateur employed in making sketches of the Abbey, and thought no more about the matter. He went to London, and was absent for some time. In the interim, his sister, who was newly married, came with her husband to pass the honey-moon at the Abbey. The Little White Lady still resided in the Weir Mill farmhouse, on the border of the haunted wood, and continued her visits daily to the Abbey. Her dress was always the same, a white gown with a little black spencer or bodice, and a white hat with a short veil that screened the upper part of her countenance. Her habits were shy, lonely, and silent; she spoke to no one, and sought no companionship, excepting with the Newfoundland dog, that had belonged to Lord Byron. His friendship she secured by caressing him and occasionally bringing him food, and he became the companion of her solitary walks. She avoided all strangers, and wandered about the retired parts of the garden; sometimes sitting for hours, by the tree on which Lord Byron had carved his name, or at the foot of the monument which he had erected among the ruins of the chapel. Sometimes she read, sometimes she wrote with a pencil on a small slate which she carried with her, but much of her time was passed in a kind of reverie.

The people about the place gradually became accustomed to her, and suffered her to wander about unmolested; their distrust of her subsided on discovering that most of her peculiar and lonely habits arose from the misfortune of being deaf and dumb. Still she was regarded with some degree of shyness, for it was the common opinion that she was not exactly in her right mind.

Colonel Wildman's sister was informed of all these circumstances by the servants of the Abbey, among whom the Little White Lady was a theme of frequent discussion. The Abbey and its monastic environs being haunted ground, it was natural that a mysterious visitant of the kind, and one supposed to be under the influence of mental hallucination, should inspire awe in a person unaccustomed to the place. As Colonel Wildman's sister was one day walking along a broad terrace of the garden, she suddenly beheld the Little White Lady coming towards her, and, in the surprise and agitation of the moment, turned and ran into the house.

Day after day now elapsed, and nothing more was seen of this singular personage. Colonel Wildman at length arrived at the Abbey, and his sister mentioned to him her rencounter and fright in the garden, It brought to mind his own adventure with the Little White Lady in the wood of Undine, and he was surprised to find that she still continued her mysterious wanderings about the Abbey. The mystery was soon explained. Immediately after his arrival he received a letter written in the most minute and delicate female hand, and in elegant and even eloquent language. It was from the Little White Lady. She had noticed and been shocked by the abrupt retreat of Colonel Wildman's sister on seeing her in the garden walk, and expressed her unhappiness at being an object of alarm to any of his family. She explained the motives of her frequent and long visits to the Abbey, whhich proved to be a singularly enthusiastic idolatry of the genius of Lord Byron, and a solitary and passionate delight in haunting the scenes he had once inhabited. She hinted at the infirmities which cut her off from all social communion with her fellow beings, and at her situation in life as desolate and bereaved; and concluded by hoping that he would not deprive her of her only comfort, the permission of visiting the Abbey occasionally, and lingering about the walks and gardens.

Colonel Wildman now made further inquiries concerning her. and found that she was a great favorite with the people of the farmhouse where she boarded, from the gentleness, quietude, and innocence of her manners. When at home, she passed the greater part of her time in a small sitting-room, reading and writing.

Colonel Wildman immediately called on her at the farmhouse. She received him with some agitation and embarrassment, but his frankness and urbanity soon put her at her ease. She was past the bloom of youth, a pale, nervous little being, and apparently deficient in most of her physical organs, for in addition to being deaf and dumb, she saw but imperfectly. They carried on a communication by means of a small slate, which she drew out of her reticule, and on which they wrote their questions and replies. In writing or reading she always approached her eyes close to the written characters.

This defective organization was accompanied by a morbid sensibility almost amounting to disease. She had not been born deaf and dumb; but had lost her hearing in a fit of sickness, and with it the power of distinct articulation. Her life had evidently been checkered and unhappy; she was apparently without family or friend, a lonely, desolate being, cut off from society by her infirmities.

"I am always amongst strangers," said she, "as much so in my native country, as I could be in the remotest parts of the world. By all I am considered as a stranger and an alien; no one will acknowledge any connection with me. I seem not to belong to the human species."

Such were the circumstances that Colonel Wildman was able to draw forth in the course of his conversation, and they strongly interested him in favor of this poor enthusiast. He was too devout an admirer of Lord Byron himself, not to sympathize in this extraordinary zeal of one of his votaries, and he entreated her to renew her visits to the Abbey, assuring her that the edifice and its grounds should always be open to her.

The Little White Lady now resumed her daily walks in the Monks' Garden, and her occasional seat at the foot of the monument; she was shy and diffident, however, and evidently fearful of intruding. If any persons were walking in the garden she would avoid them, and seek the most remote parts; and was seen like a sprite, only by gleams and glimpses, as she glided among the groves and thickets. Many of her feelings and fancies, during these lonely rambles, were embodied in verse, noted down on her tablet, and transferred to paper in the evening on her return to the farmhouse. Some of these verses now lie before me, written with considerable harmony of versification, but chiefly curious as being illustrative of that singular and enthusiastic idolatry with which she almost worshipped the genius of Byron, or rather, the romantic image of him formed by her imagination.

Two or three extracts may not be unacceptable. The following are from a long rhapsody addressed to Lord Byron:

"By what dread charm thou rulest the mind
It is not given for us to know;
We glow with feelings undefined,
Nor can explain from whence they flow.

Not that fond love which passion breathes
And youthful hearts inflame;
The soul a nobler homage gives,
And bows to thy great name.

Oft have we own'd the muses' skill,
And proved the power of song,
But sweetest notes ne'er woke the thrill
That solely to thy verse belong.

This—but far more, for thee we prove,
Something that bears a holier name,
Than the pure dream of early love,
Or friendship's nobler flame.

Something divine—Oh! what it is
Thy muse alone can tell,
So sweet, but so profound the bliss
We dread to break the spell."

This singular and romantic infatuation, for such it might truly be called, was entirely spiritual and ideal, for, as she herself declares in another of her rhapsodies, she had never beheld Lord Byron; he was, to her, a mere phantom of the brain.

"I ne'er have drunk thy glance—Thy form
My earthly eye has never seen,
Though oft when fancy's visions warm,
It greets me in some blissful dream.

Greets me, as greets the sainted seer
Some radiant visitant from high,
When heaven's own strains break on his ear,
And wrap his soul in ecstasy."

Her poetical wanderings and musings were not confined to the Abbey grounds, but extended to all parts of the neighborhood connected with the memory of Lord Byron, and among the rest to the groves and gardens of Annesley Hall, the seat of his early passion for Miss Chaworth. One of her poetical effusions mentions her having seen from Howet's Hill in Annesley Park, a "sylph-like form," in a car drawn by milk-white horses, passing by the foot of the hill, who proved to be the "favorite child," seen by Lord Byron, in his memorable interview with Miss Chaworth after her marriage. That favorite child was now a blooming girl approaching to womanhood, and seems to have understood something of the character and story of this singular visitant, and to have treated her with gentle sympathy. The Little White Lady expresses in touching terms, in a note to her verses, her sense of this gentle courtesy. "The benevolent condescension," says she, "of that amiable and interesting young lady, to the unfortunate writer of these simple lines, will remain engraved upon a grateful memory, till the vital spark that now animates a heart that too sensibly feels, and too seldom experiences such kindness, is for ever extinct."

In the meantime, Colonel Wildman, in occasional interviews, had obtained further particulars of the story of the stranger, and found that poverty was added to the other evils of her forlorn and isolated state. Her name was Sophia Hyatt. She was the daughter of a country bookseller, but both her parents had died several years before. At their death, her sole dependence was upon her brother, who allowed her a small annuity on her share of the property left by their father, and which remained in his hands. Her brother, who was a captain of a merchant vessel, removed with his family to America, leaving her almost alone in the world, for she had no other relative in England but a cousin, of whom she knew almost nothing. She received her annuity regularly for a time, but unfortunately her brother died in the West Indies, leaving his affairs in confusion, and his estate overhung by several commercial claims, which threatened to swallow up the whole. Under these disastrous circumstances, her annuity suddenly ceased; she had in vain tried to obtain a renewal of it from the widow, or even an account of the state of her brother's affairs. Her letters for three years past had remained unanswered, and she would have been exposed to the horrors of the most abject want, but for a pittance quarterly doled out to her by her cousin in England.

Colonel Wildman entered with characteristic benevolence into the story of her troubles. He saw that she was a helpless, unprotected being, unable, from her infirmities and her ignorance of the world, to prosecute her just claims. He obtained from her the address of her relations in America, and of the commercial connection of her brother; promised, through the medium of his own agents in Liverpool, to institute an inquiry into the situation of her brother's affairs, and to forward any letters she might write, so as to insure their reaching their place of destination.

Inspired with some faint hopes, the Little White Lady continued her wanderings about the Abbey and its neighborhood. The delicacy and timidity of her deportment increased the interest already felt for her by Mrs. Wildman. That lady, with her wonted kindness, sought to make acquaintance with her, and inspire her with confidence. She invited her into the Abbey; treated her with the most delicate attention, and, seeing that she had a great turn for reading, offered her the loan of any books in her possession. She borrowed a few, particularly the works of Sir Walter Scott, but soon returned them; the writings of Lord Byron seemed to form the only study in which she delighted, and when not occupied in reading those, her time was passed in passionate meditations on his genius. Her enthusiasm spread an ideal world around her in which she moved and existed as in a dream, forgetful at times of the real miseries which beset her in her mortal state.

One of her rhapsodies is, however, of a very melancholy cast; anticipating her own death, which her fragile frame and growing infirmities rendered but too probable. It is headed by the following paragraph:

"Written beneath the tree on Crowholt Hill, where it is my wish to be interred (if I should die in Newstead)."

I subjoin a few of the stanzas: they are addressed to Lord Byron:

"Thou, while thou stand'st beneath this tree,
While by thy foot this earth is press'd,
Think, here the wanderer's ashes be—
And wilt thou say, sweet be thy rest!

* * * * *

'Twould add even to a seraph's bliss,
Whose sacred charge thou then may be,
To guide—to guard—yes, Byron! yes,
That glory is reserved for me.

If woes below may plead above
 A frail heart's errors, mine forgiven,
To that "high world" I soar, where "love
 Surviving" forms the bliss of Heaven

O wheresoe'er, in realms above,
 Assign'd my spirit's new abode,
'Twill watch thee with a seraph's love,
 Till thou too soar'st to meet thy God.

And here, beneath this lonely tree—
 Beneath the earth thy feet have press'd,
My dust shall sleep—once dear to thee
 These scenes—here may the wanderer rest!"

In the midst of her reveries and rhapsodies, tidings reached Newstead of the untimely death of Lord Byron How they were received by this humble but passionate devotee I could not ascertain; her life was too obscure and lonely to furnish much personal anecdote, but among her poetical effusions are several written in a broken and irregular manner, and evidently under great agitation.

The following sonnet is the most coherent and most descriptive of her peculiar state of mind:

" Well, thou art gone—but what wert thou to me?
 I never saw thee—never heard thy voice,
Yet my soul seemed to claim affiance with thee.
 The Roman bard has sung of fields Elysian,
Where the soul sojourns ere she visits earth;
 Sure it was there my spirit knew thee, Byron!
Thine image haunteth me like a past vision;
 It hath enshrined itself in my heart's core;

'Tis my soul's soul—it fills the whole creation.
  For I do live but in that world ideal
Which the muse peopleth with her bright fancies,
  And of that world thou art a monarch real,
Nor ever earthly sceptre ruled a kingdom,
  With sway so potent as thy lyre, the mind's dominion."

Taking all the circumstances here adduced into consideration it is evident that this strong excitement and exclusive occupation of the mind upon one subject, operating upon a system in a high state of morbid irritability, was in danger of producing that species of mental derangement called monomania. The poor little being was aware, herself, of the dangers of her case, and alluded to it in the following passage of a letter to Colonel Wildman, which presents one of the most lamentable pictures of anticipated evil ever conjured up by the human mind.

"I have long," writes she, "too sensibly felt the decay of my mental faculties, which I consider as the certain indication of that dreaded calamity which I anticipate with such terror. A strange idea has long haunted my mind, that Swift's dreadful fate will be mine. It is not ordinary insanity I so much apprehend, but something worse—absolute idiotism!

"O sir! think what I must suffer from such an idea, without an earthly friend to look up to for protection in such a wretched state—exposed to the indecent insults which such spectacles always excite. But I dare not dwell upon the thought; it would facilitate the event I so much dread, and contemplate with horror. Yet I cannot help thinking from people's behavior to me at times, and from after reflections upon my conduct, that symptoms of the disease are already apparent."

Five months passed away, but the letters written by her, and forwarded by Colonel Wildman to America relative to her brother's affairs, remained unanswered; the inquiries instituted by the Colonel had as yet proved equally fruitless. A deeper gloom and despondency now seemed to gather upon her mind. She began to talk of leaving Newstead, and repairing to London, in the vague hope of obtaining relief or redress by instituting some legal process to ascertain and enforce the will of her deceased brother. Weeks elapsed, however, before she could summon up sufficient resolution to tear herself away from the scene of poetical fascination. The following simple stanzas, selected from a number written about the time, express in humble rhymes the melancholy that preyed upon her spirits:

"Farewell to thee, Newstead, thy time-riven towers
Shall meet the fond gaze of the pilgrim no more;
No more may she roam through thy walks and thy bowers,
Nor muse in thy cloisters at eve's pensive hour.

Oh how shall I leave you, ye hills and ye dales,
When lost in sad musing, though sad not unblest,
A lone pilgrim I stray—Ah! in these lonely vales,
I hoped, vainly hoped, that the pilgrim might rest.

Yet rest is far distant—in the dark vale of death,
Alone shall I find it, an outcast forlorn—
But hence vain complaints, though by fortune bereft
Of all that could solace in life's early morn.

Is not man from his birth doomed a pilgrim to roam
O'er the world's dreary wilds, whence by fortune's rude gust,
In his path, if some flowret of joy chanced to bloom,
It is torn and its foliage laid low in the dust."

At length she fixed upon a day for her departure. On the day previous, she paid a farewell visit to the Abbey; wandering over every part of the grounds and garden; pausing and lingering at every place particularly associated with the recollection of Lord Byron; and passing a long time seated at the foot of the monument, which she used to call "her altar." Seeking Mrs. Wildman, she placed in her hands a sealed packet, with an earnest request that she would not open it until after her departure from the neighborhood. This done, she took an affectionate leave of her, and with many bitter tears bade farewell to the Abbey.

On retiring to her room that evening, Mrs. Wildman could not refrain from inspecting the legacy of this singular being. On opening the packet, she found a number of fugitive poems, written in a most delicate and minute hand, and evidently the fruits of her reveries and meditations during her lonely rambles; from these the foregoing extracts have been made. These were accompanied by a voluminous letter, written with the pathos and eloquence of genuine feeling, and depicting her peculiar situation and singular state of mind in dark but painful colors.

"The last time," says she, "that I had the pleasure of seeing you, in the garden, you asked me why I leave Newstead; when I told you my circumstances obliged me, the expression of concern which I fancied I observed in your look and manner would have encouraged me to have been explicit at the time, but from my inability of expressing myself verbally."

She then goes on to detail precisely her pecuniary circumstances, by which it appears that her whole dependence for subsistence was on an allowance of thirteen pounds a year from her cousin, who bestowed it through a feeling of pride, lest his relative should come upon the parish. During two years this pittance had been augmented from other sources, to twenty-three pounds, but the last year it had shrunk within its original bounds, and was yielded so grudgingly, that she could not feel sure of its continuance from one quarter to another. More than once it had been withheld on slight pretences, and she was in constant dread lest it should be entirely withdrawn.

"It is with extreme reluctance," observes she, "that I have so far exposed my unfortunate situation; but I thought you expected to know something more of it, and I feared that Colonel Wildman, deceived by appearances, might think that I am in no immediate want, and that the delay of a few weeks, or months, respecting the inquiry, can be of no material consequence. It is absolutely necessary to the success of the business that Colonel Wildman should know the exact state of my circumstances without reserve, that he may be enabled to make a correct representation of them to any gentleman whom he intends to interest, who, I presume, if they are not of America themselves, have some connections there, through whom my friends may be convinced of the reality of my distress, if they pretend to doubt it, as I suppose they do: but to be more explicit is impossible; it would be too humiliating to particularize the circumstances of the embarrassment in which I am unhappily involved—my utter destitution. To disclose all might, too, be liable to an inference which I hope I am not so void of delicacy, of natural pride, as to endure the thought of. Pardon me, madam, for thus giving trouble where I have no right to do—compelled to throw myself upon Colonel Wildman's humanity, to entreat his earnest exertions in my behalf, for it is now my only resource. Yet do not too much despise me for thus submitting to imperious necessity—it is not love of life, believe me it is not, nor anxiety for its preservation.

I cannot say, "There are things that make the world dear to me,"—for in the world there is not an object to make *me* wish to linger here another hour, could I find that rest and peace in the grave which I have never found on earth, and I fear will be denied me there."

Another part of her letter developes more completely the dark despondency hinted at in the conclusion of the foregoing extract—and presents a lamentable instance of a mind diseased, which sought in vain, amidst sorrow and calamity, the sweet consolations of religious faith.

"That my existence has hitherto been prolonged," says she, "often beyond what I have thought to have been its destined period, is astonishing to myself. Often when my situation has been as desperate, as hopeless, or more so, if possible, than it is at present, some unexpected interposition of Providence has rescued me from a fate that has appeared inevitable. I do not particularly allude to recent circumstances or latter years, for from my earlier years I have been the child of Providence—then why should I distrust its care now? I do not *dis*trust it—neither do I trust it. I feel perfectly unanxious, unconcerned, and indifferent as to the future; but this is not trust in Providence—not that trust which alone claims its protection. I know this is a blamable indifference—it is more—for it reaches to the interminable future. It turns almost with disgust from the bright prospects which religion offers for the consolation and support of the wretched, and to which I was early taught, by an almost adored mother, to look forward with hope and joy; but to me they can afford no consolation. Not that I doubt the sacred truths that religion inculcates. I cannot doubt—though I confess I have sometimes tried to do so, because I no longer wish for that immortality of which it assures us My only wish now is for rest and peace—endless rest. 'For rest—but not to feel 'tis rest,' but I cannot delude myself with the hope that such rest will be my lot. I feel an internal evidence, stronger than any arguments that reason or religion can enforce, that I have that within me which is imperishable; that drew not its origin from the 'clod of the valley.' With this conviction, but without a hope to brighten the prospect of that dread future:

'I dare not look beyond the tomb,
Yet cannot hope for peace before.'

"Such an unhappy frame of mind, I am sure, madam, must excite your commiseration. It is perhaps owing, in part at least, to the solitude in which I have lived, I may say, even in the midst of society; when I have mixed in it; as my infirmities entirely exclude me from that sweet intercourse of kindred spirits —that sweet solace of refined conversation; the little intercourse I have at any time with those around me cannot be termed conversation—they are not kindred spirits—and even where circumstances have associated me (but rarely indeed) with superior and cultivated minds, who have not disdained to admit me to their society, they could not by all their generous efforts, even in early youth, lure from my dark soul the thoughts that loved to lie buried there, nor inspire me with the courage to attempt their disclosure; and yet of all the pleasures of polished life which fancy has often pictured to me in such vivid colors, there is not one that I have so ardently coveted as that sweet reciprocation of ideas, the supreme bliss of enlightened minds in the hour of social converse. But this I knew was not decreed for me—

'Yet this was in my nature—'

but since the loss of my hearing, I have always been incapable of verbal conversation. I need not, however, inform you, madam, of this. At the first interview with which you favored me, you quickly discovered my peculiar unhappiness in this respect: you perceived, from my manner, that any attempt to draw me into conversation would be in vain—had it been otherwise, perhaps you would not have disdained now and then to have soothed the lonely wanderer with yours. I have sometimes fancied, when I have seen you in the walk, that you seemed to wish to encourage me to throw myself in your way. Pardon me if my imagination, too apt to beguile me with such dear illusions, has deceived me into too presumptuous an idea here. You must have observed that I generally endeavored to avoid both you and Colonel Wildman. It was to spare your generous hearts the pain of witnessing distress you could not alleviate. Thus cut off, as it were, from all human society, I have been compelled to live in a world of my own, and certainly with the beings with which my world is peopled, I am at no loss to converse. But, though I love solitude and am never in want of subjects to amuse my fancy, yet solitude too much indulged in must necessarily have an unhappy effect upon the mind, which, when left to seek for resources wholly within itself, will unavoidably, in hours of gloom and despondency, brood over corroding thoughts that prey upon the spirits, and sometimes terminate in confirmed misanthropy—especially with those who, from constitution, or early misfortunes, are inclined to melancholy, and to view human nature in its dark shades. And have I not cause for gloomy reflections?

The utter loneliness of my lot would alone have rendered existence a curse to one whose heart nature has formed glowing with all the warmth of social affection, yet without an object on which to place it—without one natural connection, one earthly friend to appeal to, to shield me from the contempt, indignities, and insults, to which my deserted situation continually exposed me."

I am giving long extracts from this letter, yet I cannot refrain from subjoining another letter, which depicts her feelings with respect to Newstead.

"Permit me, madam, again to request your and Colonel Wildman's acceptance of those acknowledgments which I cannot too often repeat, for your unexampled goodness to a rude stranger. I know I ought not to have taken advantage of your extreme good-nature so frequently as I have. I should have absented myself from your garden during the stay of the company at the Abbey, but, as I knew I must be gone long before they would leave it, I could not deny myself the indulgence, as you so freely gave me your permission to continue my walks; but now they are at an end. I have taken my last farewell of every dear and interesting spot, which I now never hope to see again, unless my disembodied spirit may be permitted to revisit them.—Yet O! if Providence should enable me again to support myself with any degree of respectability, and you should grant me some little humble shed, with what joy shall I return and renew my delightful rambles. But dear as Newstead is to me, I will never again come under the same unhappy circumstances as I have this last time—never without the means of at least securing myself from contempt. How dear, how very dear Newstead is to me, how unconquerable the infatuation that possesses me, I am now going to give a too convincing proof. In offering to your acceptance the worthless trifles that will accompany this, I hope you will believe that I have no view to your amusement. I dare not hope that the consideration of their being the products of your own garden and most of them written there, in my little tablet, while sitting at the foot of *my Altar*—I could not, I cannot resist the earnest desire of leaving this memorial of the many happy hours I have there enjoyed. Oh! do not reject them, madam; suffer them to remain with you, and if you should deign to honor them with a perusal, when you read them repress, if you can, the smile that I know will too naturally arise, when you recollect the appearance of the wretched being who has dared to devote her whole soul to the contemplation of such more than human excellence. Yet ridiculous as such devotion may appear to some, I must take leave to say, that if the sentiments which I have entertained for that exalted being could be duly appreciated, I trust they would be found to be of such a nature as is no dishonor even for him to have inspired." * * * *

"I am now coming to take a last, last view of scenes too deeply impressed upon my memory ever to be effaced even by madness itself. O madam! may you never know, nor be able to conceive the agony I endure in tearing myself from all that the world contains of dear and sacred to me: the only spot on earth where I can ever hope for peace or comfort.—May every blessing the world has to bestow attend you, or rather, may you long, long live in the enjoyment of the delights of your own paradise, in secret seclusion from a world that has no real blessings to bestow. Now I go—but O might I dare to hope that when you are enjoying these blissful scenes, a thought of the unhappy wanderer might sometimes cross your mind, how soothing would such an idea be, if I dared to indulge it—could you see my heart at this moment, how needless would it be to assure you of the respectful gratitude, the affectionate esteem, this heart must ever bear you both."

The effect of this letter upon the sensitive heart of Mrs. Wildman may be more readily conceived than expressed. Her first impulse was to give a home to this poor homeless being, and to fix her in the midst of those scenes which formed her earthly paradise. She communicated her wishes to Colonel Wildman, and they met with an immediate response in his generous bosom. It was settled on the spot, that an apartment should be fitted up for the Little White Lady in one of the new farm-houses, and every arrangement made for her comfortable and permanent maintenance on the estate. With a woman's prompt benevolence, Mrs. Wildman, before she laid her head upon her pillow, wrote the following letter to the destitute stranger:

"Newstead Abbey,
Tuesday night, Sept. 20th, 1825.

"On retiring to my bedchamber this evening I have opened your letter, and cannot lose a moment in expressing to you the strong interest which it has excited both in Colonel Wildman and myself, from the details of your peculiar situation, and the delicate, and, let me add, elegant language in which they are conveyed. I am anxious that my note should reach you previous to your departure from this neighborhood, and should be truly happy if, by any arrangement for your accommodation, I could prevent the necessity of your undertaking the journey. Colonel Wildman begs me to assure you that he will use his best exertion in the investigation of those matters which you have confided to him, and should you remain here at present, or return again after a short absence, I trust we shall find means to become better acquainted, and to convince you of the interest I feel, and the real atisfaction it would afford me to contribute in any way to your omfort and happiness. I will only now add my thanks for the little packet which I received with your letter, and I must confess that the letter has so entirely engaged my attention, that I have not as yet had time for the attentive perusal of its companion.

Believe me, dear madam,
with sincere good wishes,
Yours truly,
LOUISA WILDMAN."

Early the next morning a servant was dispatched with the letter to the Weir Mill farm, but returned with the information that the Little White Lady had set off, before his arrival, in company with the farmer's wife, in a cart for Nottingham, to take her place in the coach for London. Mrs. Wildman ordered him to mount horse instantly, follow with all speed, and deliver the letter into her hand before the departure of the coach.

The bearer of good tidings spared neither whip nor spur, and arrived at Nottingham on a gallop. On entering the town a crowd obstructed him in the principal street. He checked his horse to make his way through it quietly. As the crowd opened to the right and left, he beheld a human body lying on the pavement.—It was the corpse of the Little White Lady!

It seems that on arriving in town and dismounting from the cart, the farmer's wife had parted with her to go on an errand, and the White Lady continued on toward the coach-office. In crossing a street a cart came along driven at a rapid rate. The driver called out to her, but she was too deaf to hear his voice or the rattling of his cart. In an instant she was knocked down by the horse, the wheels passed over her body, and she died without a groan.

THE END.

www.ingramcontent.com/pod-product-compliance
Lightning Source LLC
LaVergne TN
LVHW010130110826
845151LV00002B/314

* 9 7 8 1 4 2 5 5 4 0 4 8 7 *